# Seeking the
# TRUTH
## About Money

To Liana - Anthony:

   May God richly bless
every dimension of your lives!

            Love Karen

Karen Henein has also published:

*Counsel of the Most High:* Receiving God's Guidance for Life's Decisions

*Bent Out of Shape:* Reshaping our Emotional Lives

# Seeking the
# TRUTH
## About Money

## Karen Henein

SEEKING THE TRUTH ABOUT MONEY

ISBN: 978-1-77069-287-9

Printed in Canada.

Word Alive Press
131 Cordite Road, Winnipeg, MB R3W 1S1
www.wordalivepress.ca

Library and Archives Canada Cataloguing in Publication

Henein, Karen
    Seeking the truth about money / Karen Henein.

ISBN 978-1-77069-287-9

    1. Money--Religious aspects--Christianity.
    2. Finance, Personal--Religious aspects--Christianity. I. Title.

BR115.W4H45 2011        241'.68        C2011-903572-3

# CONTENTS

---

# THANK-YOU NOTES

First and foremost, I thank God for helping me to bring this book to full fruition. I thank Him for the time, strength, energy, inspiration, guidance, and knowledge He so graciously and generously gave me. May this book be used for His purposes.

I next express my deepest thanks to the multitude of people who have helped to make this book possible and who have journeyed with me as an author. I wish I had the space to name and publicly thank every supportive person.

I thank my precious husband, Sam, who encouraged me and supported me along the way. He once again took the time to provide suggested revisions and wise comments regarding my entire manuscript.

I also thank my son, Darrin, my daughter, Samantha, and my daughter-in-law, Alicia, for their love and encouragement. I am so proud of them.

I am once again grateful to Shirley Hutchison for her careful review of my full manuscript, for her insightful suggestions, and for her many prayers over the years. I also thank Eleanor Morrison and Julie Dietrich for reviewing my whole manuscript and for providing useful feedback and Derrick Milne, David Milne, and Anne Milne for their helpful comments on portions of my manuscript. I thank those who have given me permission to use their personal stories.

Thanks to the staff at Word Alive Press for the parts they played in bringing this book to print, especially Jen Jandavs-Hedlin, Larissa Bartos, and Nikki Braun.

I am grateful for every reader of my first two books, particularly those who have taken the time to write, e-mail, phone, or speak with me in person, offering kind words about what I have written. I pray that this third book is of some worth to many readers too.

# 1

---

# In Pursuit of Balance

*Jesus answered, "…For this purpose I was born and for this purpose I have come into the world—to bear witness to the truth. Everyone who is of the truth listens to my voice." Pilate said to him, "What is truth?"*

John 18:37b–38a

*Money is like a foreign film with no subtitles.*

From the movie *Matchstick Men*[1]

A few years ago, the global economy began spinning in a destructive downward spiral. Millions lost their jobs. Many also lost their homes. Great banks and blue-chip companies struggled and some collapsed. In a few astonishing months, trillions of dollars vanished from stock markets around the world. The nest eggs of individuals shrunk to sorry shadows of their former selves.

Even after governments pumped trillions of dollars into their banking systems and national economies, the downhill ride continued.

---

[1]  *Matchstick Men*. Directed by Ridley Scott. 2003. Hollywood, CA: Warner Brothers Pictures, 2003.

Mercifully, the dizzy tailspin has lost some of its ferocious velocity. A fragile measure of recovery has occurred, but many financial hopes and plans remain severely shaken.

All of us have, in some way, been impacted by the recent global financial meltdown. In the aftermath, we find ourselves wondering if there is any sound financial wisdom or truth about money that we can rely on.

## Tackling the Topic of Money

Many Christians don't like to think or talk about money. We sometimes perceive contemplating or discussing money to be unspiritual and worldly. Furthermore, focusing on money can generate unpleasant feelings ranging from worry to jealousy, insecurity, and guilt. Financial matters often remain quite private—to the point that even married couples or adult siblings don't talk about them.

In some churches in North America, pastors hesitate to preach about money, apart from an occasional sermon to encourage giving. This has always puzzled me, considering that one out of every fifteen verses in the Bible has something to say about money and possessions (or our lack thereof). The silence on this topic from many pulpits (a silence so prevalent it was noted in a 2006 *Time* magazine cover story[2]) is also remarkable in light of the fact that we all need *some* measure of money to buy our daily bread. After I began tackling the topic of money, I quickly encountered the complexities and controversies that abound. I've since become more sympathetic to the pastoral reticence to address this touchy topic!

Pastors who *do* talk about money often come across as being unbalanced in what they teach. Some preach the prosperity gospel. Some forcefully bash it. Some criticize the rich while crusading for the poor. When pastors do speak up, it seems that money is either too venerated or too vilified, a commodity to be either acquired in abundance (in pursuit of the good life) or sacrificially disposed of (before it can corrupt us).

---

[2]   Van Biema and Chu article.

As a result of the recent financial crisis, it seems to me that many Christians are becoming more interested in financial matters. Whether to make sense of what has been happening in their own lives (in their workplaces, bank accounts, and retirement savings), to understand what has been happening to the world around them, or perhaps to find some comfort for the future, most Christians are now willing to more meaningfully and more deeply focus on the topic of money.

If you are one of them, may I engage your company for a while?

## God Cares About Money

I am thoroughly convinced that God cares a great deal about money. In His Word, He has so much to say about greed and generosity, poverty and prosperity, needs and desires, gaining and giving, and many other money-related themes.

Jesus considered the topic of money to be so significant that He spent about half of His parables addressing it. Jesus spoke more on the subject of money than on any other topic. In the Bible as a whole, around two thousand verses address money-related matters out of a total of just over 30,000 verses, outnumbering verses about prayer by a ratio of almost four to one.[3] From God's point of view, money is not a peripheral matter. How we value, acquire, save, invest, spend, and give away money interests Him greatly.

## Finding Clear Principles

Studying biblical principles on the topic of money can be confusing, however, because at first glance they can appear inconsistent with one another. On one occasion, Jesus told a rich man to sell everything he owned and to give the proceeds to the poor. On another occasion, Jesus criticized a man who had not carefully invested the money entrusted to him. Jesus also talked about how He came to give us an abundant life without clearly defining what that meant.

---

[3]   March 11, 2009 episode wrap, www.listenuptv.com; Alcorn book.

In one of his letters, the apostle Paul assured Christians that God wants to meet our every need. In other letters, Paul wrote about working hard, providing for our own families, and sharing with others in the Christian community. Paul also talked about richly enjoying all things.

The Bible warns about the sin of loving money while also assuming that we will accumulate sufficient money to both meet our own earthly needs *and* be able to give generously to others. Sometimes the Bible focuses on the legitimate reality of our temporal needs and at other times it encourages us to invest primarily in that which has eternal value.

This book will attempt to reconcile all these seemingly competing—even contradictory—ideas, images, and principles. We will try to figure out together how these concepts are interconnected and how each one finds a meaningful place within the whole biblical truth about money.

## Balancing All Principles

In writing this book, I have tried hard to avoid addressing too narrow a view on the subject of money. What I have earnestly searched for is a sense of *well-rounded* and *well-grounded* biblical balance.

I believe that when a pastor only preaches about prosperity, he promotes an imbalanced and incomplete approach to money. The Christian who focuses all of their attention on accumulating wealth and managing investments lives with lopsided intentionality. If a speaker suggests that our singular Christian duty regarding money is to help the poor, they are ignoring many other necessary, complementary facets of handling money.

When any of us apply only one passage or concept in the Bible on the topic of money while side-stepping other passages and concepts, we invite deception, distortion, error, and confusion. We short-change ourselves if we live by a selective and skewed version of the truth. Latching on to a few favourite verses or sticking to a few palatable principles will never be a magic cure-all for the financial issues in our lives. Financial wisdom is simply not that simple.

I invite you to journey with me, to see if together we can find some better sense of balance regarding such money-related biblical subtopics as provision, prosperity, materialism, investing, spending, managing debt, helping the poor, and other key issues. Let's seek to find and follow as *complete* a truth as possible.

## The Art of Presenting the Whole Picture

As a trial lawyer for twenty years, I learned much about seeking truth by taking a carefully focused look at the whole picture.

I know what some of you may be thinking. I am forever being told that the term "Christian lawyer" is an oxymoron. Friends keep sharing with me the newest lawyer jokes, which do nothing to dispel the supposed oxymoron. Maybe you have heard this one: not all lawyers are crooks—it's the other 99% that give the rest of us a bad name! I humbly profess to be one of the good guys.

During my years of practice, whenever I presented any matter to a judge or jury, I always tried to be accurate, thorough, and balanced. Of course, I wanted to deal primarily with the evidence in favour of my client, but I also had to address the evidence I was *not* so thrilled about. I had to present my own experts' opinions but also had to fairly comment on the opinions of my opponent's experts. In addressing issues of law, I had to take into account *all* of the law pertinent to the case. Any lawyer of good faith and integrity would do this.

By the end of a case, the *whole* body of evidence and law had to be reasonably placed before the judge or jury. And certainly, other lawyers had their part to play in this too.

It was then up to the judge or jury to carefully consider the whole picture. They had to consider what *weight* (or degree of importance) they would attach to every fact, witness, document, or legal principle. After assigning each aspect of the case some weight, they had to place each aspect inside the bigger picture. Some aspects of the case were more significant (or weightier) than others. Ultimately, finding some semblance of the truth involved weighing, balancing, and counter-balancing *all* relevant matters.

Given this kind of training, and a few decades of professional practice trying to apply it, you can understand why I am uncomfortable every time I hear a preacher present only the Bible verses pertaining to prosperity as if they were the whole gospel about money—or, conversely, whenever I hear a critic forcefully trash the prosperity gospel as if the Bible never mentions the word prosperity in a positive light.

I have tried my best not to support these kinds of simplistic, polarized views. In Proverbs 11:1, God reveals that He detests false balances when goods are being weighed and measured on the scales of the marketplace. I imagine that He also hates false balance in the teaching of His principles or undue weight being given to just one aspect of His truth. Of course, I concede that no one will ever perfectly comprehend or communicate truth, but surely the task of seeking truth requires *our* best efforts, yours and mine.

Let's pursue sound and balanced doctrine. The apostle Paul warned us in 2 Timothy 4:3–4 that "the time is coming when people will not endure sound teaching, but having itching ears they will accumulate for themselves teachers to suit their own passions, and will turn away from listening to the truth…" In light of that wise warning, let's tackle the subject of money as holistically as possible instead of just focusing on those verses that most appeal to our human nature.

## Integrating the Principles

The different principles we will consider and weigh must also be integrated. Learning how to bring together the various principles regarding money is not easy. Maybe you have been frustrated in the past in this endeavour. I know that I have.

You have probably worked hard to earn whatever money you have. You have likely prayed, asking in faith for God's material provision. Perhaps you have tried to save and invest. Perhaps you have been a faithful giver.

Some of you might be somewhat cynical or confused because none of these biblical concepts appear to have "worked" for you so far or they have not worked as well as you thought they would. You may feel that, financially, you are no better off than you were before you made the effort to engage in some of these activities. It is quite possible that you are even worse off today than you were a few years ago.

Or maybe you have figured out how to make a lot of money, but life itself does not feel very rich. Something seems to be missing. You might be financially rich yet feel spiritually poor.

Often the problem we face is that we have not, over a long enough period of time, tried *all* of the key biblical principles *working together* as they are meant to. Instead of being discouraged about what you have already tried, I invite you to give thought to what principles you have not yet put into consistent, continual practice, whether they pertain to actions you are biblically instructed to take or to prescribed attitudes of the heart.

A car will not move forward unless there are four wheels ready to roll, fuel in the tank, a key in the ignition, disengaged brakes, a gearshift set on drive, *and* a foot pressing the gas pedal. We are foolish to think that we can leave out even one of those factors and still be able to go somewhere. Of course we cannot drive a car if the key is still sitting on the kitchen counter or if the gearshift remains in park mode—even if we are doing everything else right. Similarly, biblical financial principles are meant to work together as a fully integrated process.

## What I Will Offer You

Have I nailed this subject of money perfectly? Absolutely not! Let's get that straight from the outset. I have *some* knowledge on the subject. I took economics courses in university, and real estate, taxation, and business courses during my legal training. Because those qualifications do not confer financial expertise, I have sought the counsel of various professionals in connection with my own finances and have learned much from them. I have read the Bible cover to cover dozens of times over more than three decades and have, with great interest, noted what it says about money; I have made this particular subject an area of granular study over the past three years. I have heard what various pastors have preached on the subject (although, as I lamented earlier, not often enough nor as comprehensively as I have wanted to hear). As a result, I have sought out Christian books on the subject. Notwithstanding all of that formal and informal education, I cannot promise a flawless treatise on this subject.

I cannot offer you instant solutions to whatever your money issues might be. I will not attempt to outline ten simple steps to follow. I do not know five hidden secrets or three grand principles that will automatically conjure up financial health. I have no get-rich-quick scheme to sell. I have no pat answers. I do not pretend to be a financial expert. I am not a super-spiritual know-it-all.

But here's what I *will* promise to offer you:

- I will refer to almost one thousand pertinent Bible verses.

- I will offer interesting stories and insights from the lives of many well-known Christians, past and present. These men and women come from diverse denominations, different nationalities, assorted careers, various periods of history, and the whole range of social classes.

- I will also share money-related stories from my own life involving both struggles and successes. As further contemporary illustrations, I will tell stories from the lives of people I personally know.

Hopefully, all of this content will shed some light on how we, as Christians, can practically apply what God has to say about money. We need all the light we can get!

### What You Can Give Yourself

Instead of passively reading this book, I hope that you will thoughtfully and prayerfully consider each biblical principle I present. You do not have to agree with everything I say. Instead, one chapter at a time,

I trust that you will determine what *you* believe God's perspective is on each subtopic.

I will place a lot of material before you but, at the end of the day, *you* get to be the judge of what is true and right. Ultimately, you will have to figure out for yourself how to fully balance and integrate biblical truth and how to practically apply it to your own financial affairs. I trust that you will add your own life lessons, experience, wisdom, knowledge, insight, and discernment into this process.

I challenge you to be open to changing some of your views, and maybe even your lifestyle, as you meditate on what God has to say about money. Finding and applying truth is a life-long process. We all need to constantly renew our thinking and recalibrate our actions, in every aspect of our lives, as we mature in stages in our Christian faith.

For some, the pages ahead might help to create a brand new roadmap for living in the area of finances. Others will be reminded of great truths and principles they already know. Be encouraged to press on in the light of these thoughts.

On a different note, I am increasingly convinced that handling money by right principles is a practical life skill that God wants us to teach to our children. In this modern world, such tasks as acquiring and investing money and avoiding unwise debt or out-of-control spending are perhaps more complicated than they were for us (or our parents and grandparents) when we emerged into adulthood in simpler times. Aside from what you might personally gain from this book, I invite you to thoughtfully consider how you can pass on foundational financial principles to your teens and young-adult children.

## What God Has to Offer Us

Thankfully, we have a gracious God willing to help us! He wants each one of us to grasp and apply the *full* spectrum of His principles pertaining to every aspect of life, including our money. God wants to counsel, challenge, and change each one of us as we explore what He has to say.

As we deal with money, God's first priority is to transform us from within, to properly set our hearts and minds in the right direction. God is also willing and well able to help us transform our external financial circumstances, but we cannot expect Him to bless us in areas such as our work or our investments unless (and until) we develop the right attitudes towards money. For that reason, we will begin our study by giving due weight to biblically-advocated attitudes about money. After laying that necessary foundation, we will move on to discuss what God has to say about: acquiring money; giving back to Him; saving and investing; spending; managing debt; and helping the poor.

The world at large often seems negative and dysfunctional in the material realm. In times of plenty, greed and materialism dominate. In economic downturns, fear, panic, despair, and stress prevail. Whether the market is up or down, billions suffer in dire poverty and billions of others don't seem to care about them.

In contrast, *God* emphasizes productivity and provision combined with generosity and sharing so that the less fortunate can be compassionately lifted out of poverty. God's intended outcome is on the positive side of the ledger for each one of us, spiritually and financially. No matter how shaky the rest of the world appears, Christians can look forward to a brighter financial future for ourselves and for those we aspire to help.

The very best part of all is that, for the Christian, material wealth does not even represent the finest riches in life. Jesus advises: "...real life and real living are not related to how rich we are" (Luke 12:15c TLB). I pray that we filter everything we learn about money through that exquisite truth. We cannot really gain, save, invest, spend, or give in right fashion without this larger truth permeating our thoughts and actions. As a result, this key truth will weave in and out of the various sections ahead and will be duly highlighted at the end of our journey together.

I pray that we all emerge at the end of this book with richer attitudes, sounder financial lives, and enhanced relationships with God and others as we jointly seek a reasonably comprehensive, balanced, and integrated approach to the biblical truth about money.

> *I will ask the Father, and he will give you another Helper,*
> *to be with you forever, even the Spirit of truth....he will*
> *teach you all things...*

John 14:16–17a, 26

# ATTITUDES ABOUT MONEY

# 2

---

# THE LOVE OF MONEY

*People who want to get rich fall into temptation and a trap
and into many foolish and harmful desires that plunge men
into ruin and destruction. For the love of money is a root of
all kinds of evil. Some people, eager for money, have wandered
from the faith and pierced themselves with many griefs.*

1 Timothy 6:9–10 (NIV)

*Whoever loves money never has money enough; whoever
loves wealth is never satisfied with his income.*

Ecclesiastes 5:10a (NIV)

*Keep your life free from love of money, and be
content with what you have…*

Hebrews 13:5

Catherine the Great, an Empress in 18th-century Russia, loved
material possessions and acquired them on an extravagant scale.
Flaunting her vast wealth, she lived in grand palaces and rode around

in golden carriages pulled by horses with bejewelled bridles. She wore most of her ornate gowns only once before casting them aside. Today, visitors to her Summer Palace at Pushkin or her Winter Palace in St. Petersburg can view the giant chandeliers, gilded doorframes, masterpiece paintings, fairy-tale beds, and massive tapestries that adorned her imperial living spaces.

In our present world, many still accrue enormous wealth. An Indian billionaire just finished building a twenty-seven-story skyscraper in Mumbai for his family of six to live in. It overlooks the desperately poor slums of Mumbai so poignantly portrayed in the movie *Slumdog Millionaire*. The building boasts 168 parking spaces, an entertainment centre seating fifty, three roof-top helipads, a swimming pool and health centre, outdoor garden terraces, and guest floors. Construction costs have been estimated at about one billion dollars, making this the world's most expensive private residence. It will take about 600 staff to maintain it. One guest has called it the Taj Mahal of the 21st century.[4]

Even as a child, another modern business tycoon treasured his treasure. He hand-washed his dollar bills, hung them up to dry, and then painstakingly iron-pressed each bill until it was perfectly flat and unwrinkled (creating an alternative meaning to the expression "money laundering"). Not surprisingly, as an adult, he has eagerly accumulated homes, cars, and businesses around the globe.

While most of us will not amass wealth on that scale, all of us must guard our hearts from the human weakness of loving money and material possessions. Who among us can say they have no love for money? Who has never felt a keen desire to acquire? This inquiry leads to another crucial question…

## Is the Love of Money Compatible with Christian Faith?

Several years ago, I acted as legal counsel for an author, defending a libel lawsuit against him initiated by a wealthy business titan named Conrad Black. The author had written about Black's decision

---

[4] Fatah article; www.bbc.co.uk/news/world-south-asia-11854177, last accessed Feb. 8, 2011.

to embrace the Catholic faith. The author queried the level of Black's spiritual sincerity in light of his alleged love of money. Two issues I had to explore were whether Conrad Black's life did indeed demonstrate a love for money and whether his alleged love of wealth was compatible with his professed Christian faith.

In my early case preparation, I served Black's lawyer with notice of our intention to rely on various verses from the Bible. The point of collecting all those biblical references was *not* to use them to criticize or condemn Black. I was not the judge of his lawsuit, his life, or his relationship with God. The verses would simply serve to present our position as to what the Bible teaches about how Christians should relate to money. I personally learned a lot while framing that position.

Soon after receiving that list of verses, Black's lawyer asked me whether we would consent to the case ending at that point. Of course we agreed. As a result, I never did get to question Black about his faith and how it impacted his attitudes and actions regarding money.

As I later watched Conrad Black's life unfold, I have often wondered what he would have answered if I had been able to ask him this question: is it possible for a person to love money and still authentically live by the principles of the Christian faith?

*Good question for all of us.* How do *we* answer it?

## Money Itself Is Not Inherently Evil

First of all, let's make a clear distinction between money and the concept of the love of money. The Bible teaches that the *love* of money, not money itself, is the root of all kinds of evil. Money is neutral—neither good nor bad all on its own.

Consider 1 Timothy 6:9–10: "...People who want to get rich fall into temptation and a trap and into many foolish and harmful desires that plunge men into ruin and destruction. For the love of money is a root of all kinds of evil. Some people, eager for money, have wandered from the faith and pierced themselves with many griefs" (NIV). Paul's words make it clear that it's the love of money that sets one on a path full of pitfalls.

In contrast, simply *having* money is not a sin. Some people are born into a wealthy family. For others, money arrives as a windfall, such as an inheritance, or perhaps it compounds in wise investments. Yet others receive money as the product of hard work; the financial rewards are often especially high for those who work with excellence, distinction, and diligence in their field. None of this is wrong.

Furthermore, those who have a lot of money are not ineludibly in love with it.

Possession of some money is necessary to sustain life. As the Israelites passed through lands occupied by others, Moses instructed them: "You shall purchase food from them for money, that you may eat, and you shall also buy water of them for money, that you may drink" (Deuteronomy 2:6).

Jesus acquired money and He spent money. He even paid taxes. Although He never aspired to be rich in this world, money was an everyday reality to Him.

On a similar note, the apostle Paul pragmatically made money and spent money, but he did not *live* for it. Sometimes Paul possessed a significant amount of material wealth. He wrote: "…I have learned how to be content with whatever I have. I know how to live on almost nothing or with everything. I have learned the secret of living in every situation, whether it is with a full stomach or empty, with plenty or little" (Philippians 4:11–12 NLT).

Elsewhere, Paul acknowledged that, while *most* Christians were neither wealthy nor powerful, some *were* (1 Corinthians 1:26). Paul did not condemn those who had wealth. Instead, he challenged those who had wealth to share it and to use it to do good works (1 Timothy 6:18).

Simply *having* money and *handling* money cannot automatically be equated with *loving* money.

The possession of an abundance of money does not tell us much about the heart of its owner. A person can love money whether they have a little or a lot, whether they earned it themselves or not. I have known rich people who are admirably *not* attached to their money and poorer folk who won't let go of a dime. God's primary concern is not the size of our bank account; He cares more about the state of our heart. The critical issue is not how much we own but whether what we own owns us. Do we possess our money and our possessions—or do they possess us?

God does not despise money. It can be used for so many good purposes. I believe that God has two main objectives for money: (1) the responsible support of our families and our own selves; and (2) the advancement of His Kingdom through our investment in people, churches, and ministries. Chapters on saving, investing, and spending will address that first purpose. Chapters pertaining to giving will address the second.

In summary, it is not a sin to have money. Even being rich is not a sin. Striving to be rich above all else and hoarding riches for purely selfish consumption are what God detests.

## At What Price Will We Sell Our Souls?

How can we tell if we love money? We will examine this from several angles throughout this book, but for starters, here is one way we can know. Is there a price at which we will sell our soul? I'm not talking about selling our soul in the sense of changing our eternal destiny. I'm referring to doing something that compromises our spiritual integrity.

Matthew 26:14–15 records how Judas, one of the disciples, was willing to betray Jesus for thirty pieces of silver. How cheaply he sold his soul! How cheaply he sold out the Son of God.

When I first asked myself whether I would ever compromise my conscience for money, I immediately responded: "Of course not! I would never sell my soul, not at any price!"

But then I remembered this story.

While backpacking around Europe in my late teens, my sister and I were the victims of petty theft on a few occasions. During our stay at a German youth hostel, someone stole the butter knife I kept in my backpack. That knife had been very useful for spreading peanut butter and grape jelly on slices of bread (a backpacker's staple).

After that theft, we wandered around a large department store in search of a new knife. Noticing that the cutlery aisle was totally deserted, I briefly considered shoplifting a knife. I rationalized that in the big scheme of things it would not be wrong. After all, I reasoned, we ourselves had been victims of crime; maybe the universe owed us a knife. Besides, such a large store would never miss one knife.

To this day, I thank God that I had the sense to think these next thoughts: Was it worth selling my soul for a mere butter knife? If I was going to become a thief, why not plan a more ambitious crime, like stealing a million dollars from a bank? This wasn't exactly flawless moral reasoning, but at least I realized that by stealing the knife I *would* compromise my soul. That would be a pretty steep price to pay just to save a dollar. I promptly abandoned my foolish plan and have never again been tempted to steal.

In my law career, I saw many people sell their souls for money. I remember one court case involving a man who had been in a terrible accident years ago. While walking at the side of an unlit highway late at night, he was struck from behind by a vehicle rounding a corner. He *almost* died from multiple injuries to his internal organs but mercifully recovered, except for an alleged back injury that supposedly prevented him from returning to work. During the trial of his lawsuit, he showed up in court each day in a wheelchair, dramatically grimacing every time he shifted his body weight.

He might have fooled the jury except for one revealing piece of evidence. While concealed behind a hedge, our investigator had filmed a surveillance tape of the plaintiff working in his backyard. His video showed the unaware plaintiff merrily performing all kinds of heavy chores. For example, the plaintiff climbed up and down a large pile of firewood with ease. Each time, he picked up an impressive armload of logs and then agilely balanced himself as he walked back down the unsteady pile. He carried all that firewood down into his basement. Needless to say, after viewing that film, the jury did not believe that the plaintiff had a serious back injury. They awarded him absolutely nothing for that claim.

I am sad to say that this was not the only time I saw lust for money affect individuals in court and beyond. Perhaps you recently read about the healthy young woman who lied about having cancer so she could raise some funds for herself.

When it comes to money, is there a price tag on your soul? Have you told a waitress that your eleven-year-old child is only ten to take advantage of the cheaper prices on the kiddie menu? Have you ever failed to declare purchases at customs when returning home from abroad? Are you tempted to fudge figures on your income tax form? Have you ever bought an item with the intention of using it and then returning it? What do you do when you receive wrong change from a cashier and the error rests in *your* favour?

The answers to these kinds of questions tell each one of us something about whether or not we have a spiritual problem with the love of money. Even the fact that a mere dime or dollar is at stake does not absolve our crime. The smallness of the amount just shows us how *cheaply* we will sell out.

Too many in our society are willing to sell their souls to *make* or to *keep* or to *save* a buck. Whether we're talking about petty shoplifting, little white lies, unjustly keeping wrong change, or the massive corporate frauds that brought down WorldCom and Enron—the love of money is, for many, the root of all kinds of evil.

## Harmful Consequences of Loving Money

### Leading a Self-Centred Life

Eighteenth-century economist Adam Smith observed in his classic book *The Wealth of Nations* that the prime motivation for economic growth is selfishness. Those who love money tend to lead self-centred lives. Some eventually recognize that there must be something more meaningful in this life than spending their best energy making and multiplying their wealth. Throughout this book, you will read about many rich, successful people who eventually grew tired of their quest for money and self-gratification. They searched for that "something more" and ultimately found it in a relationship with God.

## Anxiety

Those who have little money might understandably be anxious about how they will make ends meet from day to day. Perhaps they worry about losing the roof over their head or the jacket off their back. A common notion persists that, in contrast, wealthy people enjoy lives of carefree ease. Do you believe that money can buy freedom from worry? When the market takes a downturn, which person tosses and turns at night: the rich person or the poor one? The more one owns, the more there is to be anxious about losing. This anxiety is multiplied many times over for the person who really loves their money. Ecclesiastes 5:12 observes that "…the abundance of a rich man permits him no sleep" (NIV). People can become ridiculously anxious about shifting electronic numbers, stressing about every downtick in their digital accounts even if the decrease will not affect their everyday living.

## Time Loss

It takes time to make money, manage money, and spend money. We then expend further time and *more* money to maintain our possessions, repair them, insure them, protect them, dispose of them, and replace them. Our money and our possessions can become enormously time-costly. Most of us learn this the hard way.

Of course, *some* time needs to be spent on investing our money, buying things, and then taking reasonable care of what we own. For the lover of money, however, an excessive and disproportionate amount of time gets spent on money-related and possession-related matters.

Unlike money, time is a finite resource. All the money in the world cannot buy extra minutes in the hour or extra hours in the day. No matter how rich a person becomes, they still get the same number of hours in the day as the poorest pauper.

Although the point is obvious, I will state it anyway: the more time we spend on our money and our possessions, the less time we have for more important matters.

### Hurting Others

Have you ever watched reality television shows such as *The Amazing Race* or *Survivor*? Isn't it fascinating to observe what people will do in their quest to be the winner of a million-dollar prize? Ordinary people readily badmouth or betray their fellow competitors. Such shows starkly capture some ugly truths about human nature.

Some people perceive themselves as playing the game of life for the grand prize of a bundle of money. How many others do they maul as they fight dog-eat-dog in the marketplace or perhaps in the legal system? I thought about that afresh the other night while watching *The Social Network*, a movie about the men who battled over the billions of dollars generated by Facebook.

Lovers of money create casualties on the family front too. Conflict over money hurts many marriages and vies as a leading cause of divorce; some say it's the number one cause. Sibling relationships can tear apart when parents die and war erupts over the assets left behind. Many lawyers who specialize in either family or estate law have noted that the recent recession caused a sinister spike in those kinds of strife.

Love of material wealth often goes hand in hand with cruelty. In fact, it has led to some of the worst atrocities in history. Slavery became rampant a few centuries ago because it helped plantation owners to maximize their financial gain. Colonial empires sentenced many to death in their pursuit of profits. Pizarro, for example, slaughtered the Incas of Peru so he could obtain their silver and gold to fill the coffers of Spain. Many wars have been waged for the purpose of profit. Perhaps you remember Iraq invading Kuwait for its oil.

### Gambling Addiction

In their quest to get rich, some turn to gambling. In the US, commercial casino revenue topped $34 billion in 2007. In Canada, government-run casinos and lotteries have annually accrued over $13 billion in recent years.[5] Christians can get caught up in this. In Las Vegas, some church-goers put casino chips in the offering plate. The church officials entrusted to cash in the chips have been nick-named "chip monks."

It's no joke, however, that many people develop an out-of-control addiction to gambling. My husband, Sam, and I once knew a neighbour who lost his marriage and his home after his compulsive gambling destroyed his finances.

### Choking Out the Word of God

Jesus told a parable about a farmer who sowed seed on four different kinds of ground (representing four kinds of people who hear the Word of God). Some seed fell on ground covered with thorns. In Matthew 13:22, Jesus explained: "As for what was sown among thorns, this is the one who hears the word, but the cares of the world and the deceitfulness of riches choke the word, and it proves unfruitful."

The prophet Ezekiel, writing about the Israelites of his time, lamented about that same problem: "…they sit before you as my people, and they hear what you say but they will not do it…their heart is set on their gain" (Ezekiel 33:31).

What is your heart set on? Do you prioritize reading the financial section of your newspaper over reading your Bible? Those who prioritize their wealth risk losing sight of God's truth.

### A Futile Finish

At the end of it all, what can the person who lived for money say about their life? What has their consuming passion for money achieved beyond piling up wealth? Of what benefit is their money to them when they cross life's finish line?

---

[5]   www.statcan.gc.ca, last accessed on October 18, 2010.

The apostle James cautioned: "But the one who is rich...will pass away like a wild flower. For the sun rises with scorching heat and withers the plant; its blossom falls and its beauty is destroyed. In the same way, the rich man will fade away even while he goes about his business" (James 1:10–11 NIV).

Psalm 49:16–17 counsels: "Do not be overawed when a man grows rich, when the splendor of his house increases; for he will take nothing with him when he dies, his splendor will not descend with him" (NIV).

Psalm 39:6 sums it up: "We are merely moving shadows, and all our busy rushing ends in nothing. We heap up wealth, not knowing who will spend it" (NLT).

You might have heard about the man who asked his wife to bury all his money with him when he died. She sweetly promised to do so. After his death, she remembered his request. She approached his coffin in the funeral home and slyly slipped a useless cheque beside his still corpse.

John Jacob Astor, the richest man in the world in 1912, was a passenger on the *Titanic*. Along with many others, he lost his life at sea when the ship sank. He had tried in vain to buy a seat in a lifeboat, but soon discovered that his money could not save him. On that tragic night, his vast personal fortune was worth absolutely nothing to him. None of it went down into the dark ocean with him.[6]

### Our Eternal Destiny

The Bible reveals the eternal destiny of those who spend their lives on earth in self-centered pleasure, loving money instead of loving God: "Now listen, you rich people, weep and wail because of the misery that is coming upon you. Your wealth has rotted, and moths have eaten your clothes. Your gold and silver are corroded. Their corrosion will testify against you and eat your flesh like fire. You have hoarded wealth....You have lived on earth in luxury and self-indulgence" (James 5:1–3, 5a NIV).

---

[6] Adams book, p. 18.

Zephaniah 1:18a similarly noted: "Neither their silver nor their gold will be able to save them on the day of the Lord's wrath" (NIV).

One Psalmist warned: "They trust in their wealth and boast about how rich they are, yet not one of them, though rich as kings, can ransom his own brother from the penalty of sin! For God's forgiveness does not come that way. For a soul is far too precious to be ransomed by mere earthly wealth. There is not enough of it in all the earth to buy eternal life for just one soul…" (Psalm 49:6–9 TLB).

Our money cannot connect us with God. It cannot put us in right relationship with Him. It cannot pardon our sins or purchase our salvation. Neither can it buy us a ticket to heaven.

We must all address these matters before it is too late. All of us will have to stand before God someday and give an account of our lives. For better or worse, we will then move on to our assigned eternal destiny.

Everyone, rich or poor, can enter into a relationship with God that will last beyond this life, if they are prepared to love and serve Him instead of bogus gods such as self or money.[7]

## The Noble Few

Some people don't have an issue with loving money. But I suspect their numbers are few.

Genesis 13 tells the story of Abraham and his nephew Lot settling down with their flocks and herds near Bethel. Abraham generously told Lot that he could take first pick of the acres of land surrounding them. Lot chose the best piece of land, the well-watered plain by the Jordan River. Even though Abraham was the elder relative, he graciously accepted second-best. Abraham's counter-cultural action revealed that material wealth did not have a strong grip on his heart.

I discovered some men and women with the heart of Abraham while researching the lives of well-known Christians. Florence Nightingale, for example, grew up in a very wealthy family. In her younger years, she travelled around Europe in great style. Back in England, her family enjoyed both a summer home and a winter estate, and on

---

[7]  See Appendix A.

weekends they often visited friends who were entertaining as many as eighty other houseguests.

Florence was not attached to her wealth. In fact, she found the social whirl of high society to be frivolous, boring, and oppressive. Drawn instead to helping the sick and the suffering, she left her family home to live and work in poor communities. Reading through her diaries, I was quite amazed at the incredible ease with which she abandoned her money and her social station. I was further astonished at the appalling conditions in which she was freely willing to live during the gruelling years she nursed the wounded and dying in the Crimean War.[8] She was the Mother Teresa of her century, a woman with no attraction to money who selflessly served the suffering.

Cut from the same cloth as Nightingale, William Whiting Borden grew up with a blueblood pedigree. Borden acquired an elite education alongside wealthy peers at Yale and Princeton. But in his early adult years, instead of pursuing a profitable profession or spending his inheritance, he started a mission for the poor. He dreamed of reaching the Muslim population in northwest China. Unfortunately, he never made it there. He died of meningitis in Egypt at the age of twenty-five. Although his life was so short, he left behind an enormous legacy. His will bequeathed his inherited fortune to a variety of Christian ministries.[9]

Billy Graham has always struck me as a man who lives above money. Having read several biographies about his fascinating life, it seems to me that his heart has always been primarily focused on knowing God and on leading men and women to Christ. He has travelled to countries all over the globe, preaching to hundreds of millions of people in person (more than anyone else in history) and to hundreds of millions more through media such as television.

He has never sought wealth. On the contrary, he has always earned a modest income and lived in a humble home, unlike other famous preachers who have built mansions.

---

[8]   Wellman book.
[9]   Wiersbe book, p. 32.

Early on, he resolved that money would not be a temptation for him or his team. While creating the Modesto Manifesto in 1948, Graham and his colleagues agreed to avoid even the appearance of financial impropriety or excess. From 1950 on, everyone received a set salary. Graham's salary remained in the five figures for several decades regardless of how high donations tallied each year. His salary did not climb above $100,000 until 1993, almost a half-century after he started his ministry.

Graham advocated financial transparency for both his own ministry and other ministries in America. He set up a Board made up mainly of individuals outside his ministry so he could be held fully accountable for ministry finances.[10]

Strikingly, Billy Graham has still been able to enjoy some of the wealth of this world. As a guest of others, he has golfed some of the finest golf courses and dined in some of the best restaurants. He has even stayed overnight countless times at the White House. He has had personal audiences with the last twelve Presidents of the United States, from Harry S. Truman to Barack Obama. Graham has not stressed or strained to receive those blessings. While simply being faithful and obedient to God's call on his life, he has encountered others who have been willing to share their worldly blessings with him.

Graham's example brings to life the apostle Paul's comment: "We are poor, but we give spiritual riches to others. We own nothing, and yet we have everything" (2 Corinthians 6:10bc NLT). Similarly, Graham has preferred to travel lightly. He has either declined or given away many of the gifts offered to him. When he received two homes as gifts, for example, he promptly donated them to Christian causes.[11]

**The Rest of Us**

What about the rest of us—we who have struggled with the seduction of money? How can we detach ourselves from its lure? We can start the process by turning our struggle over to God. Detaching ourselves

---

[10]  Gibbs and Ostling article.
[11]  Gibbs and Ostling article.

from the love of money will take time, firm resolve, and ongoing reliance on God.

Rees Howells, an exemplary prayer warrior (best known for regularly gathering with a hundred men during World War II to pray for the defeat of the Nazis), humbly understood his need for God's help.

Howells had once dreamed of acquiring a lot of money. Also wanting to serve God, Howells eventually recognized that his strong desire for money was an encumbrance to his nobler pursuit. He decided at one point in time to fully surrender his money-seeking self-nature to God. Howells sensed an inner assurance that God would fill his surrendered soul with His own divine nature.

Over time, as Howells prayed about his hunger for money and worked at adjusting his own heart, God did remove Howells' appetite for riches. It is important for us to see that Howells, by his own admission, was not able to leave his love of money behind without God's help and grace.[12]

Most of us don't seek God's help in this matter so early and so fully in our faith journey. We are not willing to embark on the process of detaching ourselves from the love of money until we encounter some of the snares, destruction, and grief that the apostle Paul warned about in 1 Timothy 6:9–10. The late Millard Fuller, the CEO of Habitat for Humanity for almost three decades, was one such late-bloomer.

I had the privilege of hearing Millard tell his remarkable story in person. He shared about how he grew up in a Christian home and decided in his youth to become a Christ follower himself.

While still a young man, Millard considered Mark 10:24, the Bible verse in which Jesus commented on how difficult it is for a rich man to enter heaven. Millard noted that Jesus said it was difficult, but not impossible, for a rich man to get to heaven. Instead of perceiving the verse as a warning, Millard interpreted it as a challenge. He decided then and there that he would accept that formidable challenge and perform that unusual feat. Using that single verse to convince himself

---

12  Grubb book, p. 37.

that he could freely chase money, Millard resolved that his main mission in life would be to get *very* rich.

By the time he was thirty, Millard had earned his first million dollars. He went on to accumulate all of the properties, cars, speed-boats, and other luxuries he had dreamed of, but his relentless pursuit of money nearly destroyed his family. Along the way, he had paid scant attention to his wife Linda and their children. After Linda left him, he finally woke up to the fact that his marriage was in serious jeopardy.

Millard pursued his wife. He talked her into reconciliation, promising to work hard at rebuilding their marriage on higher principles. They jointly agreed it was time to pursue God above all. Millard asked God to help him let go of his love of money.

Soon after their fresh start, Millard and Linda decided to give away most of their money, change their lifestyle, and commit themselves to full-time Christian service. They started Habitat for Humanity in 1976. Millard no longer dreamt of building his own self-serving business empire; instead, he wanted to build as many decent homes for as many people as he could. During the following decades, his organization built homes for over one million people in about one hundred countries.[13] I invite you to contrast Millard's legacy with the man in India who recently built a one-billion-dollar home for himself.

Millard exchanged his love of money for a deep love for people, including his own wife and children, emanating from a growing love for and reliance upon God.

By giving this example, I am not suggesting that we must all move from a marketplace position to ministry as our primary career or that we must all give away most of our money at a certain point in time. God needs Christians working and ministering in all good professions. What God cares about most is our inner transformation. Among other necessary changes, He wants us to get rid of our natural human instinct to love money, replacing it with a love for God and others.

---

[13]   From a talk given by Fuller at the Ontario Prayer Breakfast in Toronto, Canada on May 14, 2008.

Each one of us can undergo this particular transformation if we combine our own steady resolve with an ongoing plea for God's gracious help.

These are not the last words on the critical subject of relinquishing our love for money. This important topic needs to be approached from different angles as we move on to other facets of what God says about money.

*...in the last days there will come times of difficulty. For people will be lovers of self, lovers of money,...lovers of pleasure rather than lovers of God...*

2 Timothy 3:1–4

*Do not love the world or the things in the world. If anyone loves the world, the love of the Father is not in him. For all that is in the world—the desires of the flesh and the desires of the eyes and pride in possessions—is not from the Father but is from the world. And the world is passing away along with its desires, but whoever does the will of God abides forever.*

1 John 2:15–17

# 3

---

## SERVING GOD OR GOLD

*No one can serve two masters, for either he will hate the
one and love the other, or he will be devoted to the one and
despise the other. You cannot serve God and money.*

Matthew 6:24

*The idols of the nations are silver and gold,
the work of human hands.*

Psalm 135:15

*Turn my heart toward your statutes and
not toward selfish gain.*

Psalm 119:36 (NIV)

No one grows up yearning to serve a master. Instead, our human
instinct drives us to want freedom and self-rule. Yet, eventually, all of
us *do* serve someone or something. Matthew 6:24 (above) asserts that
we cannot serve both God and money. In that regard, we must make
a clear-cut choice.

## Serving the Idol of Money

Some translations of Matthew 6:24 refer to the choice between serving God or serving Mammon. I used to think that Mammon was synonymous with money. Not so. Scholars believe that Mammon was an ancient man-made deity, an idol, believed to have some power over material wealth.[14]

God does not want us to worship idols of any sort. The prohibition against worshipping false gods ranks as the *first* of His Ten Commandments. Yet throughout history, some of God's people have disregarded this prohibition.

On one dramatic occasion, the Israelites worshipped a golden calf they made while Moses was up on the mountain receiving the Ten Commandments from God. When Moses came down from the mountain, he angrily destroyed the golden calf. Then he declared to God: "Alas, this people have sinned a great sin. They have made for themselves gods of gold" (Exodus 32:31).

Over the years, the Israelites kept foolishly believing they could serve idols *and* God simultaneously. Time and again, God warned them about the price they would pay for serving idols. "With their silver and gold they made idols for their own destruction….they sow the wind, and they shall reap the whirlwind" (Hosea 8:4c, 7a).

In Psalm 106:39, the psalmist equated worshipping idols with committing adultery. Believing you can love God and money at the same time is like believing you can get away with loving your spouse and another lover.

Isaiah warned: "All who fashion idols are nothing, and the things they delight in do not profit" (Isaiah 44:9). Paul instructed: "Don't be greedy, for a greedy person is an idolater, worshiping the things of this world" (Colossians 3:5c NLT). Paul further advised: "Therefore, my beloved, flee from idolatry" (1 Corinthians 10:14).

We are to serve God and God alone. However, people continue to worship and serve gold. No one consciously worships Mammon

---

14　Hill and Pitts book, p. 14.

anymore, but many still serve loyally at the pagan altar of materialism. They don't actually bow down to worship before a pile of dollar bills or bricks of gold—their idolatry is more subtle, usually consisting of placing too high a value on material possessions and perhaps the high-octane careers that power the purchase of more possessions.

## How Do We Serve God?

When we think of serving God, we often think of church activities such as cutting carrot sticks for a banquet, taking shifts in the nursery, or teaching a Sunday school class. Valuable as all those acts of service are, I've come to see that serving God cuts a much broader swath across our lives. God wants us to serve Him 24/7 in every facet of our lives.

How does a servant serve any master? In simplest terms, a servant obeys the commands and demands of the master. Or, put another way, a servant follows the instructions of the master. If God is our chosen master, what commands are we expected to obey and what instructions are we to follow? In broad terms, we are to obey the instructions God has given us in the Bible. Of course, we do not have the space here to address all of God's commands! So let's zero in on two of them.

In Matthew 22:37–40, Jesus revealed the two *most important* commandments. Firstly, we must love God with all of our heart, mind, and soul. Secondly, we must love others as we love ourselves. We may never understand the entire Bible, but I suspect that every one of us can understand those two clear commands.

In this chapter, we will seek to integrate Matthew 6:24 (serving God or gold) with obeying the two supreme commands of Matthew 22:37–40.

## Where Career Fits In

At some point, most of us will pursue a career. We all need to support ourselves financially unless someone else is appropriately supporting us.

The apostle Paul had a career as a tent-maker. He continued with this trade even while he was travelling around developing and encouraging churches.

Jesus worked in the trade of carpentry for many years. As was the custom in those days, He likely began apprenticing in His early teens. He did not begin His life of public ministry until He was thirty. Have you ever stopped to consider that Jesus had a marketplace career for most of His adult life?

Work is one significant dimension of our personal purpose for being on this earth. Just because we work, and make an income doing so, doesn't necessarily mean that we are serving gold instead of God.

Having said that, there's clearly a big difference between working to live and living to work. We are not meant to idolize our careers or the money they make for us. We should not become career-crazed.

I invite you to reflect on your answers to the following questions. Consider how you are presently living your life in regard to the Matthew 6:24 choice (choosing to serve God or gold) and the two key commands of Matthew 22:37–40. Your answers will help you honestly assess the place that career/income generation actually holds in your life compared to serving God by loving Him and loving others as you love yourself.

- Do you regularly make the time to attend church services and other church events? Or are you usually too tired after a busy day/week at work?

- Do you ever work on Sundays, at home or at the office? How often? Are you a nurse, an emergency physician, or a pastor with no choice in the matter?

- Do you set aside time each day for meaningful spiritual devotions?

- Do you take time to serve in some form of volunteer ministry, whether at church, with a parachurch organization, and/or in the marketplace?

- Can you put the brakes on your work? Can you sometimes say "no" to your boss? Could you turn down a promotion (assuming good reasons for doing so)?

- Do you feel called or driven? Do you feel God is in charge of your career path, or are you obsessed with self-motivated ambition? Are you stressing, straining, and striving to get ahead in your career or calmly, prayerfully, and peacefully putting one foot in front of the next? How would you describe your career pace?

- In your career, do you care more about pleasing God or pleasing people?

- Does the thought of further material acquisition/ consumption routinely motivate you to keep at it or to step it up?

- Do you routinely work more than forty to fifty hours a week? If so, have you had a sincere discussion with God about whether this is really necessary?

- Does your spouse complain about how much you work?

- Do you often miss significant events in your children's lives (parent-teacher meetings, sports games, birthday parties, awards ceremonies, graduations, etc.)?

- Do you take regular holidays with the people you care about? Do you take work with you? Do you constantly check your cell phone or your laptop for work messages? Can you focus on your loved ones?

- Have you ever been able to put your career on the back burner in order to pursue priorities such as raising children or caring for a sick family member?

- Do you socialize with mostly work colleagues? Do you genuinely care about them or are you using them to advance your career?

- How often do you socialize with non-work-related friends? How often do you visit extended family? How well do you know your neighbours?

- At social events, do you talk most often about your career or your latest purchases or your spiritual journey?

- Does it matter to you that new acquaintances learn what kind of work you do? Do you tell them at the very earliest possible opportunity? Are you more eager to tell them what you do for a living than to identify yourself as a Christian?

- Is your physical or emotional health suffering because of work? Is your work interfering with your sleep or with your ability to pay proper attention to exercise and nutrition? Do you work so hard you have no time to visit your doctor, your optometrist, or your dentist?

- Do you measure your self-worth by your income or your career achievements and advancement?

Matthew 22:37–40 *unequivocally* establishes that the first and greatest commandment is to love God with all of our heart, mind, and soul. Loving and serving God involves being in a *relationship* with Him. All relationships take time and commitment. Do your answers to the questions above indicate that you are regularly giving your relationship with God adequate time and sincere commitment? Can you honestly say that your relationship with God is your highest daily priority? Is God clearly more important to you than your career and your income?

If you are not yet in a relationship with God (or not sure if you are), have you been setting aside any time to explore what it means to enter into such a relationship?

Loving others and properly loving our own selves also takes quality time and authentic commitment. What do your answers to the above questions tell you about the degree of attention you are giving to your relationships with others and to your personal self-care relative to career advancement and income generation?

I invite you to notice that there's *nothing* in the Matthew 22:37–40 passage about career or money. In eternity, only God and people will remain. If we truly obey the two most important commandments, and genuinely prioritize relationships ahead of career and money, we set the right foundation for serving God instead of gold.

## Easier Said Than Done

Living according to right priorities can be a real challenge in this hectic modern world. This was the realization that greeted me the moment I entered the career world in my mid-twenties. I will briefly share with you three circumstances I encountered, back in my early days of practicing as a trial lawyer on Bay Street, which tested my priorities. (I will tell you about tests which I "passed," although I must humbly confess that I did not pass *every* test of priorities I faced!)

The first situation tested whether my primary allegiance was to God or to my career. A senior lawyer asked me to come in to the office on a Sunday for a client meeting. I knew this kind of request would crop up again. With God helping me to have bold resolve, I said no.

This senior lawyer had just seen the movie *Chariots of Fire*[15], the true story of runner Eric Liddell. Liddell, a strong Christian, refused to run his Olympic qualifying heat on a Sunday, a decision which could have cost him his opportunity to compete. In fact, Liddell was later offered the chance to run in a different length of race on another day and, although he was not trained to run that particular distance, he

---

[15]  *Chariots of Fire*. Directed by Hugh Hudson. 1981. Hollywood, CA: Twentieth Century Fox, 1981.

won an Olympic gold medal. My senior colleague loved the movie. Thankfully, Liddell's story helped this colleague to respect my decision regarding working on Sundays. In fact, this lawyer respected my Christian convictions so much that he sometimes thereafter allowed me to leave work early for charity board meetings and on a few occasions extended my vacation time so I could participate in mission trips overseas. I'm glad I spoke up about the Sunday issue.

The second early test of my priorities involved whether or not I would put my career ahead of a significant relationship. One afternoon, a senior lawyer I was assisting announced that we would have to work late into the night. I nervously told him that I had promised to attend my mom's birthday dinner that night. Ranting and raving, he told me that it was not appropriate for the junior person on the file to skip out of the office for a few hours. He was offended that I would be leaving him to slave over the documents while I went out and partied. How unprofessional of me!

I will never forget the incredulous look on his face when I held my ground and announced firmly (although my knees were knocking!) that I was stepping out for dinner. I prayed under my breath as I left his office. He told me not to bother coming back at all that night and that I would not have a job to come back to in the morning.

I wasn't sure how serious his threatening words were—I remember thinking that if this unpleasant incident was any indication of the way my career was going to play out, maybe I didn't want to keep this job. I refused to value my career more than the people I love. I had no problem working into the evening some nights, but that night I had to draw a line.

I dared to show up at the office the next morning. The senior lawyer rather sheepishly carried on working with me as if nothing had happened. Ironically, I outlasted this lawyer at my firm.

Soon after, I faced a third situation that tested whether my career had become more important than taking proper care of my own self. On the first day of a trial I had been asked to junior, the senior lawyer asked me to use my lunch hour to run case-related errands. After court resumed that afternoon, I wrote a note to my colleague, telling him I was going to slip out for a quick bite. He scribbled a note back. Court was in session—being hungry was no excuse to leave! With an apologetic smile, I quietly stood up, bowed respectfully to the Judge, and left the courtroom.

I went to the court cafeteria and ordered a tuna sandwich. I felt some trepidation as I wolfed down my meal, but I also felt a sense of indignation. I knew that this was not just about one missed lunch. I knew that if I didn't take this stand to take care of myself, I would miss many more lunches over the next weeks, months, and years.

I expected the lawyer to berate me after court ended that afternoon. Instead, he grinned, pleased that I was made of tougher stuff than he had thought. Over the following days, I usually had to use my lunch hour to prepare for our afternoon witnesses. My colleague graciously allowed me to take time for lunch afterwards, even if that meant slipping into court a little late.

I cannot think of a single day I missed lunch in all my later years of practice. It's not that food is so important to me. The lunch habit was always about taking good care of my health, on every level, in the midst of pursuing the high-stress career I felt called to work in. God has made us all stewards of our bodies, minds, and emotions, and we need to take loving care of ourselves. Is any job worth compromising our physical, mental, or emotional health?

The above episodes provide just three examples of work situations in which I had to decide whether I would put God, other people, and proper care of my own self ahead of career success. In each case, I knew my decisions put my fledgling career at risk along with the income it made me. I believed then, and still believe now, that I made the right decisions in accordance with Matthew 22:37–40. In each case, God protected my career and my ongoing relationships with the three lawyers involved.

Although they were not major crises, learning to stand up with backbone in those situations helped me to stand up tall when tougher decisions came along. When we learn to be faithful to our Christian priorities in simple everyday matters, we are more likely to be faithful to God when much bigger issues are at stake. In making decisions, large or small, we must be true to our Christian convictions and priorities *above* being loyal to our careers and the money they make us.

Of course, I fully understand that at times we have to work on a Sunday, or cannot attend a special event for someone we care about, or have to skip a meal. But shouldn't those times be the exception, not the rule?

In your career, I encourage you to be bold and brave about Matthew 22:37–40 priorities in your numerous daily decisions. In doing so, you will prove to God that you are willing to serve Him and His principles instead of serving gold. Have faith that God will honour every right choice you make in this regard and that your career will be enhanced, not harmed over the long haul. Even if you end up having to look for a new job, trust that God will help you to find a position that is more conducive to right priorities.

## Curtailing Career Aspirations

After I married and had children, I faced the toughest choice of my career: whether to cut back on my full-time law practice to be home more with my kids. Figuring out my priorities had become a lot more complicated. After much thought, prayer, and discussion with my husband, I negotiated a part-time work arrangement with my firm, an arrangement that was not common in my profession. The senior lawyer who had respected my decision not to work on Sundays championed my family priorities and spearheaded the approval process. My new reduced-hours arrangement allowed me to take on fewer client files than most of my colleagues, although thankfully the work continued to remain appropriate to my increasing level of seniority. It was a miracle of sorts that my firm graciously allowed me to work on this "mommy track" for the following sixteen years.

Reduced hours (and reduced billings) came at a price. I thereafter made a lot less money than I could have made and I never moved into a corner office.

My husband, Sam, made some counter-cultural career decisions too, reflecting his own Matthew 22:37–40 priorities. Way back when Sam and I decided to embark on familyhood, Sam gave up his residency in pediatrics, which had been at a prestigious children's hospital. He started a general medical practice so he could devote more hours to priorities other than work.

I'm not trying to put Sam and myself up on some pedestal. I know many other couples who have made similar career cut-backs while raising their families.

Nor do I wish to criticize those who currently work hefty hours in law, medicine, or any other career. No cookie-cutter solution fits everyone in this matter of how much time and energy gets spent on career. The fledgling stage of a career may demand more than forty hours a week. It did for me. Furthermore, not everyone will marry. Not everyone will have children. Those with children may have a different kind of support system in place than I had. Hearing God's voice regarding our individual career trajectory is a very personal matter. Most Christians, however, will find that at *some* point they will have to navigate their career path differently than their non-believing colleagues if they want to authentically live by the supreme priorities described by Jesus in Matthew 22:37–40.

## Moving from the Marketplace

God may call some of us (not all of us) to serve Him by switching from a marketplace position to ministry as our primary career. My sister, for example, chose to give up her successful career in film production years ago in order to start afresh in media work for Christian organizations. I suspect she took a big cut in pay. She later gave up her film career altogether to engage in full-time humanitarian work. She has been an aid worker in Afghanistan for over sixteen years.

Many well-known Christians have sacrificially moved from a marketplace career to a full-time ministry career.

As a young man, legendary evangelist D. L. Moody worked long hours as a salesman. He aspired to become rich. In 1856, he set the lofty goal of making $100,000 (a *lot* of money in that century). On Sundays, he taught a Bible class to slum kids.

Eventually, he faced a pivotal choice. He was offered a new, better-paying job that would involve considerable travel. He would have to give up his Sunday class. Moody saw the value of the job offer, but he also highly valued his Bible class. Moody talked to a business friend about his agonizing decision. The friend provided an unexpected solution to the situation; he generously gave Moody a railroad pass, which enabled Moody to travel home every weekend. God thereafter helped him to prosper in his new sales position *and* still minister to the one thousand slum children who showed up for his class each Sunday.

Over time, Moody found his financial ambitions waning. He finally lost all interest in making a personal fortune. After praying about it, Moody quit his sales job and from that day forward worked in full-time ministry.[16] Moody travelled one million miles as an evangelist, preaching to about 100 million people and leading at least 750,000 people to Christ. These numbers are remarkable, considering that 19th-century global travel would not have been easy.

Billy Sunday, born a generation after Moody, made a substantial income as a professional baseball player. After playing in the major leagues for eight years, he felt God call him into career ministry. He also became an evangelist, travelling far and wide, living on what he received from free-will offerings. Early on, Billy and his wife often had little to eat. As Sunday's ministry became better known, the offerings became larger, but they never came anywhere near the income he could have made had he carried on as a pro baseball player. Like Moody, Sunday preached to 100 million people and won about one million souls to Christ. These numbers are enormous when we consider that he preached in the years before media facilitated reaching large audiences.[17]

Several decades later, Bill Bright (founder and long-standing leader of Campus Crusade for Christ) also began his adult life seeking to achieve success in the secular world. In 1943, Bright started a company

---

[16] Bailey book, (*D. L. Moody*), pp. 53–65; Petersen book, p. 41.
[17] Petersen book, pp. 92–98.

that provided gourmet food items to upscale stores in Los Angeles. His new business rapidly achieved financial success.

While attending a Navigator Bible study, Bright realized that something was missing in his life. His business success was not meaningful enough. Money no longer dazzled him. Eventually, he gave his life to Christ and decided to leave the business world. In the early 1950s, he started a ministry on college campuses, wholeheartedly resolving to serve God, not gold.

Campus Crusade for Christ has grown, over the past fifty years, to become one of the largest interdenominational ministries in the world.[18] Originally focusing on college students, it now ministers to business leaders, professionals, athletes, ambassadors, and many others. Although he himself had left the business world, Bright recognized that God wanted others to *remain* in secular careers. Bright spent most of his life spiritually supporting and enriching those Christians. Grateful wealthy donors offered him luxury vehicles and high-end homes; he repeatedly refused such offers.[19]

Contemporary ministry leader Bob Buford enjoyed a very successful first career as a cable television magnate. In mid-life, he left that business to start The Leadership Network, an organization that nurtures church growth. He has also spent time authoring best-selling Christian books such as *Half Time,* (a great book aimed at those searching for significance in mid-life, especially those wanting to add more of a ministry dimension to their lives).

I had the privilege of meeting the late Sam Ericsson, a graduate of Harvard Law School. He left a prestigious law practice in Los Angeles to lead the Christian Legal Society. In 1991, he started Advocates International, an organization which now networks tens of thousands of Christian lawyers in over 130 countries around the world and which operates task forces that seek to fight corruption, uphold the sanctity of life, protect family values, advocate for the poor, and promote freedom of religion.

---

[18]   Rusten book, pp. 482–483.
[19]   Lindsay book, p. 168.

In my mid-forties, God came knocking on my own heart.

After twenty years of practice, I felt called to leave my law career to spend more hours on various Christian ministries. Most of my time now is spent on my writing and speaking ministries and serving on the Boards of Christian organizations.

Many ask me how I could walk away from a career I spent years training for and which paid me hundreds of dollars per hour. How could I trade a career that I loved for ministries that pay significantly less, if they pay anything at all? Money-wise, there's simply no comparison between my law career and my present ministries. In some ways, it *was* hard to walk away from my practice. I resolutely made this change, however, because I believed that God was asking me to serve Him in a new way *and* because decision after decision over the years had kept me free from golden handcuffs. I was encouraged by the examples of so many others who had made a similar transition.

### The Marketplace Still Matters

The above stories are not intended to elevate ministry-as-career above marketplace careers. Nor do I suggest that everyone will be called to move from the marketplace to ministry as primary vocation. One calling does not rank higher than the other.

I believe that our responses to the questions posed earlier in this chapter hold greater significance than where we work. I concur with Bill Bright, who opined that God needs people in both the marketplace and ministry careers. God cares that we serve Him and His priorities first, whatever our specific calling may be.

It takes a very strong Christian to serve God in the marketplace, in the midst of so many material temptations. Perhaps God places some of His strongest servants there.

I have met many in the marketplace who clearly give God highest priority in their lives. They have found manifold ways to minister *in* the marketplace. Furthermore, they give much time, money, and energy to churches and charities. Who can measure the impact Christian marketplace leaders have across our nation and around our world?

Throughout this book, I will attempt to balance examples of Christians who serve God in the secular world with those who have chosen ministry as their primary career. Wherever we work, whether in the marketplace, in a ministry career, or in the home, we *all* have to make frequent decisions that determine whether we are serving God or gold. The state of our heart will govern these decisions, not our job description.

## God Will Test Us

Along the way, God will test all of us to see whether we are serving Him or serving money. Our decisions will show Him who or what we are really serving.

For some, obeying and serving God might mean turning down an attractive new job offer if, for example, God does not want them to leave their church or uproot their family to move across the country. For others, obeying and serving God might mean just the opposite — accepting a promotion in a new city with its own costs: family upheaval and leaving valued friends and fellowship behind. For yet others, obeying and serving God might mean giving up career altogether to stay home to raise children.

We need to watch out for the tests that will come into our lives — the tests that will determine whether we care most about money and career (even if that career is full-time ministry) or care most about loving and pleasing God in the way that we live our lives. As we respond to those tests, I can pretty much guarantee that choosing to serve God above all else will cost each one of us something.

## Other Idols of Gold: Material Possessions

Careers are not the only golden idols of this age. Our possessions can also be golden idols. We can easily deify our homes, cars, clothes, golf clubs, and tennis racquets just as much as we deify our careers.

God warned the Israelites about adopting the idols of the surrounding cultures: "You must burn their idols in fire, and you must not covet the silver or gold that covers them. You must not take it or it will become a trap to you…" (Deuteronomy 7:25 NLT).

Moses, who recorded those words, had to choose between his possessions and his God. Because he stood up for God's people in Egypt, Moses had to flee, leaving behind the treasures of Pharaoh's court (Hebrews 11:24–27). For the next four decades, he lived with meagre possessions on the backside of the desert.

We all own *some* material possessions. While travelling for long periods, I still owned a backpack, clothes, books, and toiletries. Even the homeless can often be seen pushing their possessions around in stolen shopping buggies. However much we own, let's remember that whatever we own can, in some measure, own us. Our possessions can too easily become snares. We need to be prayerful about what we accumulate. Maybe we should think twice before we buy a bigger home, another car, a vacation property, or a leisure boat. Our possessions *will* cost us more than money. We have to use up precious time (and money) maintaining and repairing what we own. Sometimes our possessions create extra hassles in our lives. "Better is a little with the fear of the Lord than great treasure and trouble with it" (Proverbs 15:16).

We are not meant to serve material things. They are meant to serve us while we serve God.

## Not Judging Others

How human it is to judge one another! It's too easy to make negative assumptions about a fellow Christian who is the CEO of a big corporation, especially if he drives a nice car, lives in an upscale home, and wears expensive suits. How quickly we might think of him as a mere pew-warmer, less spiritual than others.

As I talked with many wealthy Christians in the course of writing this book, they complained about the unfairness of facing this attitude of judgment all the time. Many of them are sincere Christians who are doing much to advance God's Kingdom.

In Matthew 7:1, Jesus told us to stop judging one another. Appearances don't always tell the whole story. Only God truly knows the inner attitude of the heart. Man is prone to look at the outward appearance, whereas God looks into the heart (1 Samuel 16:7). Not one of us is in a position to judge the decisions that others make regarding their careers, incomes, lifestyles, or possessions. Only God knows who is truly serving Him above all.

## In Closing

Albert Einstein once said that anyone who isn't lost in awe at the wonder of the universe is like a burned-out candle. Is that what many of us have become, he wondered? Have we become like candles without flames, toiling in darkness—and all of that for the sake of mere money? Have we so lost ourselves in our laborious quest for money that we have lost our awe for the vast, magnificent universe?[20]

Let's reframe Einstein's query: have we lost our awe and reverence for the *Creator* of our amazing universe—all because we are too focused on toiling for money?

It's not too late to recover our awe and reverence for our Creator. We can choose each day, first and foremost, to love and serve God instead of gold. I do not want to be a candle without flame, toiling in the darkness for lifeless gold.

God or gold: we must declare our prime allegiance to one *or* the other.

> *The Lord your God will soon bring you into the land he*
> *swore to give you…It is a land with large, prosperous*
> *cities…When you have eaten your fill in this land, be*
> *careful not to forget the Lord…You must fear the Lord your*
> *God and serve him.*
>
> Deuteronomy 6:10–13a (NLT)

---

[20]  Kullberg book, p. 90.

*And the devil took [Jesus] up and showed him all the kingdoms of the world…and said to him, "….If you, then, will worship me, it will all be yours." And Jesus answered him, "It is written, 'You shall worship the Lord your God, and him only shall you serve.'"*

Luke 4:5–8

*…serve the Lord with all your heart. And do not turn aside after empty things that cannot profit or deliver…*

1 Samuel 12:20b–21

# 4

---

# Our Security System

*Trust in your money and down you go!*

Proverbs 11:28a (NLT)

*Look here, you who say, "Today or tomorrow we are going to a certain town and will stay there a year. We will do business there and make a profit." How do you know what your life will be like tomorrow?*

James 4:13–14a (NLT)

*Enjoy prosperity while you can, but when hard times strike, realize that both come from God. Remember that nothing is certain in this life.*

Ecclesiastes 7:14 (NLT)

*Where will your treasures be safe?*

Isaiah 10:3c (NLT)

On the infamous day now known as 9/11, business executives had gathered together to sign paperwork pertaining to a deal that would merge two companies. Expensive due diligence had been performed. Everything was set to close the deal. My personal stake in the deal was an anticipated shareholder pay-out in a six figure amount.

Before the deal could be consummated, however, two hijacked planes flew into the World Trade Towers. Along with the history of humankind taking a dramatic turn that day, my personal history took an unexpected hit.

As soon as they heard about the tragedy in Manhattan, the executives stopped signing the paperwork. The deal was put on hold. No one could predict how the events of 9/11 would impact the two companies involved in the deal. What did appear crystal clear on that day was that the economy of the whole world would be severely shaken. Financial confusion and instability would reign for a while.

The deal never did close. My cheque never arrived and life went on.

I was not alone in my financial loss. Most people perused an altered balance sheet. Even before 9/11, some had lost a portion of their net worth when the dot.com bubble burst. On the financial front, 9/11 delivered the second blow in a row. At least it was just money—I am profoundly grateful that neither I nor any of my loved ones lost life or limb on 9/11.

Over the next few years, many people got back up on steadier financial feet. Spending resumed. People felt safe incurring further debt. The future looked rosier.

Just as people began to enjoy a greater sense of financial security (or perhaps a little financial amnesia), the housing bubble burst in America. New trouble began as the subprime mortgage crisis caused another round of turmoil in markets around the world.

By mid-2008, the global financial crisis became full-blown. Described as the greatest economic meltdown since the stock market crash of 1929 (and the consequent Great Depression), the rapidly deteriorating situation began to impact everyone everywhere. The media bombarded us with news about factory shutdowns, escalating unemployment, home foreclosures, record numbers of bankruptcies, devalued pension funds, a massive credit crunch, banks going under, and deeper nosedives on the stock market. Most people began to feel very vulnerable.

The wealthy and the powerful were not exempt from the stress. Hank Paulson, who formerly held a prominent position at Wall Street investment bank Goldman Sachs, had been Secretary of the U.S. Treasury since 2006. When the global meltdown heated up in the fall of 2008, Paulson apparently stressed to the max. He slept only three hours each night. He gulped down diet soda for breakfast. He either vomited or dry-heaved in between the many meetings he attended during long, hectic days. He lived this way for weeks, worried sick over financial matters.[21]

The situation became so grim that on September 24, 2008, American President George Bush went on television to alert Americans that they were perilously close to the collapse of their banking system. On a larger scale, America stood on the very brink of total economic disaster. Here are some excerpts from his astonishing speech: "This is an extraordinary period for America's economy....We're in the midst of a serious financial crisis....[O]ur entire economy is in danger....The market is not functioning properly. There has been a widespread loss of confidence, and major sectors of America's financial system are at risk of shutting down. The government's top economic experts warn that, without immediate action by Congress, America could slip into a financial panic and a distressing scenario would unfold."

Soon after, the U.S. Congress began taking drastic measures, including an unprecedented $700-billion bail-out of failing companies. World leaders met with urgency. In unison, they poured mega-billions into their economies to stave off shipwreck.

By the second quarter of 2009, governments had injected an unthinkable fifty trillion dollars into the ailing global economy. Yet still, the foreclosures, insolvencies, and market free-fall continued. In

---

[21] Timm article ("An insider...").

America, the Big Three auto makers publicly cried out for help. We all watched in shock as many other venerable corporate giants floundered. Trillions of dollars of corporate assets evaporated into thin air. Ordinary people struggled and suffered.

Fresh waves of financial insecurity kept washing around the globe as nations staggered through the ongoing recession, still fearing an all-out financial depression.

Although some recovery is now in progress, the world economy still stands on shaky ground. America is now trillions of dollars in debt to countries such as China. Many European countries have also assumed catastrophic levels of debt. Natural and man-made disasters, from earthquakes to tsunamis, hurricanes, volcanic eruptions, and massive oil spills, have further exacerbated the economic havoc.

2000–2010: it was quite a decade.

As we ponder all of that loss, instability, and ongoing financial uncertainty, we may pause to ask ourselves the following questions. On what do we base our personal financial security? Is it even possible to feel financially secure these days?

## The Two Alternatives

Only two real options exist when it comes to financial security. We can choose to base our primary security on that which seems tangible: our jobs, bank accounts, insurance policies, retirement funds, other assets, government spending, and the whole financial system undergirding those things. Or we can find our ultimate security (financial and otherwise) in our relationship with, and obedience to, our God.

Those of us who embrace the Christian faith will hopefully choose the second option. Yet *knowing* where our true security rests does not necessarily translate into actually *living* by that knowledge.

America, for example, considers itself the most Christian nation on earth It also ranks as one of the wealthiest nations on earth and, relatively speaking, one of the safest nations. Harvard professor Niall Ferguson notes, however, with irony, that Americans are also the world's most insured people.[22] Is it possible that many Christians trust in their insurance policies more than in their God? I am not bashing insurance—it's wise to have *some* coverage. However, having spent years litigating insurance matters, I can tell you that insurance policies cover a lot less than we might assume.

To reveal where our security actually rests, let's dare to ask ourselves some probing questions. Is *all* of our personal wealth deposited in treasuries and storehouses in *this* world? Or have we made substantial eternal investments by giving money to advance God's purposes? In which realm do we hold the greatest deposits? What ratio exists between our earthly deposits and our eternal deposits?

We all tend to store up a lot of our treasure here on this earth, even though it can quickly dissipate in so many ways. Material assets can be destroyed in a matter of minutes in fires and floods. We can be robbed on the street. Our homes can be broken into. These days, money can also be stealthily stolen through identity theft. Harvard professor Niall Ferguson points out that we all face unknowable futures, which have the constant ability to take us by surprise.[23]

Even what we safely keep does not stay new and shiny forever. My husband learned this lesson when, shortly after buying a new sports car, he sat down in the driver's seat with a screwdriver in his pocket, ripping the expensive leather. I learned a similar lesson when I drove through an automated car-wash without first putting my aerial down…oops!

Our sense of material security ends up resting in the same place where our prime assets reside. If most of our wealth is stored in a bank somewhere, then our faith and trust and security must rest in this world's man-made financial systems.

Jesus told us, in Matthew 6:19–21, that heaven is the *only* place where our assets can be truly secure. He instructed: "Do not lay up for yourselves treasures on earth, where moth and rust destroy and where thieves break in and steal, but lay up for yourselves treasures in heaven,

---

22   Ferguson book, p. 5.
23   Ibid., p. 178.

where neither moth nor rust destroys and where thieves do not break in and steal. For where your treasure is, there your heart will be also."

If we have given much to advance God's purposes and bless others, then we can enjoy the inner stability and sanity that flow from security in God Himself. He has promised to safeguard all that we have given to Him. In John 14:2, Jesus promised that He will prepare a room for us in His mansions in heaven. Such material security can also rest on the premise that all of our ongoing income and all of our future assets in *this* world ultimately come from the hand of God, not from a particular job or a particular person or a particular investment.

No one develops this kind of financial peace and security overnight. I certainly didn't. When my butter knife was stolen during my teen-age year of back-packing, I was discombobulated for days by that violation of my material security. You will recall that I came close to shop-lifting a replacement knife. How deeply the loss of a small stainless steel utensil rocked my soul! A few years later, when I had trouble finding work one summer (work that I needed so that I could pay my university tuition) I burst into frantic tears at the end of one unsuccessful job interview.

Over the years, as Sam and I invested in God's purposes, a sense of financial security developed that did not depend on the current state of our investments or on the stability of our jobs. Slowly, my security switched from those tangible things to my evolving trust in a loving God. No matter what Sam and I gave away, God continued to bless us with more than enough to meet our needs.

My growing trust in God also became the basis for my ability to make decisions such as refusing to work on Sundays, attending my mom's birthday dinner, and walking out of court to buy a tuna sandwich, even though I thought that those decisions could jeopardize my embryonic career in law. Even by then, I was beginning to recognize that my *real* financial security rested in God, not man. We cannot truly learn to serve God instead of gold unless we concurrently learn that our long-term financial security rests in God's hands. These two concepts need to be closely integrated.

When my anticipated cheque did not materialize after the business deal suddenly collapsed on 9/11, I took it in stride. I'm neither super-spiritual nor dim-witted. I had simply settled in my mind, over decades of living, that my true financial security rests in God alone. I felt strangely peaceful after the hijacked business deal, knowing that my well-being still safely resided in the One who guards all that has been entrusted to Him.

Let's stop seeking *any* security in the institutions in this world, our personal assets, or any particular source of income. We can still use those institutions, own some assets, and earn an income, but our security does not have to be based on those entities.

Everyone has heard about the safety of the venerable Swiss banks; they seem to have been sturdy bastions for eons. Did you know that even the Swiss National Bank has only been around since 1907—just over a century?[24] It's probably a lot less sturdy than we might suppose. Why should any of us look for our financial security in our governments or our banks or the companies that employ us instead of in the living God, who has been around since the beginning of all time?

The Book of Revelation warns us that the world is moving toward a time when there will be one central world government and one integrated economic system. Ultimately, Christians will not be able to participate in buying and selling unless they are willing to deny their faith. Only those whose security is unshakably in God will be able to stand firm in their faith in that coming era.[25]

On the back of the American ten-dollar bill are the words "In God We Trust." In dealing with our financial affairs and otherwise, let us resolve anew to ultimately trust in God alone. Although He may allow some financial endeavours to fail, He will, by His grace, cause others to prosper. No matter what tough times we travel through, He will never fail us or forsake us.

---

[24]   Ferguson book, p. 58.
[25]   Revelation 13:5–10, 16–17.

*In the blink of an eye wealth disappears, for it will sprout wings and fly away like an eagle.*

Proverbs 23:5 (NLT)

*...whoever listens to me will dwell secure and will be at ease, without dread of disaster.*

Proverbs 1:33

*You shall do my statutes and keep my rules and perform them, and then you will dwell in the land securely. The land will yield its fruit, and you will eat your fill and dwell in it securely.*

Leviticus 25:18

*As for the rich in this present age, charge them not to be haughty, nor to set their hopes on the uncertainty of riches, but on God, who richly provides us with everything to enjoy. They are to do good, to be rich in good works, to be generous and ready to share, thus storing up treasure for themselves as a good foundation for the future, so that they may take hold of that which is truly life.*

1 Timothy 6:17–18

# 5

————

# OUR ETHICS

*If you are faithful in little things, you will be faithful in large ones. But if you are dishonest in little things, you won't be honest with greater responsibilities. And if you are untrustworthy about worldly wealth, who will trust you with the true riches of heaven? And if you are not faithful with other people's things, why should you be trusted with things of your own?*

Luke 16:10–12 (NLT)

*I always take pains to have a clear conscience toward both God and man.*

Acts 24:16

*But as for me, I shall walk in my integrity…*

Psalm 26:11

We learn in the Bible that, by nature, the heart of man is desperately wicked and that even the hearts of little children are bent towards folly.[26] I know that's true because as a young child I made some wrong decisions.

When I was six years old, I was allowed to walk down my street to a store called Larry's Confectionary, just so long as someone else came along. On the afternoon that I committed my first (and last) criminal offence, I walked to Larry's store with a friend.

We entered the store, excited about buying a nickel's worth of candy. I picked out some jaw-breakers. They were round black candies, the size of a marble. When you sucked on them, the black colour disappeared, uncovering successive layers of other colours. Jaw-breakers lasted such a pleasurably long time.

I went over to the cash register to pay my nickel, but Larry was nowhere to be seen. My friend and I quickly conspired to rush out of the store without paying for our candy. We could save our nickels for another day!

We made a run for it, thinking we were making a clean getaway. What a perfect crime! Unknown to us, Larry had been watching from the storage room.

We sat for a while on a neighbour's front lawn, savouring our candies. We didn't go home until we had finished our last jaw-breakers; intuitively, we knew we should get rid of all of the evidence of our theft.

As soon as I walked into my house, I could tell from the looks on my parents' faces that I was in *big* trouble. Larry had apparently phoned them. When confronted with the accusation that Larry had made, I compounded the awful situation by lying to my parents. I denied that I had even gone to Larry's store, not realizing that my tongue and lips were stained a tell-tale dark black—I had not destroyed all of the evidence after all!

I deserved the royal spanking I received. I also had to "serve time" in my bedroom that whole evening. Thankfully, those punishments reformed my delinquent heart. I never stole anything again.

---

[26] Jeremiah 17:9; Proverbs 22:15.

Later, while still a six-year-old, I literally ran down the aisle in a church service to accept Christ. When the pastor talked about all of us being sinners, even as a young child I *could* relate to that. With the stolen candy episode still fresh in my mind, I realized that, on occasion, I had more than a black tongue—I sometimes had a black heart. As a six-year-old, I did not have full understanding of what it meant to commit my life to Christ—I later made a more mature adult commitment at the age of nineteen. I did, however, comprehend that I needed God's forgiveness and His help to resist the temptation to sin.

Numerous biblical accounts portray unethical conduct in connection with money. John 12:6, for example, reports that the disciple Judas dipped into the contents of the money-bag that Jesus had put him in charge of, thus becoming a thief before he became a betrayer. Matthew 28:11–15 describes how the soldiers guarding the tomb of the crucified Jesus were willing to lie—to falsely say that the disciples snuck in to take the body of Jesus—in exchange for a "sufficient sum of money" (v. 12).

For all of man's supposed progress through the ages, not much has changed on the ethics front. Basic human nature has not evolved. This past decade, the news has been full of stories of terribly unethical behaviour. Bernie Madoff, for example, is alleged to have perpetrated the largest investor fraud ever committed by an individual, ripping numerous people off to the tune of more than $50 billion.

Ethical issues don't just reside in the CEO suite. The ethics of the average worker are also sliding. In the television show *The Office*, the character Dwight lies, tricks, manipulates, and profits off of those around him with devilish glee. Yet he has been a popular cultural icon.

In the business world, there's a new version of the "golden rule": He who has the gold can make up the rules!

## Biblical Ethical Principles

To address our base human nature, the Bible contains many ethical principles regarding money. We can choose whether or not we will live by them. People with a heart to serve God will try to make right ethical decisions, even when it costs them. Those who choose, above all, to love and serve gold will likely make some wrong decisions. Sooner or later, they will sneak a forbidden little treat out of life's cookie jar.

What is it that the Bible disapproves? Unethical financial behaviour can involve theft, fraud, cheating, extortion, bribery, and other dubious activities—in the workplace or otherwise. I invite you to ponder these verses pertaining to financial ethics:

- You shall not steal; you shall not deal falsely… (Leviticus 19:11)

- You shall not oppress your neighbor or rob him… (Leviticus 19:13)

- You shall have just balances, just weights…. (Leviticus 19:36)

- Honesty guides good people; dishonesty destroys treacherous people. (Proverbs 11:3 NLT)

- Treasures gained by wickedness do not profit… (Proverbs 10:2)

- Better to be poor and honest than to be dishonest and rich. (Proverbs 28:6 NLT)

- A good name is to be chosen rather than great riches… (Proverbs 22:1)

- Like a partridge that hatches eggs she has not laid, so are those who get their wealth by unjust means. At midlife they will lose their riches; in the end, they will become poor old fools. (Jeremiah 17:11 NLT)

- What sorrow awaits you who build big houses with money gained dishonestly! You believe your wealth will buy security, putting your family's nest beyond the reach of danger. (Habakkuk 2:9 NLT)

- What shall I say about the homes of the wicked filled with treasures gained by cheating? What about the disgusting practice of measuring out grain with dishonest measures? How can I tolerate your merchants who use dishonest scales and weights? The rich among you have become wealthy through extortion ....Therefore, I will wound you! I will bring you to ruin for all your sins. You will eat but never have enough. Your hunger pangs and emptiness will remain. And though you try to save your money, it will come to nothing in the end. You will save a little, but I will give it to those who conquer you. You will plant crops but not harvest them. You will press your olives but not get enough oil to anoint yourselves. You will trample the grapes but get no juice to make your wine. (Micah 6:10–15 NLT)

- Bread gained by deceit is sweet to a man, but afterward his mouth will be full of gravel. (Proverbs 20:17)

- Such are the ways of everyone who is greedy for unjust gain; it takes away the life of its possessors. (Proverbs 1:19)

Spend a moment also pondering how angry Jesus was at the money-changers and pigeon-sellers in the Temple (see Matthew 21:12–13). Jesus dramatically overturned their tables to show His disapproval. He was upset that His place of worship had become a "den of robbers" instead of a place of prayer. Notice that He said "robbers," not merchants. There seems to have been an element of dishonest gain in their activities.

Godly character is more important than financial success. Yet some people remain irresistibly tempted by the lure of success. A prominent Canadian judge, presiding over the trial of two well-known business titans charged with fraud and forgery, compared the two accused men to athletes who resort to taking performance-enhancing drugs. The corporate successes of the businessmen were spectacular, she noted; too bad that the foundation of their achievements was unscrupulous cheating.

Becoming a Christian does not automatically reform our hearts. The wise among us diligently study the ethical principles in the Bible *and* purpose to obey them. They deliberately set high standards for themselves that they will not compromise.

Perhaps we need to gain a better grasp on how much God *hates* dishonesty. The Book of Acts, chapter 5, tells the story of Ananias and Sapphira. They sold some land and then lied to their fellow Christians about the amount for which they sold it. Both of them died that very evening. The ending of this story is very sobering. God was not upset that they had sold some land and made some money. The real issue was their lack of honesty and integrity before God and man.

Sadly, we still hear from time to time about professed Christians who violate ethical principles. One notorious example is the late Ken Lay. The son of a Baptist preacher, and a Christian himself, Lay became well-known in evangelical circles as a prominent philanthropist who contributed more than $25 million to charity. He rose to the position of CEO at Enron. His dramatic downfall is a tragic story. On his watch at Enron, the company's books became scandalously inaccurate. Accountants wildly inflated the company's assets and profits. Over a five-year period, they overstated profits to the tune of $567 million; they understated long-term debt by $25 billion. Investors and employees suffered losses of billions of dollars when Enron went bankrupt in 2001. In 2006, Ken Lay was found guilty of all ten charges against him, which included making false statements, bank fraud, and securities fraud. Perhaps mercifully, he died of a heart attack at age 64, before he could be sentenced to a long jail term.[27]

Bernie Ebbers provides another shocking example. He presided as CEO of Worldcom during the time it perpetrated the largest corporate fraud in U.S. history. He once taught a Sunday school class and had

---

[27]   Ferguson book, pp. 172–174; Johnson article.

also generously supported many Christian charities. Where did he go off the rails?[28]

Every one of us has likely lied, stolen, or cheated at some point, even if it was back in our childhood. St. Augustine of Hippo, a great theologian whose brilliant writings have influenced many centuries of Christians, once admitted that for a time even he was enmeshed in habits of theft and dishonesty.[29]

Thankfully, there is hope for all of us who are willing to change our ways. God promises to forgive all of our sins, including ethical errors, if we confess them to Him and repent. True repentance means turning our wills one-hundred-and-eighty degrees, purposing to thereafter walk in the opposite, superior direction. If we repent of lying, stealing, or cheating, we must deliberately resolve never to engage in these kinds of behaviours again. Perhaps we will stumble and fall a few more times (as I almost did when I flirted with the thought of shoplifting that knife in a German department store), but with God's help we *can* live by a much higher standard. It's never too late to change our ways. "Let the thief no longer steal, but rather let him labor, doing honest work with his own hands..."(Ephesians 4:28).

The late Peter Drucker, who was a Christian, has been called the greatest business management expert of all time. He often discussed ethics. Drucker opined that sometimes we can't clearly see what the right thing is—but we *can* see what the wrong thing is or at least what is questionable. If the behaviour is wrong, or even questionable, then we must avoid it. At times, we may intuitively know what is wrong more easily than we can discern what is right.

After years of being a management consultant for some of the largest corporations in the United States, and after authoring almost forty books and numerous articles for prestigious journals, Drucker spent the last years of his life helping non-profit organizations through his Foundation. He also mentored church leaders such as Rick Warren, who used to meet with him twice a year over a two-decade period.[30] To

[28]   Lindsay book, p. 174.
[29]   Article by unspecified author ("Self-Examination...").
[30]   Karlgaard article.

the end, Drucker taught with authority that great success in the world of finance and beyond can be achieved without ever compromising ethics and integrity.

Being ethical encompasses keeping one's word. Whether we write our words in a formal contract or speak them alongside a simple hand-shake, we must honour our promises and commitments. Numbers 32:24 simply instructs us: "…do what you have promised."

Being ethical also involves treating employees fairly and giving them a decent wage. I love Loren Cunningham's advice: we must love people and use things, not love things and use people.[31]

Being ethical also involves small everyday decisions such as not overlooking a mistake in our favour on a restaurant bill.

## In Closing

I am deeply grateful that my childhood candy theft was discovered and that my wise parents suitably punished me. In my later years as a lawyer, millions of dollars of clients' money passed through the trust accounts I was responsible for. Thankfully, I had learned to live by high standards of ethical integrity.

Let's pay serious heed to the ethical dimension of our financial lives. We are warned in verses such as Proverbs 11:3 that our dishon-esty *will* destroy us if we carry on with a corrupted attitude of heart. High ethical principles must be integrated into all of the other finan-cial principles we live by if we hope to see God's blessing upon our finances.

> *Better is the little that the righteous has than the*
> *abundance of many wicked.*
>
> Psalm 37:16

> *…a poor man is better than a liar.*
>
> Proverbs 19:22

---

[31] Cunningham book, (*Daring…*), p. 107.

*...he is a shield to those who walk in integrity...*

Proverbs 2:7

*Whoever walks in integrity walks securely, but he who makes his ways crooked will be found out.*

Proverbs 10:9

*...he who hates unjust gain will prolong his days.*

Proverbs 28:16

# 6

---

## HOLDING MONEY TIGHTLY

*A stingy man hastens after wealth...*

Proverbs 28:22

*...if your wealth increases, don't make it*
*the center of your life.*

Psalm 62:10b (NLT)

*It is possible to give away and become richer! It is also*
*possible to hold on too tightly and lose everything.*

Proverbs 11:24–25 (TLB)

In 2008, Harvard Business School professor Niall Ferguson published a fascinating best-seller called *The Ascent of Money: A Financial History of the World*. His book explores the thesis that money has been the back-story behind all the major historical events that have shaped the world. In studying the significance of money throughout various periods, Ferguson noted the fluctuations between greed and fear that money provokes. As business cycles move from bullish times to bearish times, greed turns to fear until a bullish cycle reoccurs and greed resurfaces.

This chapter will examine three reasons why we sometimes hold onto our money too tightly. I will add the sin of pride to the greed and fear factors.

## Greed

Greed forms part of our sinful human default setting. If we want to live by God's financial principles, greed is an attitude of heart and mind that we must uproot.

Jesus despised greed. He spoke angrily against the Pharisee religious sect because they were "full of greed and self-indulgence" (Matthew 23:25b).

The apostle Paul also spoke stern words about greed: "Do you not know that the unrighteous will not inherit the kingdom of God? Do not be deceived: neither the sexually immoral, nor idolaters, nor adulterers,…nor thieves, *nor the greedy*, nor drunkards…will inherit the kingdom of God" (1 Corinthians 6:9–10). In 1 Corinthians 5:11, Paul taught that we should not associate with fellow Christians who are greedy. Clearly, greed is a sin of serious magnitude.

The apostle James warned: "Look here, you rich people: Weep and groan with anguish because of all the terrible troubles ahead of you. Your wealth is rotting away, and your fine clothes are moth-eaten rags. Your gold and silver have become worthless….This treasure you have accumulated will stand as evidence against you on the day of judgment….You have spent your years on earth in luxury, satisfying your every desire. You have fattened yourselves for the day of slaughter" (James 5:1–3, 5 NLT).

Greed is closely connected to coveting—wanting what others have. God was so against coveting that He plainly prohibited it in the Ten Commandments: "you shall not covet your neighbor's house…or anything that is your neighbor's" (Exodus 20:17). In Ecclesiastes 4:4, King Solomon warned about envying what others possess. Jesus cautioned: "…Take care, and be on your guard against all covetousness, for one's life does not consist in the abundance of his possessions" (Luke 12:15).

Notwithstanding these powerful biblical admonitions, the world often treats greed nonchalantly. At the start of a revolving cycle, society initially permits greed and perhaps even glorifies it. At the close of the cycle, society then reviles those who have been greedy. Harvard professor Niall Ferguson wrote, for example, about the dazzling rise of the Medici banking family in 15th-century Italy. After a period of admiring the Medicis, the population developed resentment towards their enormous wealth. In the Bonfire of the Vanities, an inflamed mob stormed the Medici palace and burned paintings, sculptures, clothing, books, and banking records.[32] That angry mob foreshadowed later uprisings against outrageously wealthy elites during the French and Russian Revolutions.

Greed remains a part of the human story in modern times. American President Carter said this in 1979: "In a nation that was proud of hard work, strong families, close-knit communities, and our faith in God, too many of us now tend to worship self-indulgence and consumption. Human identity is no longer defined by what one does, but by what one owns. But we've discovered that owning things and consuming things does not satisfy our longing for meaning. We've learned that piling up material goods cannot fill the emptiness of lives which have no confidence or purpose."[33] Much scorn was heaped on Carter for this speech. Not many took his words to heart. In fact, the ridiculously greed-ridden 1980s began just months after Carter's speech.

In 1987, the movie *Wall Street* portrayed an unscrupulous corporate raider named Gordon Gekko, whose motto was that greed is good. At times, it was hard to tell whether Gekko was meant to be a villain or some kind of twisted hero.[34] Michael Douglas, the actor who played Gekko, recently commented that he often runs into people who consider Gekko a hero.

---

[32] Ferguson book, p. 48.

[33] From President Carter's infamous "malaise" speech of July 15, 1979.

[34] *Wall Street*. Directed by Oliver Stone. 1987. Hollywood, CA: Twentieth Century Fox, 1987.

In 1987, Tom Wolfe published his best-selling novel *Bonfire of the Vanities,* describing a modern version of the greed that the public had revolted against in the original Bonfire centuries before. In Wolfe's novel, bond trader Sherman McCoy thought of himself and other Wall Street titans as Masters of the Universe. By the novel's end, the mighty bond trader had, prophetically, fallen.

Throughout history, the church has not been immune to greed. In our times, some televangelists and mega-church pastors have faced accusations of material excess in both their personal and ministry lives. A few well-known Christian leaders have been found legally guilty of financial wrong-doing.

Corporate greed has run rampant during this past decade. Barack Obama (then a Senator) noted that, in the year 2005, the average CEO in America earned 262 times what the average worker earned.[35]

In Canada in 2008, the top one hundred CEOs earned over $7 million each, about 174 times the amount the average wage-earner received ($42,305). If you were to consider only the top fifty CEOs in Canada, the ratio was even more ridiculous: 243 to 1. Now consider this snapshot of January 4, 2010: by the time the lunch hour rolled around on the *first day* back to work in that new year, the top Canadian CEOs had each already raked in the total amount the average worker would make in the whole year to come.[36]

In recent years, we all watched as Wall Street imploded under the weight of the unprecedented greed of its bankers and executives. Michael Moore's provocative 2009 documentary *Capitalism: A Love Story* depicted the ferocious Main Street backlash against Wall Street greed.[37] I confess that I found some moments in that documentary quite humorous. In one scene, Moore dramatically unspooled yellow crime-scene tape around the offices of a Manhattan investment bank. He then tried to make citizen's arrests of the executives leaving the building. He had arranged for a Brink's truck to back up to the front

---

[35]   Obama book.

[36]   Flavelle article.

[37]   *Capitalism: A Love Story.* Directed by Michael Moore. 2009. Hollywood, CA: Overture Films, 2009.

doors of that skyscraper and, with a bullhorn, he asked the bank executives to give back the billions of bail-out dollars. Of course, none of
the theatrics accomplished anything in those moments, but Moore got
his point across.

I attended a reception at the Canadian Embassy in Washington D.C.
not long after I saw Moore's documentary. Our ambassador shared how
much anger he had sensed in many of the Americans he had met—
anger at the blatant excesses of Wall Street, the government bail-out of
big banks and big corporations, and the outrageous bonuses the fat cat
executives had taken even after their firms had received bail-out dollars.
It seems that no lesson was learned. The *Wall Street Journal* reported
that, in 2010, the pay and benefits doled out at the top 25 publicly traded
Wall Street banks and security firms added up to a record-breaking
$135.5 billion.[38] Of course, executives should be well-compensated for
their hard work, but not with over-the-top salaries and bonuses.

Greed is so easy to spot in others but often difficult to detect in
our own selves. Why? We compare ourselves to those *above* us on the
social ladder. We see some people in our churches driving nicer cars
than us, living in fancier neighbourhoods, and taking more exotic vacations. We smugly console ourselves by believing that *they* are the
greedy ones. If we have the courage to change the optics, to begin
looking at those *below* us on the social ladder, we might see ourselves
in a more painfully revealing light. Let's dare to change the optics. Let's
stop comparing ourselves only to the titans of Wall Street. Let's also see
ourselves relative to Mother Teresa and the poor masses she served.

Further warnings about greed will weave through later pages.
God's indictment of greed must stand as a *weighty* counterbalancing
principle to what God says about meeting our needs, granting our
good desires, investing our money, prospering, and spending.

## Pride

Pride can cause us to hold onto our money very tightly, especially if
we take particular pride in our possessions and our status in society.

---

[38]   Article by an unspecified author ("Bankers...").

Pride can prompt us to flaunt our wealth, sometimes insufferably so. Who likes to be around someone who is perpetually in boast mode?

To some extent, money *does* buy worldly admiration. Our money and our possessions can attract attention and recognition. To ratchet up the "cool" quotient in our lives, we may be tempted to wear the hippest clothes, show off the latest home decor, and own the newest toys. While there's nothing wrong with occasionally updating what we own, an ever-present compulsion to buy things to impress others is a spiritual danger sign. It can also become a fast-track to racking up a lot of unmanageable debt.

The Bible warns us that negative consequences follow this kind of prideful lust for social esteem and worldly approval. In Isaiah 39:1–6, for example, we learn about how King Hezekiah foolishly showed off all his treasures to envoys from Babylon. Not pleased with King Hezekiah's pride in his possessions, God told him that everything the King had so proudly boasted about would soon be carried off to Babylon. There's a powerful lesson here about resisting the urge to be show-offs with a "look-at-me" or "look-at-my-car" or "look-at-my-ring" attitude.

The apostle John also cautioned against having pride in our worldly possessions: "Do not love this world nor the things it offers you, for when you love the world, you do not have the love of the Father in you. For the world offers only a craving for physical pleasure, a craving for everything we see, and *pride* in our achievements and possessions. These are not from the Father, but are from this world. And this world is fading away, along with everything that people crave…"(1 John 2:15–17a NLT).

**Fear**

Fear also tempts us to hold onto our money very tightly: fear of economic downturns; fear of losing our jobs; fear of our investments shrinking; fear of not having enough; and fear of living longer than our savings last. All of this is undergirded by an insidious general fear of somehow losing all of our money if we dare to loosen our grip.

Fear is fed when we immerse ourselves in the media. In striking contrast, the apostle Paul advised that faith comes by immersing ourselves in the Word of God (Romans 10:17).

Fear also ties in with the source of security we have chosen. If we have decided to base our security on our job, our insurance, our government, and/or our investments, then we are sitting ducks for episodic bouts of fear. In contrast, if we have firmly decided to see God as the ultimate source of our security (financial and otherwise), we will be far less prone to fear, even when circumstances take a negative turn.

If we are bound by fear with regards to our money, we will not be able to handle our careers properly. We will not be able to say no to excess work or take the risk of making a career change. Fear will sorely shackle us to our jobs. Fear can literally enslave us. Golden handcuffs can snap on just as readily from fear as they can from greed or from pride in our financial status.

Those who harbour a lot of fear in connection with their money have trouble investing wisely. They often panic as soon as bear markets come along and hastily sell their investments at a loss. The fearful tend to re-invest during a bull market when prices are up; the investments seem safer but they are acquired at a high cost. Successful investors do not let fear rule their decisions.

When a lot of people fear and panic (as they did at the outset of the Great Depression), the entire economy can be badly shaken. Fear multiplies. For instance, fear and panic—even hysteria—once again fastened a grip on the masses when the recent global recession first hit. People wanted to stock up on whatever they could while they could. In late 2008, a Walmart employee was trampled to death by a frantic bargain-hunting crowd that ran wild on a sale day.

When financial calamity strikes, our knees do not have to buckle. To overcome our fears, worries, and anxieties regarding money, we can follow the advice Jesus gave in Matthew 6:25–34. In that passage, Jesus told His followers not to be worried about material needs but instead to put God first and then all their needs would be met. He also advised us to live one day at a time, not concerned about tomorrow.

If we learn to do that, we will be better able to live peacefully in the present, not worrying about worst-case scenarios that might happen in the future.

## Facing the Consequences

Ambitiously acquiring more money than we need, and then holding onto our money too tightly, impacts our physical and mental health. It does not matter if the tight hold derives from greed, pride, or fear. It is highly stressful to slave in the proverbial salt mines each day, when gold is our master, and just as stressful to ensure our hoarded stores of wealth are tightly guarded. What does stress lead to? Migraines, high blood pressure, digestive problems, insomnia…

Society at large will suffer when its citizenry is afflicted by greed, pride, and fear. The recent global crisis freshly demonstrates that this toxic trio can create an incredibly potent weapon of economic mass destruction.

> *At the time that he was the wealthiest man in the world,*
> *John D. Rockefeller was asked how much money was*
> *enough. He replied: "Just a little bit more."*[39]

> *They will throw their money in the streets, tossing it out*
> *like worthless trash. Their silver and gold won't save them*
> *on that day of the Lord's anger. It will neither satisfy nor*
> *feed them, for their greed can only trip them up.*
>
> Ezekiel 7:19 (NLT)

---

[39]    Robertson book, p. vii.

# 7

————

# HOLDING MONEY LIGHTLY

*...if riches increase, set not your heart on them.*

Psalm 62:10

Instead of holding tightly, we can learn to hold our money and possessions lightly. I have benefited enormously in this regard from the deep insights of the late Chinese author and church leader Watchman Nee. His classic book, *Love Not the World*, gave me much to think about when I first read it during my twenties. I've since re-read that book several times to the point where my only copy is falling apart.

Before I came across Nee's book, I used to be perplexed by the story in the New Testament in which Jesus told a rich young man that he should sell everything he had and give the proceeds to the poor. Could it be that God requires this of *all* of us right *this* moment? Is giving literally everything away the *only* alternative to holding onto our money too tightly?

## Examining the Story of the Rich Young Ruler

Perhaps that story has unsettled you too. Let's be brave enough to examine it. Matthew 19 records the full account of the rich young man who came to Jesus, asking what he must do to inherit eternal life. Jesus told him that he must keep the commandments. The young man said that he was already keeping the commandments; he asked Jesus what else he must do. Jesus responded: "If you would be perfect, go, sell what you possess and give to the poor, and you will have treasure in heaven; and come, follow me" (Matthew 19:21). That struck a sensitive nerve in the rich young man.

In Christian circles, I don't think we will ever reach a complete consensus on the exact meaning and application of this passage. Some take the passage very literally. They believe they should live with next to nothing. I do not judge them. Most Christians, however, do not agree with such an extreme interpretation or such radical practical application.

Let's examine the Matthew 19 story from three different angles.

As the conversation with the rich young man unfolded, I imagine that Jesus looked into the heart of the specific individual to whom He was talking. He knew this young man was generally able to follow the commandments. To his credit, this young man was willing to turn over a substantial part of his life to God. I suspect, however, that Jesus knew in advance that this young man was spiritually vulnerable and non-committal in one key area: he was too attached to his wealth.

When Jesus raised the issue of money, the young man ended the discussion. He walked away from Jesus sadly, but nonetheless abruptly. He could submit all the other areas of his life to God, but when it came to money…that was the deal-breaker.

Perhaps he was still placing all of his security in his wealth. Perhaps he had issues with greed, pride in his possessions, or money-related fear. We don't really know what was going on in his heart. But Jesus did. Jesus knew that He had to get this young man to unclench the tight grip that he had on his wealth.

God didn't need the young man's money. God already owns everything—the whole world is His. Even the richest person on earth possesses (on temporary loan) a very tiny drop in the universe-sized bucket of what God owns. God is not primarily interested in any of our wealth *per se*. He is far more interested in our *attitude* towards whatever money we have. The more tightly our hand clenches our money, the more painful it will be for God to pry our hand open. However, it is important to point out that not every rich person holds their money in a tightly-closed fist.

Here's a second angle from which to consider the Matthew 19 story. In his final statement to the young man, Jesus addressed what it takes to be "perfect." By that point, Jesus was no longer talking about the minimum threshold standard expected of us. Instead, He was talking about the highest possible standard, indeed the standard of perfection.

Notice that Jesus did not initially mention this matter of selling possessions and giving the proceeds away. I do not think Jesus absent-mindedly forgot to mention this matter at the outset. Jesus told the young man to sell his possessions only after the man said that he had met the threshold matters already outlined by Jesus. Jesus then went on to describe what was needed to *perfect* this young man's soul. Perhaps we can compare this to the difference between what is expected of a student to pass a test and what is required to achieve a perfect mark. Most of us do more than pass, but we do not necessarily achieve perfection.

Let's move on to my third angle on this story. Jesus treated the rich young man differently than He treated some others. Jesus did not consistently tell the various people He met to sell everything they owned and then give the proceeds to the poor. We can contrast the story of the rich young ruler with the story of Zaccheus, who was also a rich man. His story unfolds in Luke 19:1–10. To better see Jesus in the midst of the crowd, Zacchaeus climbed up into a sycamore tree. Jesus, knowing that Zacchaeus had a hungry heart, stopped beside the tree and paid personal attention to him. Jesus told him that He wanted to visit his home. Zacchaeus was so impacted by Jesus that he voluntarily promised to give half of his belongings to the poor and to restore fourfold any monies he had defrauded. Note that Zacchaeus did not promise to give everything away. Zaccheus offered to part with *some* of his money, but not all. Jesus commended Zaccheus's gesture: "Today salvation has come to this house..."(v. 9).

We can also contrast the story of the rich young ruler with the surprising story of the woman who poured a bottle of very expensive perfume on Jesus. Here's what happened after she did that: "The disciples were indignant when they saw this. 'What a waste!' they said. 'It could have been sold for a high price and the money given to the poor.' But Jesus, aware of this, replied, 'Why criticize this woman for doing such a good thing to me? You will always have the poor among you, but you will not always have me....I tell you the truth, wherever the Good News is preached throughout the world, this woman's deed will be remembered and discussed'"(Matthew 26:8–13 NLT).

Jesus treated this woman as a unique individual. He looked into *her* heart and approved *her* motive. The fact that the perfume was expensive and that it could have been sold to help the poor was not on the front burner for Him at that time.

We cannot read one passage in Scripture (e.g. the story of the rich young ruler) and assume it applies to everyone everywhere in exactly the same way. Each story in Scripture needs to be weighed and balanced alongside the rest of Scripture. One thing I get out of comparing these three stories is the consistent inference that Jesus primarily cared about the state of each person's heart in regards to what they owned. He responded to them dissimilarly, according to what He discerned.

## What About Us?

God cares about all of our hearts. He will do whatever it takes—ask for whatever He asks for—to get each one of us to grow more mature and more willing to fully commit everything to Him (our money included). Because each one of us is in a different place spiritually, God will deal with each one of us differently. Not everyone has a problem with loving money or with holding onto it too tightly. Furthermore, God has different plans and purposes for each one of us. Some individuals will need to keep a portion of their money to fulfil their destiny. We are all placed in various positions in the world, financially and otherwise.

God deals with each one of us both intimately and individually, but always lovingly.

Watchman Nee's book helped me to see that God may not require each one of us to literally give everything away. Nee taught me that God does, however, want each one of us to be *willing*, in our *hearts*, to give what we have, if and when He does ask us. God wants all of us, at a minimum, to be generous givers. In the process of giving, we actually do have to let some of our money and possessions go. And we constantly have to be ready to give more—whatever He asks.

That's the nub of it. We must be sincerely willing, in our hearts, to part with our wealth (in whole or in part). That's why we must hold onto our money and our belongings very lightly. We can *touch* the material world; indeed, we must touch it to survive. But touching or handling money and possessions is not synonymous with grasping them tightly.

John the Baptist taught that when we turn to God we must bear fruit in keeping with repentance. It is interesting that the three examples John then provided had to do with money (Luke 3:8–14). An authentic signature of faith is a heart truly willing to be set free from money's grip. That is not, however, the same thing as totally releasing all of our money at a particular point in time.

Imagine that we all *did* give everything away this very hour—our homes, our cars, our business wardrobes, our laptops. In the short term, churches and Christian organizations would be flush with cash. This year would be a great year for ministry and missions—but what about next year, and the year after? Many of us could not carry on working without our cars or laptops or business suits. The great ministries would soon grind to a halt. After a season of plenty, famine would set in. Common sense alone tells us that, obviously, not all Christians are meant to literally and simultaneously give away everything this very moment.

## God Will Test Our Hearts

Just as Jesus tested the heart of the rich young ruler, God will, at various points in our lives, test all of our hearts. Such tests are more for our sakes than for His. God already knows how tightly or how lightly you and I hold onto our money and our possessions. By testing us in some fashion, He wants *us* to see the state of our own hearts.

I have failed some tests and passed some tests along the way. At times, I have felt clearly led to give away some money or one of my possessions and I did not. Usually, it wasn't an out-and-out refusal. Most often, I promised myself I would give *later* that week or that month, but time passed and I never got around to it. I have learned that, in God's eyes, good intentions are worth absolutely nothing. If they are not promptly acted upon, good intentions are nothing but self-comforting, self-delusional thoughts that make us feel good and noble—but they don't deceive God.

Other times, I have passed the test. I have been willing to give what God has asked me to give. Here's one highly memorable example. When my husband and I still had a large mortgage and a young family, we heard God unmistakably tell us to write a cheque for a certain sum to help an individual at our church. We knew that this person, by doing something very wrong, had been the cause of his own financial trouble. It would have been so easy to justify why we should not help this person.

We could not, however, dispute God's clear tug on our hearts to give that specific sum. We prayed about it and discussed it. In unity and at peace about the issue, we wrote the cheque. We were not rashly or irrationally giving our money away on sudden impulse or in the emotion of the moment.

Whenever any of us are in this kind of situation, we must thoughtfully and prayerfully decide what God would have us do. We must mix wisdom and prudence into the process, bearing in mind that we must always maintain appropriate financial responsibility for ourselves and our families. Holding onto our money lightly must not be confused with letting it go randomly or carelessly.

I can't leave the above story without telling you about its conclusion. Our financial gift helped the individual climb out of the hole he had dug for himself. We later heard that he was greatly encouraged that anyone in the church wanted to assist him notwithstanding his wrong behaviour. We did not expect that our financial gift would ever be repaid. It had been given as an anonymous gift. That very same month, however, our investment account went up by *just over* the sum we had given. God—not the individual—paid us back in full almost immediately. God doesn't always work exactly like that, but I feel compelled to report that He did on that particular occasion.

Our hearts are also tested when we are robbed or cheated. I was robbed in a crowded marketplace in India when a pack of pushing children distracted me and one of them grabbed a small amount of cash, an old watch, and some cheap sunglasses out of my purse. (He thankfully missed taking the folder containing my passport, plane ticket, and traveller's cheques.) I felt violated and incensed. Later, I was able to recognize that the children needed the money a lot more than I did. My initial upset and pathetic lack of compassion told me a lot about how tightly I was holding onto my money and my possessions.

Willing. We must be willing. We must always be ready to part with our material assets. We must hold them very lightly. If we don't have a strong and tight grip on our money, it will never have a strong and tight grip on us. I don't apologize for hammering home that point with re-emphasis. Be ready—God *will* ask for something. He will likely ask on many occasions. Take time to learn how to hear His voice clearly.

He may even ask you to give up the career that generates your money in the first place. We need to be ready on that front too. Maybe the day will come, maybe not. Jesus asked His first disciples to give up everything, including (and especially) their marketplace careers. Peter, for example, was a fisherman. Matthew was a tax collector. Both walked away from their homes, their possessions, *and* their livelihoods. In Mark 10:28, Peter remarked on how he and the other disciples had given up "everything," leaving it all behind to follow Jesus. D. L. Moody, Billy Sunday, and Bill Bright also walked away from profitable careers to follow the call of Jesus.

In this book, we will also talk about many others who have *stayed* in high-paying positions—with God's blessing and for His purposes.

They feel called to minister where they are. They have not, as physical fact, given up everything. To remain sincere and authentic Christians, however, those holding such positions must always be ready and willing to give up anything or everything (whether money or position or both).

We must relinquish any right we think we have to our money or our material goods. Hmmm…relinquishment…not a word we hear very often these days!

## Look Into Your Heart

Aside from observing our own reactions when God individually tests us, how do we know if we are holding onto our wealth lightly or not? Let me ask you this: How were you feeling as the global economy started to unravel at high speed a few years ago? Think back to the great financial meltdown of 2008–09. As you followed the media reports during that scary roller-coaster ride, what were you thinking and feeling? Did you experience worry and anxiety? Did your spirit sink every time you opened your investment statements? How closely and how uncomfortably were you monitoring the stock markets?

Honestly recalling what we were thinking and feeling during that recent meltdown will tell each one of us a lot about how tightly or how lightly we hold onto our worldly wealth. This, of course, integrates with the issue we discussed earlier regarding in what/whom we place our security.

## Eternal Focus

The more that we focus on eternity, the more lightly we can hold onto our money and material possessions. I have always loved the psalmist who called himself "a traveler passing through" this life (Psalm 39:12d NLT). In my two years of backpacking, I always travelled very lightly. In those days, I thought twice about owning *any*thing because I had to carry its weight on my back from place to place. If we remember that we are simply pilgrims on this earth, bound for another place, the less attached we will be to anything in this world and the less weight we will want to carry.

We can also benefit from occasionally reminding ourselves that we will have to leave everything behind when we leave this world. You have probably heard the old saying: On the way to the cemetery, we can't drag a U-haul behind our hearse.

## Gratitude and Contentment

To hold on lightly, we need to displace greed with attitudes such as gratitude and contentment. Greed focuses on what we don't have; greed wants more and more. Greed has no idea how to curb its voracious appetite. Greed prevents generosity from taking root. On the other hand, gratitude and contentment focus on what we already have and help us know how to decide this is enough. Those who are grateful and content can readily give and share. When possessions or money are given away, gratitude and contentment can easily adjust to having less.

God loves an attitude of gratitude. How *deeply* grateful each of us ought to be for everything—from the food on our table to the clothes on our back to the roof above our heads.

Regarding contentment, the apostle Paul wrote: "…I have learned to be content whatever the circumstances. I know what it is to be in need, and I know what it is to have plenty. I have learned the secret of being content in any and every situation, whether well fed or hungry, whether living in plenty or in want" (Philippians 4:11–12 NIV).

Paul shared another perspective on contentment in 1 Timothy 6. In that chapter, he exhorted us to be content if we have food and clothing. In my years on the road, living out of a backpack, I learned a lot about how to be sublimely content with very few worldly possessions. It *is* possible to be wonderfully content with simple food and a small amount of clothing and not much else.

We can learn to be more and more content. We can learn how to accept financial ups and downs in life without letting them affect us. We may never achieve perfection in this area, but we can all benefit from improving on this front.

I admire the attitude of the prophet Habakkuk, who penned these words: "Even though the fig trees have no blossoms, and there are no grapes on the vines; even though the olive crop fails, and the fields lie empty and barren; even though the flocks die in the fields, and the cattle barns are empty, yet I will rejoice in the Lord! I will be joyful in the God of my salvation!" (Habakkuk 3:17–18 NLT). Like Paul, Habakkuk knew how to be content in any situation.

## In Closing

The Israelites were taught that they were not the owners of their wealth. God spoke, for example, regarding the land He had given them: "The land must never be sold on a permanent basis, for the land belongs to me. You are only foreigners and tenant farmers working for me" (Leviticus 25:23 NLT). We, too, are trustees and beneficiaries, not owners, of all that God has temporarily loaned to us.

From time to time, let's genuinely ask ourselves the following questions. Are we willing, in our hearts, to relinquish our material wealth? Are we willing to give, give up, let go, leave behind…whatever He asks of us? Can we be grateful and content with whatever is left? Can we delicately hold whatever passes through our hands in sacred trust?

> *I came naked from my mother's womb, and I will be naked when I leave. The Lord gave me what I had, and the Lord has taken it away…*
>
> Job 1:21 (NLT)

# 8

---

## SURROUND SOUND

*Train a child in the way he should go…*

Proverbs 22:6 (NIV)

Our unique personal backgrounds influence the way we view and handle money. In dealing with all of the inner attitudes we have discussed, it helps to understand what has shaped us.

### Childhood Influences

We learned our very first lessons about money while listening and observing in our family homes. We discovered soon enough whether our family was rich, poor, or middle class. We noticed how our parents acquired money, spent money, and saved money, and whether or not they ever gave any of it away. We picked up on whether they held onto their money and possessions tightly or lightly.

We also heard stories about grandparents, aunts, and uncles. We visited their homes. We learned about their work, play, and travel. Perhaps we wanted to grow up to be just like some of them—or not.

Our family histories have strongly impacted us, for better or worse. Even though we now live as adults in a universe bigger than our family of birth, we all still carry some attitudes towards money and material things that began forming long ago.

## My Family Background

My parents were born on the Canadian prairies at the start of the Great Depression. One of my grandfathers worked as a tailor during those hardscrabble years. The other rode freight trains, looking for farm work at harvest time, and also worked for a while on a General Motors assembly line. His factory switched to manufacturing guns once World War II broke out. One grandmother, known in the rodeo circuit as Holywood Rose, rode bucking broncos to help support her children. My parents grew up in tough times.

High school sweethearts, my parents married in the 1950s. By then, Canada had recovered from the Great Depression and the Second World War. The postwar economy, humming with relative prosperity, allowed most people to enter the newly-burgeoning middle class.

My dad worked, for the most part, as a salesman during my growing-up years. By the time I started school, my mom had stopped working outside of the home. For many years, the four of us kids enjoyed the privilege of having a stay-at-home mom. I will always be grateful for the financial sacrifice my parents made in this regard. Mom's example undergirded my strong feelings about not working full-time during the years I was raising my children.

Even though my father was the only breadwinner for several years, we lived comfortably enough. We acquired a television soon after the first black-and-white sets came out. Each child owned special toys. I loved my prized collection of fuzzy animals and my rocking horse. We also invented our own fun. We created puzzles out of the dry, cracked summer earth and chased the prickly tumbleweeds that blew down our street on windy days. In the winter, we made snow igloos.

As I got older, my favourite possession was an old typewriter. I loved to write, even back then. I also loved to read books and to draw. Those absorbing, enriching interests cost very little. Not having too many possessions to distract me allowed my natural creativity to develop without hindrance.

My dad was paid mostly on commission, so our family income was not predictable. Whatever the monthly income, bills relentlessly arrived in the mail. A debt load had to be shouldered. Sometimes money was tight.

My parents knew how to stretch grocery money. On school days, we came home at lunch-time to hot bowls of chicken noodle soup or macaroni and cheese. At dinnertime, we feasted on spaghetti or hamburger and beans. I consider those dishes comfort foods to this day, never forgetting the years in which they were prepared with great love.

Mom was very handy with her sewing machine, a talent she probably inherited from her tailor father. It's nice to look back at old photos of the velvet dresses with silver-ribbon trim or rabbit-fur cuffs that she sewed for my sister and me so that we would have special outfits for Christmas.

When I was twelve, my mom went back to work as an executive secretary. From that point on, my sister and I kept an eye on our younger brothers after school and made dinner before my parents arrived home. As a family, we learned how to work as a team. We were all expected to pitch in.

Gathering together for dinner each evening was a very important part of each day, generating some of my most precious memories. I loved our family conversations around the kitchen table. If you were to ask me the very best part of growing up in my family, that would be my answer—talking together at dinnertime.

As a family, we also went to drive-in movies, had picnics in the park, skated, tobogganed, and played lots of board games together. From time to time, we enjoyed family vacations. All six of us would pile into the car and hit the road. Some summers we headed west to visit relatives. Other times we travelled to the north-eastern United States, accompanying my dad on sales trips. Through it all, we shared lots of love and fun and laughter. To this day, I firmly believe that happy family times do not depend on lots of money. In fact, sometimes money just gets in the way. Wealthy parents can be tempted to be off doing other things, often away from their kids or even their marriage partner.

I did not feel deprived in any way. We always had a warm home, cosy beds, food on the table, clothes on our backs, and adventures of one sort or another. I trust that my words do not convey any sense of complaint or any dishonour towards my parents. Though we were not the richest of families, I am grateful that my parents gave us *so much* in all the ways that mattered. Most importantly, my mom shared about her faith in Christ. She nurtured my own spiritual development more than she will ever know.

Around the time my siblings and I emerged into early adulthood, my parents' fortunes began to climb. My parents are now financially blessed far beyond their highest expectations. At the age of eighty-one, my father still chooses to work a few days a week at a large company he now partly owns.

Throughout this journey, I learned many valuable lessons from my parents regarding: working hard; spending money wisely; saving and investing; tackling debt; giving (even in tough times); always persevering; and relying on faith-filled prayer and God's limitless grace. Overall, I learned positive lessons about money and further discovered that life's best riches cannot be purchased.

## Your Own Family Background

I invite you to spend some moments thinking back over your personal family history. How did you live? What childhood circumstances shaped your viewpoint on money? What lessons did you learn?

Although we have been shaped by our past, none of us needs to remain bound by our past. We can evaluate which inherited beliefs, values, habits, goals, and attitudes we would like to keep and which ones we might want to override or modify.

## Church Background

If you were raised in church, you heard a particular viewpoint on what the Bible teaches about various matters, including money. Perhaps for years you believed that what you were taught was the only possible Christian viewpoint. Perhaps some of you still hold very fast to the earliest lessons about money you were taught by pastors or priests, Sunday School teachers or TV preachers.

I encourage you also to reflect on this aspect of your history. Prayerfully consider how your church background affects your present attitudes regarding money. Do you think they are all sound? I think it's fair to say that no denomination, no church, no pastor, no teacher, (and no author) *perfectly* presents truth. The Holy Spirit must be our ultimate teacher. God's Word must be the supreme influence in our lives.

## Our Marriage Partner's Viewpoint

As adults, we also have to come to grips with what our marriage partner (if we have one) believes about money. Our spouse also has a family background and perhaps a church background that might be very different from our own. A partner's financial philosophy will greatly impact what a couple earns, saves, spends, and gives away.

My husband, Sam, and I have similar outlooks on many financial matters, although it would not be fair to say we are totally on the same page on every money issue. In fact, in many ways, we are the opposite of one another. We have learned from each other's strengths; we have influenced one another to grow in our areas of weakness. Sometimes we stumble, struggle, and make mistakes together, but most of the time we counterbalance one another. Like every other married couple, however, we have our moments of disagreement and tension over money issues, especially spending decisions. It does not surprise me that financial conflict is one of the leading causes of divorce. Feelings about money run pretty deep in most people.

In your marriage, what issues, if any, do you fight about when it comes to money? What area has generated the most tension and resentment?

Perhaps this book can give you a third-party viewpoint on some of those issues. I pray that this book challenges each of you to consider what you believe and why, especially in light of your family and church backgrounds. I encourage you to think about your mate's background with some compassion—to seek some deeper understanding of where he or she is coming from.

Each marriage is unique. No one can offer you a prescribed formula as to how much you should make or what percentage of your money you should save, invest, spend, or give away. If you both read and discuss this book, perhaps you can find some fresh agreement on biblical principles that can guide you onwards.

## Cultural Influences

Beyond family background, church background (if any), and marriage dynamics, our personal viewpoints on money have also been influenced by the society we have lived in. The culture around us can be intriguing and enticing. We can get so easily caught up in it by reading newspapers, watching movies, enjoying television, surfing the Internet, and listening to popular music.

Not all cultural influence is bad. Sometimes culture affects us in a positive way. It's useful to make a conscious and cautious evaluation of the impact that our surrounding culture has had on our money attitudes. When have we dared to be counter-cultural?

When Joshua and the Israelites entered the Promised Land, God told them to drive out the indigenous cultures. God warned them against adopting the cultures of the lands around them. Eventually, foreigners immigrated into their midst and God once again warned His people about the dangers of everything from intermarrying to idolatry. God did not want His distinctive people to compromise their values.

You probably know how the story of the Israelites unfolded. At times they intermarried, and at times they worshipped the idols of the people around them. Those actions corrupted their values, undermined their beliefs, and displeased God.

Christians have been instructed to live amidst various cultures without carelessly assimilating. Jesus prayed that His Father would help His followers to be "in" the world but not "of" the world. In John 17:15–18, we can read this portion of His final prayer for us: "I do not ask that you take them out of the world....They are not of the world, just as I am not of the world. Sanctify them in the truth; your word is truth. As you sent me into the world, so I have sent them into the world."

The challenge that Jesus has left us with is this: How do we still live as salt and light "in" this world without this world unduly influencing us? What exactly does it mean for us to live "in" the world but not be "of" the world? How can we separate ourselves from the world's values and yet still practically live and work on this planet? Pertinent to this book, how do we differentiate ourselves from the world around us when it comes to handling money?

Western societies went through centuries of being predominantly Christian. For a long stretch of history, church steeples rose above all else. Churches usually occupied the corners of the main crossroads. Everything shut down on Sundays except for the churches. Perhaps being a Christian was easier in those times.

Obviously, things have changed a lot. The tallest buildings, located on prime urban real estate, now house our banks, investment firms, law firms, and accounting firms. Those firms handle gazillions of dollars. Long gone are the days when church spires overshadowed all other buildings and when businesses displayed a closed sign on Sundays. These days, to maintain right attitudes of heart towards money, we need to deal with the secular culture pressing in around and skyscraping above us.

Some recent decades have been easier than others. I will spend a moment contrasting the 1960s and '70s (the days of the hippies) with the 1980s and '90s (eras of excessive consumption). I will briefly share how the cultural currents of those decades helped or hindered my own faith journey and we will then briefly touch on more recent cultural trends in attitudes towards money. I invite you to remember your own journey through those years.

## The 1960s and '70s

The hippies despised materialism. They loudly rejected their parents' post-war dream of owning a nice home in the suburbs. They did not aspire to holding a life-long job in a big corporation. The Jackie Kennedy white-gloves-and-haute-couture image did not appeal to them. Instead, the hippies camped in the fields of Woodstock, wore faded jeans, revelled in bare feet, scoffed at suits and ties, and experimented with frugal communal living, all the while pledging never to be like their supposedly money-hungry parents. This stance was very easy for the hippies to take because, unlike their parents, they had not grown up during the Great Depression.

Some of that hippie-culture impact was positive. I grew up questioning materialism. I latched onto the popular belief that making money was not as important as seeking spirituality and enjoying quality relationships. I loved Joni Mitchell's song about how a person could become more "than a name on the door on the thirty-third floor."[40]

Added into the hippie mix was a renewed interest in Christianity. That *really* impacted me. When I fully committed my life to Christ, at the age of nineteen, it was not a totally counter-cultural decision. Many considered the Jesus Movement in California to be cool—"Jesus freaks" were respected as hip radicals. Young adult Christians wore blue jeans and bandanas just like the rest of their laid-back peers. They strummed their guitars and sang about love and peace and leaning on one another. While all of us were growing up, Jesus had been traditionally portrayed sporting long hair, a beard, and leather

---

[40] From Joni Mitchell's song *The Arrangement* (New York: Siquomb Publishing Company, 1969).

sandals, so He, along with His perceived anti-materialistic senti-ments, fit right in.

My friends were generally okay with my new Christian com-mitment, especially since I had seen the light while back-packing in Europe for a year. They did not agree with *all* of my new values, but the whole package was just hippie and edgy enough.

As the 1970s drew to a close, I sensed the winds of change. Peers began expressing much greater interest in acquiring money. As co-chair of the Christian Legal Fellowship student chapter during my last year in law school, I proposed that our group explore what the Bible teaches about money. Believing some challenges would soon arise for us Christians, I searched for all of the verses I could find per-taining to money. In a sense, this book was birthed way back then.

## The 1980s and '90s

Along came the 1980s. Hippie culture was quickly displaced by an era of unbridled and unabashed conspicuous consumption. The very hippie generation that once so noisily eschewed materialism bought into it big-time as they aged. Most of the boomers eventually outdid their parents on the material front, pursuing *super-sized* dreams of what they could own. For most former hippies, the years of ranting about materialism were left behind as a passing phase of adolescent rebellion.

In the 1980s, the television shows *Dynasty* and *Dallas* (prime-time soap operas about rich oil families) became big hits. Glitz and glamour became wildly fashionable. Suddenly, it was okay to want money and lots of it. Ralph Lauren encouraged everyone to look like they came from "old money," the very image that the hippies had loathed. This cultural shift posed a major challenge to my Christian faith. I knew I could not just lazily go with the flow.

I started practicing law on Bay Street in that era, surrounded mostly by a money-driven mentality. As I walked to my office each morning, I remember resolutely praying that I would only keep walking down that affluent street as long as God and I were walking in step together.

When I met my husband, Sam, a few years later, he was working as a pediatric resident at a downtown children's hospital. He lived in a posh townhouse in a chic neighbourhood and drove around town in a sleek sports car. By that point, I regularly wore power suits and pricey high heels and lived in a downtown apartment that was a walkable distance from my law firm. To some extent, the prevailing culture had already affected Sam and me. It bothered me when friends began labelling us "yuppies"—a nickname for the ambitious young urban professionals of that day.

Sam and I married in 1984 and, soon after, we were privileged to spend a sabbatical kind of year travelling around Africa. Mercifully, it was a great break from the onslaught of materialism washing over North America. To be back on the road, living simply out of a backpack, felt wonderfully comfortable. We had a long stretch of time to figure out where we, as a newly-married Christian couple, fit into the cultural shift of the '80s. We conversed about what our lives would look like when we returned. We discussed issues such as how many hours each of us would work and how much money we needed to make. We talked about whether to buy our own home, what size it should be, and where it would be located.

We came back with some shared financial goals and values. In order to work fewer hours, Sam started a family medical practice instead of resuming his specialized residency; I returned to the same law firm and, pregnant with my first child, negotiated a part-time position. We thereafter worked a *combined* total of about fifty-five hours a week—a far cry from the crazy hours we had sometimes clocked as young, single career people in the gruelling early years of training.

Those career decisions cost us a lot of potential income and spending power. We had to make some lifestyle sacrifices. We could no longer afford to live in the city core. We had to commute in from the suburbs. Over the years, we watched colleagues upgrade to increasingly upscale homes in the best urban neighbourhoods. We were still paying a mortgage when they started buying cottages or other investment properties. We could not dress, eat out, or decorate our homes in quite the same style as our professional colleagues.

I am not crying the blues here. Sam and I have always enjoyed a better lifestyle than so many other people have. I simply point out that we did significantly sacrifice our financial potential. Time is money in both of our professions. You can't slash work hours as radically as we did without also slashing income just as radically.

All of this was quite counter-cultural at that time. Working long hours, making piles of money, acquiring this-and-that, and pursuing the best that money could buy reigned as the dominant cultural norms.

As a Christian couple, Sam and I tried to stay grounded together in shared values, although no married couple is ever perfectly in sync when in comes to money. A culture that had gone berserk on material-ism *compelled* us either to give in to that culture or to keep developing a principled Christian perspective we could share. We encouraged each other in what we believed were biblical, family-oriented, and ministry-oriented values.

Was this easy? Not always. Like everyone else, we were bom-barded with marketing messages in the media. Even if we didn't see ourselves as competing and comparing with the Jones's next door (or the Jones's we knew in better neighbourhoods), we sometimes wanted what we saw in magazines and on TV ads. We all know that the media works hard to create the desire for more, better, newer, bigger. My personal weakness was evident whenever I browsed through decorat-ing and lifestyle magazines. The Bible knows what it's talking about when it refers to the lust of the eyes! For a while I stopped flipping through those magazines.

For any Christian, keeping materialism in check was further com-plicated by the emerging popularity of the prosperity gospel in the 1980s.

With respect to blatant materialism, the 1990s were no improve-ment over the previous decade. Despite some cycles of economic downturn, acquiring new toys remained in style. Two-career couples became the norm. Monster homes started to appear on the city streets of previously ordinary neighbourhoods. The status of wearing brand names prevailed, even in the playgrounds of primary schools. Instant gratification and an air of entitlement pervaded the ranks of the young and not-so-young. Across generations, an even sicker striving for excess spread like the common cold. Consumer debt started to sky-rocket. And generally, for most North Americans, the good times rolled on.

I continued to work part-time hours, even after my kids started school—in fact, even after they entered high school. In a profession where billable hours rule, I was an odd fish swimming upstream against a very strong current. I worked at my downtown office a few days a week and in my home office on the other days until the kids came home from school. I was one of the first in my firm to telecommute quite extensively once technology permitted it. That was manageable except when cases went to court.

Sam and I also took most Fridays off. Fridays started out being a family day when the kids were little but later evolved into a date day for Sam and I (after Saturdays had become a child-centric blur of driving our kids to hockey, figure skating, and birthday parties). Sunday was generally reserved for church and relaxation.

Living this kind of lifestyle was good, not just for us as a marriage and family—it was good for the spirit and the soul. It helped us to keep career and income generating in perspective. We could devote decent time to our relationships with God, family, friends, and fellow Christians. We could get involved in various ministries. We have no regrets about deliberately putting the brakes on our career ambitions during the decades we raised our kids.

As a married couple, did we become ensnared *at all* by the cultural trends of that era? I must humbly confess the answer is yes. Along with so many in the North American church, we became somewhat disoriented as to where to draw a sensible line in our spending. It was not just secular culture that kept trying to pull us from true north on this issue of materialism. Sadly, Christian culture had generally become so compromised and so heavily influenced by worldliness that it became increasingly difficult to find a spiritual port in the storm. Christians had lost too much of their distinctiveness. If we told Christian friends we were thinking about spending on this or that, too many of them, in self-validating mode, would approve and applaud anything we had in mind. Sometimes it seemed that we were all sailing along in the same leaky boat, searching for the solid shore, oblivious to how much our mutual materialism impeded our spiritual progress. God help us all, I sometimes prayed.

## The New Millenium

Money madness continued as we entered the new millennium. Many people still worked like maniacs, spent a lot, and got even deeper into debt to finance high-rolling lifestyles. All that insanity was briefly put on hold after 9/11, but then North Americans decided it was their patriotic duty to shop (or the terrorists would win). Retail therapy returned as a popular leisure activity. Many shoppers proudly turned into shopaholics. E-commerce made it even easier to shop; we could now buy almost anything, day or night, from our home computers. People wanted more than material possessions—they wanted to acquire experiences. More and more people became increasingly addicted to whatever pleasure and entertainment money could buy.

Materialism was almost rabid by mid-decade. I read a *Wall Street Journal* article about a woman, self-described as spectacularly beautiful, who had advertised in that newspaper for a mate. She was trolling for a man who earned at least half a million dollars a year. (Anything less, she noted, would not get her to Central Park West.) One investment banker replied to her ad with sarcastic rejection. He arrogantly told her that *his* assets would keep on appreciating in value while *her* beauty was destined to fade; to him, it did not make financial sense to take on a depreciating asset.[41] Materialism fosters such a peculiar shallowness of soul.

I heard about a new brand of bottled water called Bling H2O, which had Swarovski crystals imbedded in the disposable container. I read

---

41  Frank article.

about lavish birthday parties that cost tens of thousands of dollars. One night I watched a Hollywood movie called *Mad Money*; in one scene, its three female stars stood in a big pile of dollar bills, gleefully throwing them around. That caught the spirit of the age.

Then, seemingly out of nowhere, giving and volunteering suddenly became fashionable. Celebrities, from rock star Bono to Hollywood actors, publicly jumped on the bandwagon of helping the poor and disadvantaged. Business titans Bill Gates and Warren Buffett set up a foundation, worth tens of billions of dollars, committed to helping worthy causes. Gates left his full-time position at Microsoft to spend most of his time on his philanthropic endeavours. Former President Bill Clinton wrote a book called *Giving*. It was a breath of fresh air— one area of life where the values of the world at large began to mesh to some extent with Christian ideals.

After the financial meltdown in 2008, further refreshing change occurred for a while. The dark cloud of the recent recession was, indeed, haloed with a silver lining of saner values. Excess became fleetingly unacceptable. In sharp contrast, frugality came back into vogue for a season. Consumers weren't so eager to spend. Debt became another nasty four-letter word. Toxic bank debt, government debt, consumer debt—it had all spun so badly out of control. Old-fashioned financial restraint rose in esteem again. Banks stopped giving easy loans.

Articles began to discuss whether we need to buy bottled water— *any* bottled water, not just the stuff with Swarovski crystals imbedded in the container.

Thankfully, secular mass media such as television, newspapers, magazines, and radio no longer controls cultural trends. Populist media, fuelled by the Internet through sites such as Facebook, YouTube, and Twitter, has fragmented culture into thousands of niches. This shift benefits Christians, who can choose to belong to the niche of their own faith, which has developed an alternative media presence.

For all of this recent positive change, Christians must still judiciously resist being absorbed into the culture at large. As world economies sputter into further tentative recovery, attitudes about money are changing once again and not necessarily for the better. Materialism is creeping back into culture.

Who knows how the culture around us will continue to shift? As Christians moving forward, we need constantly to ask ourselves how much we are being buffeted by the prevailing world winds. We must remain vigilant regarding the cultural influences all around us, ready to become as counter-cultural as each era demands. Sometimes we can go with the current of culture, if it happens to coincide with Christian values. Most of the time, however, we must be prepared to press headlong into the winds of worldly groupthink.

> *The Israelites lived among the Canaanites, Hittites, Amorites, Perizzites, Hivites and Jebusites. They took their daughters in marriage and gave their own daughters to their sons, and served their gods. The Israelites did evil in the eyes of the Lord; they forgot the Lord their God and served the Baals and the Asherahs.*

Judges 3:5–7 (NIV)

> *Pray that you will not fall into temptation.*

Luke 22:40b (NIV)

> *Do not conform any longer to the pattern of this world, but be transformed by the renewing of your mind.*

Romans 12:2a (NIV)

# RECEIVING MONEY

# 9

---

## MEETING OUR NEEDS

*Therefore do not be anxious, saying "What shall we eat?"*
*or "What shall we drink?" or "What shall we wear?"...your*
*heavenly Father knows that you need [these things]. But*
*seek first the kingdom of God and his righteousness, and all*
*these things will be added to you.*

Matthew 6:31–33

*He who did not spare his own Son but gave him up for us all,*
*how will he not also with him graciously give us all things?*

Romans 8:32

*Fear the Lord, you his saints, for those who fear him lack*
*nothing...those who seek the Lord lack no good thing.*

Psalm 34:9–10 (NIV)

*He provides food for those who fear him;*
*he remembers his covenant forever.*

Psalm 111:5

The stunning film series *Planet Earth* wonderfully demonstrates how God sustains all living creatures. Psalm 145:15–16 affirms God's always sufficient provision: "The eyes of all look to you, and you give them their food in due season. You open your hand; you satisfy the desire of every living thing."

If God so clearly cares for fish, birds, animals, insects, and all of humankind, how much more does He care about the material needs of His people? In Philippians 4:19, the apostle Paul unequivocally taught: "…my God will supply *every* need of yours according to his riches in glory in Christ Jesus."

Jesus walked this earth and experienced the human condition. He wore clothes, ate meals, and found shelter. In Matthew 6:31–33 (above), Jesus does not rebuke us for seeking food, drink, and clothes. Instead, He confirms that God knows we need those things. He intends to provide them *if* we seek Him as our first priority.

In John 21:5–7, Jesus asked His disciples if they had caught any fish. When they answered no, He told them to cast their nets on the opposite side of their boat. When they did so, they caught so many fish that they had trouble hauling in their nets.

In Matthew 6:11, Jesus taught us to pray, asking God to give us our daily bread. We do not need to beg God *or* man for our daily bread. We simply need to ask our loving Father. In Psalm 37:25, David wrote: "I have been young, and now am old, yet I have not seen the righteous forsaken or his children begging for bread." God still lovingly assures each one of us: "The Lord does not let the righteous go hungry…" (Proverbs 10:3); "Open your mouth wide, and I will fill it" (Psalm 81:10b).

**God Has the Resources**

God does not have a limited supply of this or that. He owns all good things. In Job 41:11b, He asserts: "Whatever is under the whole heaven is mine." In Psalm 24:1, the psalmist exalts: "The earth is the Lord's and the fullness thereof, the world and those who dwell therein…" In Psalm 50:10, God declares: "Every beast of the forest is mine, the cattle on a thousand hills." In Haggai 2:8, God reveals: "The silver is mine, and the gold is mine..." Abraham called God the "Possessor of heaven and earth" (Genesis 14:22).

God's resources will *never* run out. I love the story of Elijah and the poor widow recorded in 1 Kings 17:7–16. Elijah encountered her when she had just enough food in her pantry to prepare one last meal. Even after she told him about it, Elijah asked her to feed him. He promised her that her handful of flour and few drops of oil would not run out until rain came again.

Amazingly, the flour and oil lasted beyond the dinner she prepared. In fact, the widow, her son, and Elijah continued to enjoy meal after meal. No matter how much flour and oil she used, plenty remained.

Another remarkable story can be found in 2 Kings 4:42–44. A man brought Elisha twenty loaves of bread and a sack of corn. Elisha instructed the man to feed one hundred men with it. The man protested that it was not enough. Elisha told him to start serving the men, declaring that there would even be some left over. And there was!

Along those same lines, you are probably familiar with the stories of Jesus in which, on multiple occasions, He fed *thousands* of people, starting with only a small number of fish and a few loaves of bread.

God's resources never run dry.

## God's Covenant Names

In the Old Testament, God disclosed that He has several names for Himself. One of those names is Jehovah Jireh, which has been translated as "the God who will provide." His role as divine Provider is an essential aspect of His character. Who are we to doubt this dimension of His declared identity? He has made a covenant with us, written forever into one of His names, promising us that He *will* provide. Who dares to call Him a liar?

Hudson Taylor, a pioneer missionary in China, believed that God was, indeed, Jehovah Jireh. From the outset of his long ministry, Hudson determined that he would not rely on fellow humans for his material provisions but on God alone. His organization, called the China Inland Mission, was financed entirely by unsolicited donations. Hudson never asked anyone for money, simply believing that God would move men's hearts to send him what he needed. Hudson was so confident in God's provision that he sometimes gave away all that he had in hand to help meet others' needs. Hudson delighted in proclaiming: "Can Christ be rich and I be poor?"[42]

## Need Versus Greed

When the people of Israel travelled towards the Promised Land, God supernaturally fed them with manna. Every morning, except on the Sabbath, the manna formed on the ground. Moses instructed the people: "Everyone can go out each day and gather as much food as he *needs*" (Exodus 16:4b TLB). No one was to take more than he needed for his family. The manna quickly spoiled when people tried to hoard extra amounts in their tents.

God has promised to meet our need, not our greed.

Although the manna satisfied their hunger, the people grumbled and complained, remembering the leeks, garlic, and other savoury food in Egypt. They told God they craved meat. So God gave them what they asked for in the form of a miraculous provision of quail, but many of the people died as they were eating it.[43] I don't think God had anything against meat. He was reacting to their grumbling and greed. Psalm 106:14 describes their lust for meat as a "wanton craving."

How do we draw the line between need and greed? Here's how I see it. Imagine a horizontal line. On the far left is our need zone—the area of our truly legitimate physical needs. I invite you to spend some time defining what those legitimate needs are. On the far right end of the line is the greed zone—that which is clearly excessive and purely self-indulgent. It's the middle zone that is more troublesome. In it are the many desires that cannot be so easily classified as either need or

---

[42]   Petersen book, pp. 123–142; Wiersbe book, p. 13.

[43]   See the full story in Numbers 11.

greed. What does God have to say about those? We will spend time in a later chapter looking at that middle zone of want and desire.

Suffice it to summarize here that God promises to meet all of our needs but frowns on our greed. We cannot expect God to provide for our every whim. We cannot act like spoiled children with an attitude of entitlement, demanding everything under the sun. I will later make the case, however, that God does want to grant us our *good* desires even if they transcend basic need.

## Differing Needs

Your needs and my needs may not be the same. We may have different needs depending on our life circumstances, including what God calls us to do with our lives. A couple with four children needs more money than a couple with two children or a person with no children at all. A person living in Tokyo or London or New York will require more money than a person living in a small town, because the cost of living is much higher. A person who has to commute an hour to work every day will need more money for transportation than a person who can walk to work or who works in a home office. A business executive needs to spend more on their wardrobe than a stay-at-home mom.

We must recognize these differences in our needs and not judge one another in this area. We should never try to define the line between need and greed for anyone but our own selves.

## Putting God First

God's promise to provide for our needs has one non-negotiable catch: we must make Him and His purposes our top priority. Jesus clearly stated, in Matthew 6:33 and Luke 12:31 (presented at the beginning and end of this chapter), that God will provide for our needs *if* we make His Kingdom our main concern. We must trust God in this.

From God's perspective, the spiritual dimension of life is always more important than the physical. But our physical needs still have *some* importance. They are not to be our top priority, but they still matter.

## Challenging Times

In good economic times, we can take God's provision for granted. We all know, however, that economic times are not always great. We can learn valuable lessons about God's faithful provision from the following stories of people who have lived through various kinds of challenging financial circumstances: those who have endured periods of prolonged economic downturn; those in ministry who have not relied on the committed support of others; and students who have had to fend for themselves financially (in whole or in part) while getting their education. Your present financial challenge might not match any of these, but hopefully you will still be encouraged by the examples below of God's faithful provision.

### *Times of Hardship and Famine*

God promises that He will provide for us even in times of famine. The book of Genesis includes the story of how God provided for Joseph's family's needs (indeed, his whole nation's needs) in a seven-year-long famine.

Psalm 37:18–19 states: "The Lord knows the days of the blameless,…they are not put to shame in evil times; in the days of famine they have abundance." I am particularly struck by the word "abundance." This verse does not just promise barely enough. Instead, this verse promises abundance, even in days of famine.

God took great care of my maternal grandparents, for example, while they lived through very tough times. Both of them grew up in Eastern Europe. Their families suffered through the First World War and through disease epidemics. While in their late teens, my grandparents lived for a while in Russia, experiencing the trauma and the drama of the Russian Revolution. The Revolution destroyed the old class system, stripping the rich of their wealth and ushering in decades of Communism. Both the War and the Revolution caused enormous hardships such as shortages of food and shelter. Yet my grandparents' needs were always met.

Recognizing that the new Russian regime was hostile to their Christian faith, my grandparents moved to Germany, a country in the midst of its own political and economic upheaval. Observing the alarming rise of the Nazis in the late 1920s, my grandparents decided not to settle permanently in Germany. Moving onwards to Canada, they migrated to Saskatchewan just in time for the Great Depression.

Although jobs were scarce in the Depression years, my grandfather found work as a tailor, making uniforms for the Royal Canadian Mounted Police. He also took on work as a painter. Even during the worst years of the Depression, he earned a steady income. His family lived frugally, being careful about every dollar spent, but there was always some food in the pantry and even the occasional treat. When my mom stopped by to see my grandfather at work on her way home from school, he sometimes gave her a nickel so she could buy an ice cream cone. When her older brothers found work in their teens, they generously bought her a pair of skates and a bicycle. My grandparents taught their children to recognize God as their faithful provider.

God can provide for each one of us, even in times of global economic downturn. God's economy is never in recession or depression.

### Ministering without Regular Income

The apostle Paul lived in Rome for the final years of his life, ministering to many: "He lived there two whole years at his own expense, and welcomed all who came to him, proclaiming the kingdom of God and teaching about the Lord Jesus Christ with all boldness and without hindrance" (Acts 28:30–31). It is not clear how he supported himself, because he lived under house arrest and could not go out to work (Acts 28:16). Somehow, God provided for him during those years.

George and Mary Mueller worked for decades to care for numerous orphans in England in an era when most others had no compassion for homeless children. If you've read Charles Dickens' *Oliver Twist* (published the year after the Muellers took in their first orphans), you can picture the era I'm talking about. Although they had no means of regular income, George and Mary trusted that God would provide, not only for the needs of their immediate family, but also for the needs of the growing number of orphans they took under their wings.

One day, the Muellers and their young charges were sitting around the table with empty dishes in front of everyone. There was no food in their house and no money with which to buy food. Yet George Mueller dared to bow his head to thank God, in advance, for what He was going to provide for them to eat.

Soon after, they heard someone knocking on the door. It was the local baker, bearing baskets of freshly-baked goods. The baker told the Muellers that God had awakened him during the previous night and had prompted him to bake bread for the Mueller household.

Then a second knock came. This time it was the milkman. His cart had just broken down right in front of the Mueller home. The milkman announced that the Muellers and their household might as well take all the milk in the cart before it turned sour.[44]

That food was only enough for that day. The Muellers had to trust God for the next day and the day after that. In response to their daily prayers, God amply provided the Muellers with food *and* with Bibles, clothes, kitchenware, furniture, household help, and whatever else they needed. A stream of people showed up at their door with gifts of all kinds, and envelopes stuffed with money arrived in the mail. Eventually, the Muellers ran five separate orphanages, housing over two thousand boys and girls. Those children no longer had to live on the street or in the wretched almshouses other orphans lived in alongside criminals and the mentally ill.[45]

In the early 1900s, a single young woman named Lillian Trasher travelled to Egypt. Without any mission organization supporting her,

---

[44]   Petersen book, pp. 225–226.

[45]   Peterson book, pp. 225–242; Bailey book, (*George Mueller*), especially pp. 55–57, 75–76, 96.

Lillian began to care for orphans in that country. Like the Muellers, she trusted from day to day that God would meet all of their needs. Also like the Muellers, she continued this work for over five decades, helping thousands of homeless children. One day at a time, money and provisions miraculously arrived from one unexpected source or another.[46]

Rees Howells, a well-known 20th-century Welsh Christian, dared to quit his paying job to strike out in unpaid full-time ministry. He thereafter had to trust that God would somehow provide his daily bread.

Howells considered the promises of God to be just like coins, a valuable and spendable kind of currency. Howells did not worry about carrying any tangible treasure around with him. He had learned where the ultimate Treasury is and how to access it. He saw no reason to ask anyone for money for either his own needs or the needs of his ministry. Instead, he simply asked God to meet his needs, reminding Him of His promises, each time cashing in some of that divine currency.

Armed with that mindset, Howells ministered for forty years. For some of his projects, he had to purchase and maintain properties and to construct buildings. Even in those expensive ventures, Howells trusted in God alone. He was inspired by the Muellers, who had also purchased and maintained many properties decades before him.

Howells had only two shillings in his pocket when he set out to build a Christian college in Wales. Over a fourteen-year period, God provided him with the 125,000 pounds he needed to complete the college. Every year after that, Howells had to trust God to provide him with further funds to pay for operating expenses such as taxes.

One year, Howells owed forty pounds in realty taxes. A friend needed eight pounds for his taxes. At that time, Howells did not have forty pounds; but he did have eight. God told him to help out his friend. So Howells went over to his friend's place, where he found his friend and his wife in prayer. Howells joyfully told them they could get up

---

[46]   Cunningham book, (*Daring…*), pp. 68–69.

off their knees—he was delivering the eight pounds they needed. He did not tell them about his own larger need. Upon his return to the college, Howells found a gift of money waiting for him in the exact sum of forty pounds.[47]

If you have sound reason to believe that God is calling you into some form of ministry, step out in faith and trust that He will meet your material needs too. I have watched friends and relatives do this and have been awestruck that the God of the Muellers, Trasher, and Howells is still meeting ministry needs today. I do not criticize those who ask others for committed support. The above examples simply demonstrate God's faithful provision even to those who do not have regular human support they can depend on.

### The Student Years

While still in university, George Mueller decided that he would commit his life to Christian ministry. Not supportive of this, his father promptly cut off all financial help. Resolute in his goals, George trusted that God would somehow provide all the money he needed for the rest of his education. God promptly sent along some rich Americans who were willing to pay Mueller for tutoring help.[48] Throughout his later decades of sheltering orphans, George never forgot those early lessons in God's timely and sufficient provision.

I had to trust God too as I worked every year to pay for university tuition, books, and other expenses. God did more than meet my basic needs during my undergraduate years and my three years of law school. He helped me to find jobs that paid well. I started my full-time career carrying a miniscule student debt load of about one thousand dollars.

My son and daughter have both spent years attending university. While they have not had to rely on God for the full cost of their education, they learned during those years to trust Him to meet some of their material needs.

---

[47] Grubb book, pp. 52, 71, 130, 182, 203–204.

[48] Bailey book (*George Mueller*), chapter 4.

When my daughter was in her second year of university, for example, she needed to find a new place to live. Samantha was excited when she found a decent room to sublet at a great rental price.

Soon after, I received a phone call from her. The person she was planning to sublet from had reneged on their arrangement and all of the good houses in town had already been taken. The only places left by that point in time were either not fit to live in or way too expensive.

I suggested we pray. I am delighted that my adult kids are always open to praying with me, my husband, or others about their needs. Over the phone, we began praying even though Samantha and her girlfriend were sitting in the middle of a busy café. Two students sitting close to Samantha overheard her stated need. While Samantha was praying with me, they told her girlfriend that someone in *their* house had *just* backed out of his lease, leaving a room suddenly available. As soon as Samantha said "amen" and "good-bye" to me, she learned of this amazing and timely opportunity.

The two students took Samantha to show her their house that very hour. It was huge, awesome, close to her classes, and in a safe, well-lit location. The bedroom available for her was particularly spacious and had a large window, a high ceiling, and hardwood flooring. On top of everything else, the rent was reasonable. Later that day, Samantha phoned me to tell me she had already signed a new sub-lease.

God does not always *so* dramatically and *so* immediately provide for our material needs. Samantha had to remember how wonderfully God had provided for her on that occasion when, the following year, she went through a long, frustrating, and much more arduous process of finding student housing for her exchange semester in Sydney, Australia. In the end, God met that need for housing as well.

If you believe God wants you to pursue further education, I urge you to step out in faith and trust that He will provide for your material needs along the way.

## Questioning God as Provider

Foreign as it seems to me, some people will strongly argue against the notion that God is a giving, blessing Provider who wants to lovingly care for us. They point, for example, to the many who die in Third World famines. Why doesn't God feed them? Why doesn't He care for them the way He cared for my grandparents or the Muellers or the others I have just written about?

I do not have the space to delve deeply into this issue. I do assert, however, that God *does* want to help meet the needs of everyone around this globe. I believe that He wants to use *us* to meet those needs—to be His heart and hands and feet. Instead of spending time arguing about why God isn't doing anything about starving children, why don't *we* do something in His name? God has commanded us to help the poor. He wants us to share the resources He has given to us. In addressing the needs of the starving and the suffering, God hasn't dropped the ball. We have.

## Pride as a Barrier to Receiving from God

We talked earlier about the sin of pride in the context of having too much pride in our possessions and sometimes even flaunting them. It is also wrong to be "proud" in our time of need. The sin of pride can show up as a resistance to receiving financial or material help from others. Pride can block the gifts God wants us to receive.

When we're in need, let's never be too proud to accept help.

## My Prayer

As the Israelites finished their four decades of wandering in the desert, their leader Moses pointed out to them: "These forty years the Lord your God has been with you. You have lacked nothing" (Deuteronomy 2:7c–d). I pray that this becomes the life testimony of every one of us as we press on, trusting that God will meet our needs.

*The Lord is my Shepherd; I shall not want.*

Psalm 23:1

*Don't be concerned about what to eat and what to drink. Don't worry about such things. These things dominate the thoughts of unbelievers all over the world, but your Father already knows your needs. Seek the Kingdom of God above all else, and he will give you everything you need.*

Luke 12:29-31 (NLT)

*They feast on the abundance of your house, and you give them drink from the river of your delights.*

Psalm 36:8

# 10

---

# THE FAITH FACTOR

*Therefore I tell you, whatever you ask in prayer, believe that
you have received it, and it will be yours.*

Mark 11:24

*All things are possible for one who believes.*

Mark 9:23b

*Faith is the assurance of things hoped for,
the conviction of things not seen.*

Hebrews 11:1

W e touched on the faith factor in the last chapter. God *will* meet our
needs, but He does expect us to exercise our faith in that regard. Let's
delve in deeper. What exactly does it mean to live in faith in the area
of our finances?

I have met Christians over the years who maintain that living in faith
(some call it living "on" faith or "by" faith) in our material lives requires
us to own almost nothing and to live very simply. Those who hold this

view often travel around as evangelists, move abroad as missionaries without structured support, or live communally with other Christians. Many such Christians save up nothing for tomorrow and survive on Spartan supplies for today. They quote Matthew 10:9–11, which records how Jesus sent His disciples out with these instructions: "Acquire no gold nor silver nor copper for your belts, no bag for your journey, nor two tunics nor sandals nor a staff…And whatever town or village you enter, find out who is worthy in it and stay there until you depart."

I do not criticize Christians who live by that passage. In fact, I admire them for their mission, their lifestyle, and their edgy faith. I once lived for a number of months in a close-knit, communal Christian setting and it was an eye-opening, faith-stretching, positive experience. Should we all live so radically all of the time when it comes to our finances? Is that the only way to live in faith?

I'm not convinced. Ponder this. Even the disciples were not always instructed to live so radically. In Luke 22:35–36a, for example, Jesus said to His disciples: "… 'When I sent you out with no moneybag or knapsack or sandals, did you lack anything?' They said, 'Nothing.' He said to them, 'But *now* let the one who has a moneybag take it, and likewise a knapsack.'" The contrast between what Jesus instructed in Matthew 10:9–11 and what He later instructed in this passage from Luke underscores the importance of knowing and balancing *all* of Scripture.

That second passage affirms that it is okay to have some money and some luggage for our journey. Furthermore, I invite you to note that both of the above passages were addressed to those in full-time ministry, who were supported to some extent by those they ministered to. These verses do not necessarily apply to everyone everywhere all the time.

What about settling down in a home? Note that the disciples in the first-referenced passage above lived in the homes of others. Were those others criticized for having homes? I don't think so. The disciples would not have had any place to stay unless some fellow believers had homes large enough and with pantries full enough to accommodate guests for a while.

What about running a business? Earlier, we concluded that not all Christians are expected to work in career ministry positions. Even back in New Testament times, Christ-followers such as Priscilla and Aquila made money in the marketplace.

We require faith to live in *any* of the above scenarios. Travelling evangelists must have faith that they will find someone to stay with who will provide a room and meals for them or that others will give them money to pay for those needs. Missionaries must also have faith that their needs will be met, whether their support is formally structured or not. A person with a home must have faith that they will receive the necessary funds to pay for the mortgage, utilities, insurance, taxes, and repairs. A person who manages a business needs faith that they will be able to pay their employees, their rent, and numerous other overhead expenses every month. A person working for someone else needs faith that they will keep their job or find another job in due course.

All of this takes faith—especially in these uncertain economic times.

I strongly believe that God places His people in a wide range of professions and careers: in business, academia, politics, law, medicine, construction work, truck-driving, police work, the military, home-making, and so on and so forth. It takes faith to believe that God will provide in each and every one of these callings, on the material level and otherwise. Every person must live in faith regarding their financial affairs, whether they're a missionary overseas or the CEO of a Fortune 500 company.

No one is guaranteed a life-long paycheque. No one.

Some people think that because my husband is a doctor and I practiced as a lawyer for many years we haven't had to exercise much faith regarding our finances. That is not true. At times, due to various medical crises that have caused work interruptions, we have felt financially vulnerable. Anyone's present circumstances can change overnight. We *all* need to live continually in faith in the area of our finances.

## Prayer

Over the years, I have been surprised at the number of Christians I regularly meet who believe that it is unspiritual to pray for anything in the material realm. I believe that we can pray in faith about any aspect of our lives, including financial matters. Solomon prayed: "May there be abundance of grain in the land; on the tops of the mountains may it wave…"(Psalm 72:16). Jesus taught us how to pray, using the Lord's Prayer as a template; this powerful prayer includes asking God to give us our daily bread (see Matthew 6:11).

There are countless examples in history of great men and women of God who resolutely prayed for God to meet their material needs. I encourage you to read more about the individuals I reference in this book. All of us can learn to pray with faith, asking God to help us with our finances. Even when recession ravages the economy, stock values plummet, jobs disappear, or prices rise—even then (especially then) we can exercise our faith by praying.

## Real Faith is not Presumptive Faith

A distinction must be made between appropriate faith for our finances and the misguided presumption that God will do whatever we want just so long as we declare that we have faith.

Genuine faith is always based on the clear instructions and promises of God (such as the explicit promises that He *will* provide for our needs and good desires). The Bible is meant to be the primary source of God's revelation and the foundation for our faith. Paul taught that faith comes from taking in the Word of God (Romans 10:17). Our faith can therefore operate in confidence with respect to both our needs and those good desires we have yielded to God, desires which we have reason to believe have been God-inspired and God-approved.

Presumptive faith assumes that God will provide *anything* in the material realm that we want—even if we don't need it—just because we have prayed about it or verbalized it to others. Presumptive faith has no trouble asking for what is excessive and greedy. The "name it and claim it" (also known as "blab it and grab it") version of faith that has been around for a few decades presumes that God is a generous parent who will spoil us and indulge our every whim; all we need to do is ask for whatever we want. Does a wise and loving human parent act that way? Human parents often have to express a firm "No!" in the best interests of their child. Caring human parents never give their children every single thing they want. Is God less wise and loving?

Presumptive faith latches onto verses that state we can have whatever we ask for in prayer if we have faith. Those verses exist. I began this chapter with Mark 11:24, one of my favourite verses along those lines. Verses of that nature are *awesome* and *important* and we should all know them by heart. But let's also remember one of the over-riding principles of this book—the need to carefully balance *all* of Scripture. The verses regarding asking for "whatever" must be thoughtfully juxtaposed with verses such as 1 John 5:14, which talks about asking for anything *in accordance with God's will*. When we balance Mark 11:24 with 1 John 5:14, we see that the broad scope of Mark 11:24 has been qualified in a very significant way. If we further juxtapose some verses cautioning us about greed or self-indulgence, the scope of Mark 11:24 narrows even more. Let's also factor in James 4:3, which teaches: "You ask and do not receive, because you ask wrongly, to spend it on your passions."

The need for balance in the understanding and application of what the Bible says about money is perhaps most urgent in this particular area of asking God for things we may want but clearly don't need.

Considered in isolation, the invitation to pray for anything (in passages such as Mark 11:24) could be interpreted to apply to every-thing: a diamond necklace, a Ferrari sports car, a private jet plane, a villa in the Caribbean, or virtually anything else that the heart fancies. Instead of simply asking for the Ferrari or the Caribbean home, we need to first ask ourselves (and ask God): Is what I'm asking for within God's will for me? How do I know this?

It may be that it *is* God's will that we purchase a particular business or home or car. Dare we ask God? Dare we find out what He thinks before we start zealously praying for something and declaring to everyone that by faith we're going to receive it? Dare we search a broad range of money-related verses that might shed light on His answer?

The subject of seeking God's guidance is multi-dimensional. For those wishing to explore this subject further, you might be interested in reading my first book, *Counsel of the Most High: Receiving God's Guidance for Life's Decisions.* In this short chapter, I simply cannot repeat all of the important biblical principles that pertain to how we can discover God's will in a particular matter.

If we are exercising true biblical faith in the area of our finances, we *will* ask God what He has to say about a specific matter and we *will* also gladly filter our prayer requests through the many applicable verses about money instead of just relying on a few verses that appear to permit us to pray for anything.

We also need to note the contexts of verses we want to rely on. In John 15, for example, Jesus told His followers a few times that they could ask in prayer for whatever they wished in His name and the Father would give it to them. If you read the entire chapter, however, you will quickly see that the discussion is primarily about His followers bearing fruit for God, not shopping in luxury malls.

I have met many Christians whose faith has been derailed in the area of finances because they have failed to distinguish between appropriate faith and presumptive faith. Because God did not give them the new home, car, or vacation they were praying about, they have thrown faith out the window and have resorted to getting what they want by their own human means. They have become disappointed, disillusioned, and ultimately disinterested in praying for their material needs and good desires—all because they thought they could pray for *any* material desire and it would materialize. They leaned too hard on a few verses and never bothered to think through how those verses might be limited, influenced, and counterbalanced by their context and by other weighty biblical principles such as the warnings about coveting, selfishness, and loving money. Many have not figured out what went wrong.

Faith in God cannot conjure up a blank cheque.

I do not intend to sound judgmental. I have had my own experiences with presumptive faith. I have had moments of disappointment and confusion in this area in the past. That is one of the reasons I am so adamant, in my own life, about trying to apply what the entire Bible says, balancing all the key principles, and interpreting each verse in light of all the others.

God *does* want us to step out in bold faith to ask for our authentic needs and our good desires to be met. I strongly encourage you to do so. Let us accept, however, that He has placed some wise limits on what we can ask for in faith, especially if it is something that transcends legitimate need. I hope that by the end of this book those limits are clearer. I challenge you to come to grips with how to define true material needs and good desires.

We've all heard a lot about the Prayer of Jabez over the past decade (see 1 Chronicles 4:9–10). Among other things, Jabez asked God for enlarged territory (i.e. more land). The simple fact of the matter is that God gave Jabez what he had asked for in faith. Subject to the parameters we have just discussed, faith can and does operate in the material dimension of our lives.

## Christian Organizations

In the past, several well-known ministries operated successfully for years within a framework of faith and prayer. Corrie ten Boom's ministry is one excellent example. After being imprisoned for courageously hiding Jews in her Dutch home, Corrie survived a German concentration camp in World War II. After the war, this remarkable woman dedicated her life to delivering God's message of love and forgiveness to a hurting world.

Initially, Corrie asked others for financial assistance so she could travel to America. During that first year of speaking, however, God clearly impressed upon Corrie that she was no longer to ask anyone for money. From that point forward, while God would indeed use people as conduits of His provision, Corrie's reliance was on God alone.

Corrie needed considerable sums of money as the years progressed. She refurbished a concentration camp in Germany and used it for fourteen years to minister to many Germans who had been emotionally wounded during the war. She ran a similar home in Holland for refugees who had survived the Nazi camps.

For three decades, she travelled around the world, speaking in over sixty countries on six continents. She never stopped relying on God to supply all her material provisions. At the age of 68, for example, she believed that God was telling her to go to Denmark, Austria, Israel, and India that year. She told her assistant to arrange for the necessary tickets. Her assistant asked whether or not they had the money. Corrie responded, "Not yet," but told her assistant to never forget that God was their treasurer; they were doing God's business and He would provide the money on time. Sure enough, by the time the tickets arrived, the money to pay for them was in place.

Corrie once stated that if we insist on raising money on our own terms, God will let us. It is possible to raise a lot of money by human persuasion and perseverance, but such a fund-raiser loses the enormous blessing of watching God supply our needs from His vast resources. Corrie said that she would much prefer to be the "trusting child" of her wealthy Father than a "beggar at the door of worldly men."[49]

I personally admire Christian leaders like Corrie ten Boom and others in her class whose ministries placed great emphasis on the faith factor. Such leaders prayed fervently, trusted God, and moved forward whether or not there was much money in the bank, often receiving required funds at the eleventh hour from surprise sources. Their expenses were met without formal fund-raising swallowing up their time.

That Mueller model of ministry is becoming much less common these days, although the faith factor still plays a very prominent role in some modern Christian organizations. Youth with a Mission (YWAM) is a ministry that encourages its staff to have faith that God will provide necessary financial resources. Founded in 1960 by Loren

---

[49] Carlson book, pp.133–134, 153–154; Ten Boom book, pp. 87–88, quote from p. 88.

and Darlene Cunningham, this global ministry presently has more than 15,000 unsalaried full-time staff around the world and thousands more part-time staff. Each worker must raise their own support, ultimately trusting that God will provide funds from month to month. YWAM, which has worked in every nation of the world, continues to be one of the world's largest Christian charitable organizations.[50]

The vast majority of Christian organizations, however, have changed a lot in recent decades in the areas of planning their finances, raising money, and meeting their budgets. The trend has been for most Christian organizations to model themselves to some extent on secular business principles. They have developed financial plans and procedures that are a lot more structured and sophisticated than the simple Mueller method of prayer, faith, and waiting on God. Most ministries now employ salaried staff and rely on carefully designed fund-raising systems.

Even churches have jumped on the business-model bandwagon. Large American churches, such as Willow Creek, receive annual income of tens of millions of dollars. In the last decade, Willow Creek built a new sanctuary costing more than $70 million. In recent years, a Stanford MBA has run Willow Creek Community Church's day-to-day management.

Willow Creek also formed a separate consulting arm called the Willow Creek Association and hired Jim Mellado, who earned his MBA degree from Harvard Business School, to be its chief. The Willow Creek Association provides marketing and management advice to thousands of other churches. In 2004, for example, over 100,000 church and lay leaders attended Willow Creek conferences, bringing substantial revenue to their Association. Willow Creek recently ranked in the top 5% of the world's major brands, alongside marketing marvels like Nike.[51]

Another Harvard MBA, Stephen Douglass, has been at the helm of Campus Crusade for Christ.

---

[50]   www.ywam.org.
[51]   Lindsay book, p. 163; Symonds article.

Carson Pue of Arrow Leadership noted that Christian leaders today are sometimes "bewildered" by the two different approaches that I have described: the Mueller approach vs. the secular business model approach.[52] Are both approaches still valid? Should they be blended? I personally think a blended model is best.

The world has changed since the days of Mueller and ten Boom. Christian non-profit corporations and charities must have a formal Board of Directors. These Directors are subject to increasingly complex and stringent laws that impose a high standard of due diligence and potential liability for financial decisions. I have served on the boards of various Christian ministries, including a large church, and have been consulted by many others. I understand the need for prudent, practical, knowledgeable leadership. I recognize that some Christian ministries have suffered in the past (or have fallen apart) because of financial naïveté, mismanagement, or misguided faith.

The new highly structured, business-like approach has its necessary advantages, but I personally believe that too many Christian organizations have strayed so far from the faith-and-prayer approach that something of great value has been lost in the process. In my humble opinion, many present ministries have become too much like secular business machines. It's sad to see strategies such as marketing and branding become more important than faith-filled prayer and patient reliance on God. I wonder what God thinks about all this? How can He help us find a better balance between the faith model and the prudent business model?

As I continue to serve Christian organizations and ministries in various capacities, I want to better understand how to integrate faith, prayer, *and* business sense in the process of raising and managing financial funds.

## God's Three Ways of Responding to Our Faith for Our Finances

In their book, authors Hill and Pitts have summarized three ways in which God responds to our faith-filled prayers for our material

---

[52]  Pue book, p. 179.

needs and godly desires. Whether an individual or an organization is involved, God either provides: (a) miraculously (for example, by sending manna from heaven or an unexpected cheque in the mail); (b) by giving us a harvest we have not worked for (like when the Israelites first entered the Promised Land and ate the bounty of harvests grown from seeds they did not sow and vines they did not tend); and/or (c) by giving us a harvest that has grown from seeds we have planted and vines we have tended (in other words, arising from our own hard work).[53]

In the next chapter, we will study the most common way God provides for our material needs and good desires: our own hard work.

*Ask, and it will be given to you…*

Matthew 7:7

*I tell you the truth, if you had faith even as small as a mustard seed, you could say to this mountain, "Move from here to there," and it would move. Nothing would be impossible.*

Matthew 17:20b–21 (NLT)

*This is the confidence we have in approaching God: that if we ask anything according to his will, he hears us. And if we know that he hears us — whatever we ask — we know that we have what we asked of him.*

1 John 5:14–15 (NIV)

---

[53]　Hill and Pitts book, p. 112.

# 11

---

## THE WORK ELEMENT

*A hard worker has plenty of food, but a person who chases
fantasies has no sense.*

Proverbs 12:11 (NLT)

*Work brings profit, but mere talk leads to poverty!*

Proverbs 14:23 (NLT)

*Do you see any truly competent workers?
They will serve kings…*

Proverbs 22:29 (NLT)

While reading *Thank God It's Monday,* I came across the results of an interesting survey. Fifty percent of the Christians surveyed had never heard a single sermon about work. Over seventy percent stated that they had not been taught a theology about work.[54] Since work is the primary way that most of us acquire money, we can certainly benefit from examining the biblical framework for the activity that takes up so many hours of our days.

---

[54]  Greene book, p. 18.

## Designed for Work

God did not intend for labour to be a punishment; rather, He designed it to be fulfilling. God Himself worked hard by creating the world. He derived great satisfaction from His labour. After each stage of His work, God paused to admire His creation and to declare that it was all good.

God wanted humankind to bear His image by also working. God told Adam to rule over all living things (Genesis 1:26, 28) and to maintain the garden, "to work it and to keep it" (Genesis 2:15). Adam also had the creative task of naming all living things (Genesis 2:19–20). Eve worked alongside Adam. In our present fallen world, prickly thistles may grow in our gardens, but work is still meant to be a meaningful and productive part of our experience on this planet.

Even Jesus worked, as a carpenter (Mark 6:3). He likely spent at least fifteen years working at that trade (compared to just three years in public ministry). The fact that He did so gives great dignity to the ordinary working life.

We often think of imitating what Jesus did in His public ministry. Have you considered that putting in an honest day's work at an ordinary job, year after year, is also emulating Jesus? Have you ever thought of Jesus as an average working Joe?

I wonder what His working life was like. Did wood dealers ever try to rip Him off? Did He have to deal with complaining customers? Did He have to put up with competitors trying to bad-mouth Him? Did His hands get calloused or His throat dry from breathing in the sawdust? Was the work ever tedious?

Or did Jesus enjoy what He was doing? Did He take pride and pleasure in the sawing, hammering, sanding, and polishing? I imagine Him working with diligence and excellence, glad to be making useful items. I imagine Him charging fair prices and being helpful with customers.

Although we can only speculate about those scenarios, it is nonetheless fascinating to spend some moments pondering the conventional working period of His life.

Even after Jesus began public ministry, the task of cooking fish for His disciples was not beneath His dignity. In fact, He described Himself as a servant and told us that the greatest among us will also be servants. What do servants do? They work.

The apostle Paul laboured (in the trade of tent-making) to provide for his own needs and sometimes for the needs of others ministering with him (Acts 18:3, 20:33–35). Presumably, this work occupied many hours of his days.

Clearly, God values ordinary labour. Work is a necessary part of life.

## Sowing and Harvesting

The farmer sows seeds when he works. Later, he benefits from the great harvest that those seeds produce. When we work, all of us are sowing seeds that will allow us to reap some kind of future harvest. Work is profitable.

Some people work directly for money. Others, such as those who work full-time as parents and home-makers, certainly earn their keep. They do not earn money in those roles, but they do free up their spouses to work outside the home, facilitating their spouses' opportunities to maximize their income and career potential.

We will all eventually reap what we have sown. In fact, we will reap hopefully *much more* than we have sown. One seed of wheat turns into a head of wheat comprised of many grains. One kernel of corn becomes a stalk full of whole cobs of corn. One apple seed matures into a tree rich with apples. Genesis 26:12a records how Isaac sowed his land and reaped in the same year a hundred times what he sowed. Proverbs 12:14 declares that "the work of a man's hand comes back to him." Proverbs 13:11 asserts that: "…wealth from hard work grows over time" (NLT).

To reap a good harvest, we must aspire to live in obedience to God in every area of our lives, including our work. Deuteronomy 28:1–14 describes the blessings that befall those who love and obey God: they will be blessed in their fields, baskets, barns, and everything they put their hands to.

For those who are disobedient and rebellious, Deuteronomy 28:38–40 spells out this solemn warning: "You shall carry much seed into the field and shall gather in little, for the locust shall consume it. You shall plant vineyards and dress them, but you shall neither drink of the wine nor gather the grapes, for the worm shall eat them. You shall have olive trees throughout all your territory, but you shall not anoint yourself with the oil, for your olives shall drop off." Along those same lines, King Solomon observed the weary and fruitless toil of the fool (Ecclesiastes 10:15).

## Enjoying Work

In Ecclesiastes 1:3, King Solomon poses a fascinating question: "What does man gain by all the toil at which he toils under the sun?" In Ecclesiastes 2:11, he moans: "Then I considered all that my hands had done and the toil I had expended in doing it, and behold, all was vanity and a striving after wind, and there was nothing to be gained under the sun." Later in chapter 2, King Solomon laments that others would ultimately benefit from his toil after he was gone.

His further reflections upgrade the value of work. In Ecclesiastes 2:24–25, he opines: "There is nothing better for a person than that he should eat and drink and find enjoyment in his toil. This also, I saw, is from the hand of God…"

He repeats that upbeat theme in Ecclesiastes 3:9–13: "What gain has the worker from his toil? I have seen the business that God has given to the children of man to be busy with….I perceived that there is nothing better for them than to be joyful and to do good as long as they live; also that everyone should eat and drink and take pleasure in all his toil—this is God's gift to man." In Ecclesiastes 3:22a, he reaffirms: "So I saw that there is nothing better than that a man should rejoice in his work, for that is his lot."

In Ecclesiastes 9:10, he ultimately concludes: "Whatever your hand finds to do, do it with your might…" The apostle Paul echoes this comment in his letter to the Colossians, wherein he encourages Christians to work heartily as unto the Lord (Colossians 3:23).

It is always a pleasure to observe people who enjoy their work. I have met hair stylists, sales clerks, and taxi drivers who put their hearts and souls into their work even though their jobs are not as highly paid as other jobs. They simply love what they do, and they bless others as a result.

In contrast, too many people today don't enjoy their work. They consider it drudgery. Perhaps they suffer from cubicle coma. The popular TV show *The Office* comically depicts dissatisfied drones distracting themselves from their boring work with gossip or flirting or stirring up trouble.

If you are one of those who don't enjoy your work, perhaps it's time to: start praying about (and looking for) a new kind of job position; or seek somehow to modify the one you have; or, at a minimum, seek to change your attitude. Most of us spend far too many hours working each week to get stuck disliking what we are doing. Most of us will also spend many years at it, maybe more than we bargained for, thanks to the recent recession. I encourage you *not* to settle for work you do not enjoy. You have probably heard the expression that we should be making a life, not just making a living. Although on a certain level we work for money, we should also be working for something more.

If you are trying to figure out what work you would enjoy, I suggest reading the best-selling classic *What Color is Your Parachute?* which explores how to find work that aligns with your core values, skills, and goals. Various practical exercises are provided to help you with this process. If you browse around bookstores, you will find other good books along these lines. In addition, if you can afford it, a few sessions with a career counsellor might be beneficial.

All of us have been given skills by God—skills we can joyfully use. The Spirit of God filled Bezalel so that he had the ability, intelligence, knowledge, and craftsmanship to create artistic designs (Exodus 31:2–5). Don't you think Bezalel enjoyed putting all of that talent to work every day?

Work can potentially be so enjoyable that some do not ever want to retire. World-renowned business expert Peter Drucker wanted to work until the end of his life, just like his mother. She operated her antique shop in Vienna until her nineties. She died one morning happily sitting in her shop.[55] My own father, now past eighty, still works a few days a week in a position he enjoys.

Of course, work will never be one-hundred percent pleasurable. After Adam sinned, God decreed: "By the sweat of your face you shall [now] eat bread…" (Genesis 3:19). Realistically, work will have some moments of pure sweat, but surely it is not meant to be constant torture.

We are not meant to work endlessly in toxic work environments or for harsh taskmasters who treat us poorly. You may recall how the Israelites were mistreated by the Egyptians in the generations after Joseph. We learn in Exodus 3:7–10 that God saw their cruel taskmasters and He heard the cry of His oppressed people. He promised, through Moses, to bring them out of that slavery to a better place. I believe that God still wants to help His people break free from the shackles of heartless taskmasters and harsh working conditions.

## Working Hard

The Christian faith celebrates hard work. A great example is the Proverbs 31 woman, who personifies the virtue of hard work. Listen to this description of her average day:

> "She seeks wool and flax, and works with willing hands….She rises while it is yet night and provides food for her household and portions for her maidens. She considers a field and buys it; with…her hands she plants a vineyard….She perceives that her merchandise is profitable. Her lamp does not go out at night. She puts her hands to the distaff, and her hands hold the spindle…. She makes linen garments and sells them; she delivers sashes to the merchant….She looks well to the ways of her household and does not eat the bread of idleness… 'Many women have done excellently, but you surpass

---

[55]  Stern article.

them all'…Give her of the fruit of her hands, and let her works praise her in the gates" (Proverbs 31:13–16, 18–19, 24, 27, 29, 31).

In contrast, the Bible provides many warnings about laziness:

- Go to the ant, O sluggard; consider her ways and be wise….she prepares her bread in summer and gathers her food in harvest. How long will you lie there, O sluggard? When will you arise from your sleep? A little sleep, a little slumber, a little folding of the hands to rest, and poverty will come upon you like a robber, and want like an armed man. (Proverbs 6:6–11)

- A slack hand causes poverty, but the hand of the diligent makes rich. (Proverbs 10:4)

- A wise youth makes hay while the sun shines, but what a shame to see a lad who sleeps away his hour of opportunity. (Proverbs 10:5 TLB)

- Lazy people want much but get little, but those who work hard will prosper. (Proverbs 13:4 NLT)

- Whoever works his land will have plenty of bread, but he who follows worthless pursuits will have plenty of poverty. (Proverbs 28:19)

- Through sloth the roof sinks in, and through indolence the house leaks. (Ecclesiastes 10:18)

Perhaps you have heard about the employee who was asked by his supervisor how long he had been working at the company. The employee answered that he had been working ever since he saw the supervisor coming down the hall.

Another man was asked how many people work at his company. He answered that one out of every five of them work.

The apostle Paul was very blunt about the issue of laziness. In Romans 12:11, he taught: "Never be lazy, but work hard and serve the Lord enthusiastically" (NLT). In 2 Thessalonians 3:10–11, he instructed: "…If anyone is not willing to work, let him not eat. For we hear that some among you walk in idleness, not busy at work, but busybodies."

Let's not waste our own opportunities. Instead, let us put our hands to the plough so we can put bread on our tables. It would be nice if life could be like a Monopoly game, where all we would have to do is shake the dice. Every few turns we would pass "Go" and collect another easy $200. Every once in a while we might also land on "Chance" or "Free Parking" and obtain the windfall of another property, house, hotel, or a big cash infusion. In real life, making money takes a lot more effort!

## But Not Too Hard

We are mandated to work hard, but not *too* hard. In our present world, where a prevailing culture of long hours rules in many places, the ever-present danger of workaholism lurks. This can lead to rust-out and eventually burn-out. Rust-out involves living hollowly, robotically going through the motions of work without positive emotions. Burn-out leads to overwhelming fatigue, break-down, and perhaps total inability to carry on. If you feel on the brink of any of those conditions, I encourage you to spend serious time talking to God and others about it.

A *Wall Street Journal* article described a man who once worked on that street. Long hours of work exacted a heavy cost. He did not see his wife very often, and when he did, he was distracted. His children did not know him. His friendships did not extend beyond e-mail interaction. After finally giving up his demanding position, he now writes columns and blogs about how happiness is not to be found in work-obsession.[56]

If those around you are working like maniacs, dare to be counter-cultural. Dare to stop working *so* hard. After all, we know that promotion does not come from the east or the west, but from the hand of God

---

[56]  Newmark article.

(Psalm 75:6–7). We should put in an honest day's work, but we don't need to toil slavishly to please our employers. They may think that they have the ultimate power over us, but they don't. If they won't let us work decent hours, we can always look for work elsewhere. Paul advised in 1 Corinthians 7:23: "You were bought with a price; do not become slaves of men."

Jesus made this wonderful invitation: "Come to me, all who labor and are heavy laden, and I will give you rest. Take my yoke upon you…For my yoke is easy, and my burden is light" (Matthew 11:28–30). If our overriding desire is to please God, we do not have to be chronically overtired or overworked.

## Work/Life Balance

Perhaps you are working harder than you want to be working. Perhaps you wish you had more time for family, fellowship, friends, and fitness. Perhaps you need to somehow reconfigure your career so that your life becomes more sane.

Many businesses and professional firms are presently paying greater heed to work/life balance issues. In large American companies, there's even a growing trend to provide in-house chaplains who can counsel employees regarding a range of issues, including how to balance work and family.

At the March 2010 White House Forum on Workplace Flexibility, President Obama and his wife, Michelle, both shared about the struggles they have gone through over the years trying to balance work, home, and community with time for one's own needs. President Obama told the gathered business community that "raising the next generation is the most important job we have." The Forum demonstrated that in many families both men and women want to find the right work/life balance so that they can be more involved in their children's lives.[57]

I believe that God cares at least as much as we do about us spending more time with our marriage partner and our kids…our extended family, our best friends, and our fellow Christians…*and* with Him of

---

[57]   Friedman article.

course. He also cares that we somehow fit in ministry opportunities, home management, money management, taking care of ourselves, and all the other necessary ingredients of a well-balanced life. If you struggle with balancing all of this, I encourage you to pray about it every single day until there is some sort of breakthrough in your situation. It may not happen overnight, but ultimately, God can help each one of us to find solutions that suit each distinct phase of our lives. Because we will all likely go through a series of changes over the years, we need to keep asking God to help us fit our evolving priorities into a reasonably ordered life.

I love Matthew 7:7, wherein Jesus instructs us to ask, seek, and knock. If we do, Jesus promised that we *will* receive, we *will* find, and the door *will* be opened for us. Stand on this verse. Begin to make small changes at work. Pray. Ask God if you should consider looking for a new job. By taking these steps, you will move closer and closer to the appropriate work/life balance.

## Being Content with Our Work and Pay

Even though we do need to set boundaries at work, we should never let ourselves resent our work. In these days of high unemployment, let's remain grateful for our work and whatever income we are paid! Work may not always be fun, but it is always a *gift*.

Jesus instructed us: "…be content with your pay" (Luke 3:14c NLT). Jesus did not specify a certain amount of pay. God will call each one of us into different kinds of work, at differing rates of pay. Whether it is a little or a lot, we are to be content with it. This directive fits well with other mandated attitudes such as serving God instead of gold.

We will not be content with our pay if we fall into the mistake of comparing our salary with what others receive. Some people get paid more than we do. Some people get paid as much as we do, even though they don't work as hard or as many hours.

Jesus told an interesting parable in Matthew 20 about various workers. Some started their work in the morning. Others started at mid-day. Yet others started late in the day. Their master had agreed with each one that they would be paid one denarius. It seemed to them (and perhaps to us) that this was not fair. We can get riled up inside when we compare our income with others. Perhaps one of the lessons to be learned from this parable is that we are to be thankful that we have any work at all instead of wasting energy comparing our workload or our pay with others' workload or pay.

## Enjoying the Fruits of Our Labour

We are meant to enjoy the fruits of our labour, not just the labour itself. The Book of Ecclesiastes talks much about daily enjoying our food and our drink. Hard work can also earn for us an education, a home, and the financial ability to save, invest, spend, and give.

Aside from earning money, and what money can buy, we can also find intangible rewards from our work such as challenge, satisfaction, and fulfilment. Work is not just about making money. Having said that, there may be seasons in our lives when we have to work at *any* decent job to finance our education, pay off debt, or put food on the table. Over the long haul, however, I think each one of us should seek work that gives us a sense of meaning beyond just earning dollars.

On a different note, let's not take the Ecclesiastes "eat, drink, and be merry" message too far. Although we can appropriately enjoy the fruits of our labour, we should not become self-centred hedonists, wantonly pursuing pleasure. The Bible warns that the person who *lives* for pleasure risks eventually frittering away their wealth. Proverbs 21:17, for example, forecasts: "Whoever loves pleasure will be a poor man…" Proverbs 23:21 adds: "…the drunkard and the glutton will come to poverty…"

## Being Out of Work

Many individuals have been down-sized during the recent global recession. If you are one of these, perhaps this chapter has felt heavy. Perhaps you want to work hard and to enjoy work and excel at it, but you do not presently have the opportunity to do so.

I encourage you to trust God. I have lived long enough to see the truth in the cliché that when God closes one door, He usually opens a better door somewhere else (although not necessarily overnight). Perhaps you will look back one day and see that losing your job was actually a blessing in disguise, a stepping-stone to finding a more meaningful job.

In Matthew 20, Jesus tells a parable about the master of a vineyard who went out looking for workers to hire. The master, noticing some men who were "idle in the marketplace" (v. 3), hired them to work in his vineyard.

The master came back to the town market again later that day: "… he went out and found *others* standing. And he said to them, 'Why do you stand here idle all day?' They said to him, 'Because no one has hired us.' He said to them, 'You go into the vineyard too'"(vv. 6–7). The master even paid them what he had paid those who were fortunate enough to be hired earlier in the day. He cared that *everyone* made a living wage, enough to meet their needs that day.

Jesus was then—and is now—the master of the vineyard. He is the one who goes looking for those who stand idle in the marketplace. If you are not presently employed but wish to be, I believe that He is lovingly looking for you. Jesus *continues* to have enormous compassion for those who wait on the sidelines of the marketplace.

## A Few Comments About Women and Work

I have had zillions of challenging conversations over my lifetime about Christian women and their work roles. I don't think anybody has a problem with single Christian women working in the paid labour force. In the Western world, it is the expected norm. Once Christian women marry and have children, however, the issue of women working outside the home becomes more controversial.

I will not debate whether Christian mothers should be stay-at-home moms or whether it's fine for them to work part-time or full-time. Every woman, and every married couple, has to sort this out personally. Every woman can consider her own unique situation: her education, skills, opportunity to earn income, energy level, desire to maintain a career, the need for extra family income, and her sense that God has called her to work beyond her home. Every woman can also prayerfully evaluate whether her husband is supportive of her working and whether excellent caregivers are ready to help raise her children.

I shared earlier about my decision (made with my husband) to work on a reduced-hours basis during the years we were raising our kids. Just because that was *our* particular decision, I do not believe it is necessarily the right decision for every woman and every couple in every circumstance.

I have profound respect for stay-at-home moms. Women's work in the home (and yes, it *is* real work) needs to be more highly valued. A 2007 survey (on a website called salary.com) made this remarkable finding: if stay-at-home moms received a paid salary (including a premium for overtime) for all the tasks they perform (including being childcare specialists, chefs, housecleaners, launderers, drivers, pet-walkers, gardeners, decorators, and nurses) they would earn over $130,000 a year. When women work outside the home, some of those tasks have to be handed over to paid professionals. Stay-at-home moms save the family a lot of money!

I have learned firsthand that women involved in 24/7 hands-on parenting and home-making roles work *just as hard* as women working outside the home. During the years that I alternated shifts as a mom/homemaker and lawyer, I did not find one job easier than the other. When my kids were small, being at home was in many ways harder than working at the office (even though being a mom was so rewarding). At the office, I could drink my cup of coffee while it was still hot. I could take a refreshing lunch break and enjoy uninterrupted adult conversation. And even the most unreasonable client was a *lot* more reasonable than a toddler having a tantrum! On the other hand, it was pretty nice playing in the park with my kids on a sunny day, enjoying the pleasant company of other moms. Both kinds of work had tough moments *and* moments of enjoyment.

I also admire some of the Christian women I know who manage to work outside the home full-time yet still have lots of energy left over to spend significant time focused on their family. Women's work outside the home is worthy of respect. I believe there is sound biblical basis for such respect. The exemplary Proverbs 31 woman managed her home but also found time to buy investment property, earn profit from the vineyard she managed, and sell her handmade clothing in the marketplace. She worked diligently in her home *and* as a business-woman.

Deborah, another Old Testament woman of note, served as a judge and a military commander. Lydia, an esteemed Christian woman in the New Testament, was a seller of purple fabric in the marketplace (see Acts 16:14).

Those who say mothers should not work outside the home typically rely on these two biblical passages: 1 Timothy 5:14 and Titus 2:3–5.

The Timothy verse states that women should "manage their households." Note the word "manage." In any enterprise, managers don't do all the work themselves. They supervise others. They delegate. If a woman works outside the home and makes enough money to pay for some childcare, cleaning, and gardening services, isn't she *managing* her home and family just like the Proverbs 31 woman, who also had the benefit of household help?

In the Titus passage, older women in the church are instructed to train the younger women to work at home (or be busy at home). Even women who work at a career are busy at home for *many* hours! Career women end up working inside their home *and* beyond. Career women do not violate the spirit of the Titus passage.

These days, women's choices are expanding. It's no longer just a choice between working outside the home (full-time or part-time) or being a stay-at-home mom. An increasing number of women make money in their own homes. Some women set up their own home businesses. Others work for employers but telecommute from home.

## Conclusion

If Jesus had to work many years as an integral part of His life on earth, then it should not surprise us that we, too, have to work. This reality should not bother us. Work is a gift. It is meant to be enjoyed. If we do enjoy our work, we will likely become good at it. It is the main way that individuals and families make money. By working hard, we will reap great rewards, monetary and otherwise. I encourage you to do whatever it takes to get this dimension of your life in order. Work is a vital element of building our financial lives on a firm foundation.

*Those too lazy to plow in the right season
will have no food at the harvest.*

Proverbs 20:4 (NLT)

*Good planning and hard work lead to prosperity…*

Proverbs 21:5 (NLT)

*You shall eat the fruit of the labor of your hands; you shall
be blessed, and it shall be well with you.*

Psalm 128:2

*Plant your seed in the morning and keep busy all afternoon,
for you don't know if profit will come from one activity or
another—or maybe both.*

Ecclesiastes 11:6 (NLT)

# 12

---

# THE CHALLENGE OF CHANGE

*Praise be to the name of God for ever and ever; wisdom and
power are his. He changes times and seasons; he sets up
kings and deposes them. He gives wisdom to the wise and
knowledge to the discerning.*

Daniel 2:20–21 (NIV)

*Sometimes in the winds of change,
we find our true direction.*

Author unknown

A primary school teacher recently learned just how much our
world is changing. While teaching her class about barnyard animals,
she asked her students what noise a pig makes. "Oink, oink," they
all shouted out. "What noise does a cow make?" the teacher asked
next. "Moo, moo," they answered. "What about a duck?" the teacher
queried. "Quack, quack," was the gleeful response. Finally, she asked
the children what noise a mouse makes. "Click, click," they called out.

Change. It is an inevitable part of our lives. Soon, even the computer
mouse will be a relic of history.

The process of developing our talents, completing an education, finding quality work, becoming competent at it, and getting to the point of making a good living takes years. Some people try various educational and career paths before they discover what they are good at and will enjoy doing. Throughout this process, both the world that we journey through and our own circumstances constantly change.

Getting from seedtime to harvest takes time...lots of time. We cannot expect instant results. We all need to cultivate patience and perseverance as we press on in faith. Along the way, we will need to *initiate* change and *adapt* to whatever change intersects our path.

Ecclesiastes 9:11 talks about time and chance happening to us all. If we think of chance as opportunity, what Solomon was saying is that, *over time*, God will grant each one of us divine opportunities. In the meantime, we have to keep our hands diligently pushing whatever plough is in front of us—sometimes in the wind, sometimes in the rain, sometimes in the sunshine, sometimes in the dark.

While reading biographies, I have marvelled at how other Christians have faced the ever-changing circumstances of their lives. Here are five stories of Christians who have handled change well, at times creating it and at other times bravely reacting to it.

Colonel Harland Sanders (the Christian businessman who invented KFC chicken) lost his father when Harland was very young. His widowed mother went back to work. At only six years of age, little Harland became the family cook. During his childhood, he mastered the art of cooking. He put his whole heart into working hard at the family chore he had been assigned.

Years later, at the age of forty (after working in various jobs), Harland began operating a service station in Kentucky. In those days, service stations simply serviced the needs of cars. Still an enthusiastic cook, Harland came up with the novel idea of serving his home-made chicken to the hungry travellers who stopped for gas at his station. The customers loved his chicken.

Sometimes we have zero choice in the way that life changes. When a state highway was built over the site of his business, Harland was forced to decide what to do next. God helped him to come up with another winning idea. Instead of trying to start a new restaurant, Harland decided to sell his secret recipe to other entrepreneurs. In 1955, at the age of sixty-five, he began franchising his chicken business. It's amazing to realize that he *started* his legendary franchise business at the age when most people think of retiring.

Within less than a decade, about 600 KFC franchises began operating in North America. In 1964, when he was in his mid-seventies, Harland sold his personal interest in KFC for $2 million. His legacy carries on. Today, more than one billion KFC chicken dinners are served each year in more than eighty countries around the world.

Harland's story is a classic reminder that not one of us develops our full potential (financially or otherwise) overnight. While it's true that some people become quite successful even in their twenties, most people don't really hit their stride until a later decade. Like Harland, some of us change careers along the way.

It is never too late to start a new business, develop a new idea, or pursue a new dream. It may be that our greatest success in life is still ahead of us! And our greatest success might be in something we can't, at the moment, even imagine ourselves doing.

We can all learn a lesson in flexibility from Harland. He was content to serve his chicken, at one location, to a modest number of travellers for years. He did not stress or strain or strive to be a big success. Every day, he simply put one foot in front of the next, making the best chicken he could, pleased that his customers enjoyed his special recipe. Harland loved operating his small business until God tapped him on the shoulder with a bigger plan. When that time came, he was ready to try something new, to walk through an open door into a different kind of opportunity.

Another fascinating story can be found in the life of Christian businessman J. C. Penney. (His middle name was actually Cash!) Penney started his first business at the age of eight. Although it did not last long, he did not allow his lack of success to diminish his dream of becoming a businessman.

After a few further unsuccessful business starts in his adult life, Penney opened a dry-goods store. He purposed to run his store on the basis of the "golden rule." Customers loved the store, and before long, Penney owned dozens of stores that generated a few million dollars a year—big numbers in pre-World-War-I America. By 1917, Penney owned 1,400 stores.

Then a series of sad circumstances unfolded. Penney's wife died in childbirth. Distraught, he developed a drinking problem. In 1929, the Great Stock Market Crash destroyed him financially, wiping out a personal fortune of approximately forty million dollars. Not surprisingly, he suffered both physical and mental health problems as the Depression further shook the financial foundations of America. All of those negative changes seemed, for a while, to have shipwrecked his life on every level.

After a fresh encounter with God, Penney rebounded from his struggles. Borrowing money in his mid-fifties, he started over financially. Penney chose not to be defeated by his previous failures, difficulties, and disappointments. By pulling up the socks of his faith and by working hard, Penney became a highly successful businessman all over again. Patiently persevering in growing a whole new chain of stores, he eventually owned a store in every one of the fifty American states, employing tens of thousands of people. By 1951, the revenues of the J. C. Penney Company exceeded one billion dollars. Penney kept on working in his business into his eighties.[58]

Ed Noble, another interesting Christian businessman, mastered the art of change. In 1915, while working as an advertising salesman, Noble decided to follow his dream of developing his own business in a different field. Borrowing money to buy the rights to an unknown mint, Noble and a friend entered the candy business. The two men knew very little about that business and their venture got off to a rocky start.

At first, the men had trouble developing the right kind of packaging. They discovered that their mints lost their flavour after a short time on the store shelf. Even worse, over a longer time period, the

---

[58]   Loveless book, pp. 162–165; Woodbridge book.

mints tasted like the glue used in their packaging. Not surprisingly, the men had trouble getting repeat business.

Noble and his partner persevered. They made various changes. Progress occurred when they created tin-foil packaging that successfully preserved the strong mint flavour. By that point, Noble and his partner at least had a product worth buying. Sales increased.

Their biggest breakthrough came when Noble developed a new marketing strategy. He requested that stores and restaurants place his mints near their cash registers where customers could easily see them. Selling for only five cents a package, the mints became a hit.

Noble eventually developed a new range of candy products that he called Life Savers. These candies have a distinctive circular shape with a hole in the middle. They earned their name by preventing choking, for even if a Life Saver were to become lodged in a child's throat, the child could still breathe. In addition, the candies look like the life-preserving ring that can be tossed to a drowning person.

The initial few-thousand-dollar investment of Noble and his partner turned into a business worth hundreds of millions. A few years ago, Life Savers were the key product line in a business deal worth about $1.5 billion dollars.[59]

Condoleezza Rice has also mastered change. She planned and prepared all through her childhood and teen years to be a concert pianist on the international stage. In early adulthood, she had to accept the reality that she was not quite good enough to make it to that elite level. She wandered into political studies by default. It was later in life that Rice recognized that God had led her onto the path of His choosing. Rice became a well-respected Secretary of State during the Presidency of George Bush. She has since transitioned well back into the academic world.

Best-selling author John Grisham planned and prepared during his growing-up years to be a professional baseball player. Like Rice, he was greatly disappointed that he couldn't prevail in the final cut. He then spent four years getting an accounting degree, only to decide he did

---

[59]  Loveless book, pp. 165–167; various media reports.

not like that profession. He went into law and practiced for ten years. In the midst of that journey, he discovered his real passion: writing novels. Working from 5 a.m. until breakfast-time each day, on a type-writer perched on the narrow counter between the family's washing machine and clothes dryer, he wrote his debut novels, *A Time to Kill* and *The Firm*. He has since written several novels, sold millions of copies to date, and made many millions of dollars. It took Grisham four career changes to reach the place where he is finally really thriving.

One of the common denominators behind the enormous success of the above five Christians has been their admirable ability to adeptly handle change. Along the way, they boldly *initiated* change and mas-terfully *responded* to necessary change with courageous resolve. Many Bible characters such as Moses, Joseph, and Ruth had the same trait.

All of us need to learn how to manage change, whether we delib-erately foster it or are forced to react to it. The world around us keeps changing at breakneck speed. I have heard speakers in the workplace talk about how employees these days need to be managers of their own careers because they might find themselves changing jobs (or even careers) seven or more times during their lives.

Thankfully, the same God who helped Sanders, Penney, Noble, Rice, and Grisham deal with change can also help us and our children as we move forward in a world where companies such as Microsoft, Apple, and Google foster perpetual change.

*For everything there is a season, and a time*
*for every matter under heaven...*

Ecclesiastes 3:1

*Jesus Christ is the same yesterday and today and forever.*

Hebrew 13:8

# 13

---

# THE PROSPERITY DEBATE

*…he who trusts in the Lord will prosper.*

Proverbs 28:25 (NIV)

A few years ago, *Time* magazine ran a long cover story entitled "Does God Want You to be Rich?"[60] Its two authors explored how Christians in America have taken polarized sides in what I will call the Prosperity Debate. This sometimes fierce debate has become one of the most controversial topics in Christian circles. Some Christians enthusiastically embrace prosperity teaching. Others bash and trash that teaching. Still others watch from the sidelines, not comfortable with taking too bold a stand on either side.

I cannot write a Christian book about money without squarely addressing the subject of prosperity. Some would say this takes courage; others would say it is foolhardy to tackle such a volatile topic. No matter what I write, I am guaranteed to attract criticism.

The *Time* cover story compared the views of current mega-church pastors, such as Joel Osteen, in one camp, with those of other celebrity pastors, such as Rick Warren, in another camp. Those in the former

---

[60] Van Biema and Chu article.

camp preach that God wants all Christians to prosper, while in the opposing camp, Rick Warren calls the premise of prosperity "baloney." Another critic of prosperity teaching does not like God being treated as a "celestial ATM."

The prosperity debate has been kicking around for a few decades now. Back in the 1980s, some well-known pastors began to preach what was soon called "name it and claim it" theology. Preachers of that theology promised that if a person had faith to receive something (some went so far as to say anything they wanted, without limit), the believing person would receive it. This brand of theology was based on biblical verses which, on the surface, appeared to support that broad proposition. In Mark 11:24, for example, we read that whatever we ask for in prayer, we will receive, if we believe. You might recall that we briefly queried the scope of that verse in our section on presumptive faith.

The 1980s version of prosperity theology began to wane this past decade. It has been softened substantially by current pastors such as Osteen, who have been dubbed teachers of Prosperity Lite. They do not advocate "name it and claim it" faith, but they do continue to preach that God wants His people to prosper, to rise up out of poverty, debt, and lack. They posit that God has a purpose for prospering us — and that purpose is *not* to spend everything we receive from Him on our own selfish consumption. Instead, they proclaim that God wants to bless us so that we can be a blessing to others.

The *Time* cover story attributed this quote to Osteen: "I preach that anyone can improve their lives. I think God wants us to be prosperous....I think God wants us to send our kids to college. I think he wants us to be a blessing to other people. But I don't think I'd say God wants us to be rich."[61]

In the *Time* cover story, another well-known American pastor, Kirbyjon Caldwell, defended his present-day version of prosperity teaching: "I am not a proponent of saying the Lord's name three times, clicking your heels and then you get what you ask for. But you cannot

---

[61]  Ibid., p. 33.

give what you do not have….If I am going to help someone, I am going to have to have something with which to help."[62]

After listing some scriptural passages both for and against the premise that God wants to prosper His people, the *Time* cover story concluded that the Bible leaves lots of room for discussion on the prosperity issue. It commented, however, that most pastors are not willing to engage in such a discussion, calling this "one of the more stunning omissions in American religion."[63]

The issue of prosperity continues to generate controversy. Even the current watered-down prosperity teaching has attracted many opponents, both Christian and secular. Journalists have gone so far as to blame prosperity preachers for the recent global financial crisis. In a 2009 article called "Did Christianity Cause the Crash?" author Hanna Rosin alleged that prosperity teaching "pumped air into the housing bubble." Such teaching supposedly prompted parishioners to apply for mortgages on the basis of faith, regardless of their income or debt load. Rosin claimed that those parishioners were sitting ducks for the predatory subprime mortgage industry, which offered too-easy credit. Many home purchasers could not, in fact, afford to pay their mortgages, and they lost their homes in the recent flood of foreclosures.

According to Rosin's research, three of America's dozen largest mega-churches can be considered prosperity churches. In the next tier of churches (those with about 5,000 in their congregations), prosperity teaching dominates. She quoted a Pew study, which found that 66 % of Pentecostals and 43% of Christians from other denominations adhere to the belief that the faithful will receive wealth.[64]

The prosperity gospel is spreading worldwide. It is presently moving across Africa like wildfire.

Where do I stand in the prosperity debate? Let me begin by disclosing a little of my personal history. Soon after I became a Christian, I lived for a while in a Christian community that practiced living simply

---

[62]  Ibid., p. 36.
[63]  Ibid., p. 32.
[64]  Rosin article.

and frugally, elevating that which is spiritual and eternal far above anything material or temporal. I still value what I learned during those months. Later, in my early twenties, I went through a few intense years of listening to prosperity gospel tapes and reading books of that persuasion by American authors who were popular at that time. This was back in the early 1980s, around the time that the original version of the prosperity gospel was gaining a foothold in North America.

I spent time sifting through the prosperity gospel message, trying my best to separate the wheat of it from the chaff. I experimented with its principles, debated them, learned from what happened in my own life, and observed what happened in the lives of others who were applying this theology.

At the end of that process, I could not label myself as an advocate of the prosperity gospel, but neither could I consider myself a caustic critic. I had learned that the word "prosperity" can be found many times in the Bible, sometimes in a positive light, other times with a negative connotation. Some very wealthy men and women in the Bible were great heroes of faith; other rich folk were enemies of God. I formed the opinion that the most ardent fans of the prosperity gospel *and* their harshest critics might be equally misguided if they believe that prosperity is always a good thing or that it is always worldly and wrong. The truth is a lot more complex.

## Two Questions

Does God want His people to prosper? And what exactly does that mean anyway?

As I have pondered how to define prosperity, I have realized that it is probably impossible to define the term in a way that everyone agrees with.

Let's start with this. When words such as "prosper," "prosperous," or "prosperity" are used in the Bible in the context of earthly possessions, we would probably all agree that those words convey a sense of material abundance.

In *some* biblical contexts, these words are associated with God's blessing. In other biblical contexts, however, such words are associated with disobedient, rebellious, and greedy people. That's why we need to give the concept of prosperity very careful thought.

Trying to get a handle on prosperity is further complicated by this issue: how we define material prosperity in a purely North American context might be quite different from how we would define prosperity in a broader global context.

In North America, when we think of someone who is prosperous we often picture them living in an upscale neighbourhood, driving an expensive car, and in various other ways living a kind of affluent lifestyle that is superior to that of the ordinary person. Most North American Christians don't think of themselves as rich folk; surely biblical warnings aimed at the rich don't apply to them.

If we switch our frame of reference to consider the world as a whole, we are forced to redefine what prosperity looks like. If we in North America compare our lives to the billions of people in Third World countries, we must admit that *almost everyone* on this continent lives in *relative* prosperity. Even many of those living in slums and ghettoes in North America are much better off than billions in less fortunate nations. In North America, almost everyone has a somewhat solid roof over their head, probably more than one room in their home, running water, an indoor toilet, electricity, and close access to public services such as paved roads, garbage removal, and other amenities that would be considered luxuries in some parts of the Third World. In Canada, where I live, all legal residents have free access to public education and healthcare, and subsidies such as employment insurance payments or welfare are available for those who are not working. Even the homeless usually have some access to shelters, soup kitchens, clothing depots, and food banks.

I sometimes wonder if God is offended when He hears any North American emphatically state that they oppose the concept of prosperity, all the while still living in relatively comfortable homes, eating three meals a day, wearing clothes without holes, and walking in shoes that still have their soles intact. How can such people say that they *don't buy into* the prosperity message while they are, in fact, *living* in relative prosperity? From a global perspective, that attitude smacks of more than a *little* denial, hypocrisy, and ingratitude.

I don't have to define the word "prosperity" precisely before I can personally state with strong conviction that most North Americans live in *the most prosperous tier* of current humanity. I have travelled to almost one hundred countries, almost half of which would be considered underdeveloped. There is simply no comparison between the lives of the poor in Third World nations and the lives of most of us in North America. I will repeat a few times in this book some facts you might already know: beyond our continent, about one billion people on this planet barely survive on one dollar a day and a further billion scrape by on two dollars a day. If you have *any* money in the bank, you are rich by world standards.

Before I take a stab at more precisely defining what prosperity looks like in a biblical light, I invite you to consider whether or not you are living in the more prosperous half of humanity. If you are, I further invite you to stop attacking the notion of prosperity if you are normally prone to doing so. I suspect that most of my readers will have to own up to the fact that they *do* live in relative prosperity. Such an admission makes it all the more important to give sober thought to how the Bible deals with the concept of prosperity.

After examining the many Bible verses where words associated with material prosperity are used in a positive light, I have personally reached the following conclusion. I believe that God wants to provide His people, wherever we live, with enough money and material goods: (a) to meet our genuine needs; (b) to fulfil the good desires He approves; (c) to allow us to responsibly take care of our families now and in the future; and (d) to enable us to give a generous portion to God and to others. You will have to read this entire book to see how I biblically support the above conclusion.

When words associated with prosperity are used in a *negative* light in the Bible, they describe people who do not acknowledge or obey or thank God, who want *all* of their desires met (without yielding them to God and considering, in dialogue with Him, whether He approves of the desires), who strive to get wealthy by their own power, and who greedily consume their material wealth on themselves alone instead of generously giving and sharing to bless others. This kind of prosperity does not originate with God.

Together, let's now more specifically investigate what the Bible says about prosperity. As you consider the many verses I will present in the next chapter, I invite you to prayerfully work on *your* answers to these two questions: Do you believe that God wants to prosper His people? If so, how would *you* define the parameters of the prosperity He wants to bestow? Given the polarized debate swirling around us, I encourage you to take the time to clearly articulate what *you* believe the right answers to be.

> *Misfortune pursues the sinner, but prosperity*
> *is the reward of the righteous.*

Proverbs 13:21 (NIV)

# 14

---

# BIBLICAL PERSPECTIVES ON PROSPERITY

*This Book of the Law shall not depart from your mouth,*
*but you shall meditate on it day and night, so that you*
*may be careful to do according to all that is written in it.*
*For then you will make your way prosperous, and then*
*you will have good success.*

Joshua 1:8

*Beware lest you say in your heart, "My power and the*
*might of my hand have gotten me this wealth." You shall*
*remember the Lord your God, for it is he who gives you*
*the power to get wealth…*

Deuteronomy 8:17–18

This chapter will provide a number of biblical references, from both the Old and New Testaments, that address prosperity. Hopefully these verses will help us to better clarify how God views prosperity.

## Examples of Wealth as God's Blessing

The Old Testament contains frequent references to individuals blessed with wealth. These numerous references to God-granted material prosperity cannot be swept under the rug.

Abraham acquired large flocks and herds, many servants, and much silver and gold (Genesis 13:2, 24:35). Abraham's son Isaac was just as rich: "The Lord blessed him, and the man became rich, and gained more and more until he became very wealthy" (Genesis 26:12b–13). His material wealth is described clearly as a blessing from God.

Isaac's son Jacob declared: "…God has dealt graciously with me, and…I have enough" (Genesis 33:11b). Jacob perceived his possessions as a blessing from God.

Jacob's son Joseph eventually became one of the wealthy elite in Egypt, second in command to Pharaoh. As soon as Joseph stepped into that position, Pharaoh gave Joseph his own signet ring, beautiful clothing, a gold chain for his neck, and a chariot (Genesis 41:41–43).

Even during the subsequent years of famine, God provided for the material needs of Joseph, his brothers, their families, and his father Jacob. When everyone eventually joined Joseph in Egypt, Pharaoh offered them all "the best of the land" (Genesis 47:6).

Other Old Testament men also acquired remarkable wealth. Job was "the richest person" in his entire area, owning 7,000 sheep, 3,000 camels, and other livestock (Job 1:2–3 NLT). Through no fault of his own, Job lost his wealth for a period of time, but at the end of his trials God gave him double what he had owned before (Job 42:10, 12). Job's renewed, increased prosperity is described in verse 12 as clearly being a blessing from God.

King David lived in splendour during his decades of royal reign. According to 1 Chronicles 29:28, King David accumulated much wealth, and 2 Chronicles 7:10 reveals that this "prosperity" was granted to him by the Lord. He used a significant portion of it to honour God. In preparation for his son's assignment to build the Temple, King David amassed "several billion dollars worth of gold bullion, millions in silver, and so much iron and bronze" that he could not even weigh it.[65]

David's son King Solomon also "prospered," becoming even wealthier than his father (1 Chronicles 29:23, 25). In 1 Kings 3:13, we learn that it was God who gave Solomon such vast riches; 1 Kings 10:23 and 2 Chronicles 9:22 record that Solomon "excelled all the kings of the earth in riches…" Solomon lived in a magnificent palace and owned 1,400 chariots. During his reign, "silver and gold [were] as common in Jerusalem as stone…" (2 Chronicles 1:15).

King Hezekiah also enjoyed God-given material blessing: "Hezekiah had very great riches and honor, and he made for himself treasuries for silver, for gold, for precious stones, for spices, for shields, and for all kinds of costly vessels; storehouses also for the yield of grain, wine, and oil; and stalls for all kinds of cattle, and sheepfolds…. for God had given him very great possessions" (2 Chronicles 32:27–29).

However, not everyone in the Old Testament was wealthy. Many ordinary people worked as soldiers, servants, farmers, or shepherds. Furthermore, many of the individuals named above did not live in comfortable circumstances their whole lives. Job spent a period of time sitting in the dust, in depression and despair, struggling with the loss of his family, his health, and his wealth. Joseph spent years as a servant then as a prisoner before joining Pharaoh's circle. As a young adult, David lived in caves, on the run.

Furthermore, not *all* of the wealthy people in the Old Testament received their wealth as a result of God's blessing. Some obtained wealth by the sweat of their own brow, or by dishonest means, or by oppressing those working for them. Various Pharaohs and pagan kings had great wealth, but it was not from God's hand. In the Old Testament, material prosperity and God's blessing were not always synonymous. The Book of Job, for example, refers several times to the prosperity of the wicked (see chapters 20 and 21).

---

[65]  1 Chronicles 22:14 (TLB): note this translation has converted monetary values to current dollars.

The fact that some of the wealthy were wicked does not negate the truth that, on some occasions, God *did* bestow material wealth as a blessing from His hand. We need to conjoin two counterbalancing premises. While prosperity *can* at times be considered a blessing from God, it *cannot always* be construed as a God-given blessing.

## The Israelites: From Plenty to Poverty to the Promised Land

Jacob (later called Israel) and his sons (who fathered the twelve tribes of Israel) prospered after they came to Egypt, but circumstances eventually changed. In subsequent generations, the Israelites (the people who descended from Jacob) were enslaved and oppressed by the Egyptians for four hundred years.

Their story does not, however, end on that dismal note. Sending Moses to deliver the Israelites, God promised His people that He would lead them to a land flowing with milk and honey. God further promised Moses and the Israelites that they would be able to take some of the wealth of Egypt with them as they departed: "And I will give this people favor in the sight of the Egyptians; and when you go, you shall not go empty, but each woman shall ask of her neighbor, and any woman who lives in her house, for silver and gold jewelry, and for clothing....So you shall plunder the Egyptians" (Exodus 3:21–22). Exodus 12:36 records that this plunder did, in fact, take place.

After leaving Egypt, God led Moses and the Israelites toward the Promised Land. God specified the abundant material prosperity that awaited them there: "For the Lord your God is bringing you into a good land, a land of brooks of water, of fountains and springs, flowing out in the valleys and hills, a land of wheat and barley, of vines and fig trees and pomegranates, a land of olive trees and honey, a land in which you will eat bread without scarcity, in which you will lack nothing, a land whose stones are iron, and out of whose hills you can dig copper. And you shall eat and be full, and you shall bless the Lord your God for the good land he has given you" (Deuteronomy 8:7–10).

The promise of prosperity was followed by a warning: "Take care lest you forget the Lord your God by not keeping his commandments…

lest, when you have eaten and are full and have built good houses and live in them, and when your herds and flocks multiply and your silver and gold is multiplied and all that you have is multiplied, then your heart be lifted up, and you forget the Lord your God…Beware lest you say in your heart, 'My power and the might of my hand have gotten me this wealth.' You shall remember the Lord your God, for it is he who gives you power to get wealth…" (Deuteronomy 8:11–14, 17–18).

I draw your attention to that last sentence: God, not man, would generate their wealth. All good things were to be recognized as blessings from His hand.

This message of promised material prosperity, along with the warning to not abandon God in the midst of that prosperity, were so important that God repeated them, adding consequences: "And if you will indeed obey my commandments that I command you today, to love the Lord your God, and to serve him with all your heart and with all your soul, he will give the rain for your land in its season…that you may gather in your grain and your wine and your oil. And he will give grass in your fields for your livestock, and you shall eat and be full. Take care lest your heart be deceived, and you turn aside and serve other gods and worship them; then the anger of the Lord will be kindled against you, and he will shut up the heavens, so that there will be no rain, and the land will yield no fruit, and you will perish quickly off the good land the Lord is giving you" (Deuteronomy 11:13–17).

## The Blessings and Curses

We cannot talk about the Old Testament perspective on prosperity without specific reference to Deuteronomy 28. This chapter is all about obeying God. Its two key premises are: (1) those who obey God will prosper in various ways and be blessed; (2) those who disobey Him will suffer. Material prosperity is presented as a blessing and poverty as a curse. This passage builds on the promises and warnings Moses had previously given.

Among the many blessings promised to the obedient are these: bountiful crops and flocks, full baskets, and full barns. Deuteronomy

28:11–12 further promises the obedient: "...the Lord will make you *abound in prosperity*, in the fruit of your womb and in the fruit of your livestock and in the fruit of your ground...The Lord will open to you his good treasury, the heavens, to give the rain to your land in its season and to bless the work of your hands. And you shall lend to many nations, but you shall not borrow."

Moses later simply summarizes: "...keep the words of this covenant and do them, that you may prosper in all that you do" (Deuteronomy 29:9).

In contrast, the curses that fall on the disobedient include: failed crops, lack of rain, pestilence, having to borrow, fruitless labour, living in a desolate land overtaken by enemies, and suffering robbery and oppression.[66]

## Psalms and Proverbs

The Psalms and Proverbs refer numerous times to wealth, abundance, and prosperity. Here are some examples:

- He [the godly man] is like a tree planted by streams of water that yields its fruit in its season, and its leaf does not wither. In all that he does, he prospers. (Psalm 1:3)

- For you meet him with rich blessings...(Psalm 21:3)

- Remember me, O Lord, when you show favor to your people; help me when you save them, that I may look upon the prosperity of your chosen ones... (Psalm 106:4–5a)

- Blessed is the man who fears the Lord, who greatly delights in his commandments! His offspring will be mighty in the land; the generation of the upright will be blessed. Wealth and riches are in his house, and his righteousness endures forever....It is well

---

[66]  Deuteronomy 28:17–18, 21–24, 29–30, 33, 38, 44; also see Leviticus 26:16, 26, 32.

with the man who deals generously and lends;…He has distributed freely; he has given to the poor; his righteousness endures forever; his horn is exalted in honor. (Psalm 112:1b–3, 5, 9)

- …may our granaries be full, providing all kinds of produce; may our sheep bring forth thousands and ten thousands in our fields; may our cattle be heavy with young, suffering no mishap or failure in bearing; may there be no cry of distress in our streets! Blessed are the people to whom such blessings fall! Blessed are the people whose God is the Lord! (Psalm 144:13–15)

- Long life is in her [wisdom's] right hand; in her left hand are riches and honor. (Proverbs 3:16)

- Riches and honor are with me [wisdom], enduring wealth and righteousness. (Proverbs 8:18)

- I [wisdom] walk in the way of righteousness, in the paths of justice, granting an inheritance to those who love me, and filling their treasuries. (Proverbs 8:20–21)

- The blessing of the Lord makes rich, and he adds no sorrow with it. (Proverbs 10:22)

- A good man leaves an inheritance for his children's children… (Proverbs 13:22 NIV)

- In the house of the righteous there is much treasure… (Proverbs 15:6)

- The reward for humility and fear of the Lord is riches and honor and life. (Proverbs 22:4)

All of these passages portray prosperity as a good thing, as a blessing from God for those who are wise, God-fearing, and obedient to Him. Prosperity teachers have not taken their ideas out of thin air; they have not magically conjured up their theology out of nothing. While not all of these verses specify *material* prosperity, many of them clearly do.

## The Later History of the Israelites

The Israelites went through cycles of obeying God and then rebelling against Him. For a while, they enjoyed prosperity even while being disobedient. Biblically, their prosperity in those seasons is painted in a negative light.

In Amos 6:4–7, for example, the prophet warned the idolatrous Israelites: "Woe to those who lie on beds of ivory and stretch themselves out on their couches, and eat lambs from the flock and calves....who sing idle songs to the sound of the harp....who drink wine in bowls and anoint themselves with the finest oils....Therefore they shall now be the first of those who go into exile, and the revelry of those who stretch themselves out shall pass away."

Throughout the Old Testament, we can see this recurring pattern of rebellion, disobedience, and punishment. In the midst of enjoying the prosperity granted to them by God in their obedient years, the Israelites too often quickly forgot about God and strayed from Him. God originally intended for material prosperity to be a blessing to His people. When the people turned their backs on Him, however, God despised their prosperity. Sometimes the disobedient enjoyed wealth and ease for a *season*. But troubles of all kinds, including financial troubles, eventually caught up with them.

Just because God condemned the self-indulgent prosperity of the disobedient Israelites, however, doesn't mean He condemns all prosperity.

## Some Final Comments on Old Testament Prosperity

We should not lightly discard any part of the Old Testament unless what is written in the New Testament clearly and unequivocally overrides or replaces what is contained in the Old. We should not blithely throw away: the history of God's dealings with the patriarchs, the kings, and the nation of Israel; Moses' instructions to God's people; the Psalms and Proverbs; or the writings of the prophets. None of that content is in Scripture by accident. If we want to achieve a balanced view of what the Bible as a *whole* says about money, we need to include Old Testament passages about material prosperity in the mix. Leaving out Old Testament verses would only invite imbalance and error. The Old Testament passages discussed in this chapter need to be given some weight.

Now let's consider the New Testament perspective on prosperity.

## The Perspective of Jesus

Jesus was born in a lowly stable yet buried in a rich man's tomb. For most of His adult life, He worked as a carpenter, and was probably able to support himself. During His three years of public ministry, He relied to some extent on the support of others. Susanna and Joanna, for example, helped to support Jesus and His disciples "out of their means" (Luke 8:3). He did not own a home of His own at that point (Luke 9:58). He dined and sometimes stayed in the homes of others, including His friends Lazarus and Martha, His disciple Peter, and wealthy men like Zaccheus.

Jesus did not spend His life aspiring to be wealthy. He probably did not possess much material wealth. He did not build His Kingdom on money. As the Son of God, however, He did, in fact, have whatever material resources in the universe He wanted or needed at His constant disposal. In a flash, He could feed five thousand.

Interestingly, Jesus chose to spend a lot of time talking about money. He showed us, through His many parables, stories, and sermons, that the subject of money is multi-dimensional. He covered a wide range of topics related to money. He is, of course, the perfect model of how we should balance the many different biblical truths about money.

Here is a sampling of key principles that He taught. (I will not recite all the following verses in detail, nor discuss them at length, because they are covered in other sections of this book.)

Jesus promised that our material needs will be met if we put God first (Matthew 6:31–33). He invited us to pray to our Father, asking Him to give us our daily bread (Luke 11:3). On a much broader basis, Jesus said on various occasions that we can ask for anything and, if we believe, we will receive it (see, for example, Mark 11:24). Jesus left that last offer remarkably open-ended. None of these principles specifically contradicts the oft-repeated Old Testament assertion that God will bless His people materially if they obey His commands.

If we can ask for anything, then should we ask for the wealth of Abraham, Job, David, or Solomon?

In order to answer that, we need to factor in the other principles Jesus taught. He stated that we can't serve both God and money (Matthew 6:24). He warned that it will be hard (although not impossible) for a rich man to enter heaven (Mark 10:25). He spoke out against greed (Luke 12:15). He warned that the deceitfulness of riches can choke out the Word of God (Matthew 13:22). None of these teachings forbid wealth *per se*. They do, however, warn about the potential *snares* of wealth, just as God warned the Israelites over and over in the Old Testament.

Although Jesus did not promise us wealth or encourage us to seek it, some of His words imply that we will have some measure of money beyond that which is required to meet our needs. He told us to invest (Luke 19:11–27). He told us to share (Luke 3:11), to feed the hungry, and to clothe the poor (Matthew 25:31–46).

Jesus also declared, in John 10:10, that He had come to give us an abundant life. Abundance is not specified here to be material abundance, but let's also note that material abundance is not excluded. The statement is as open-ended as Jesus' earlier declaration that we can ask for anything and we will receive it.

Beyond all of that, Jesus elevated the importance of the spiritual dimension of our lives and our relationship with God. He posed the famous question in Mark 8:36: "What does it profit a man to gain the whole world and forfeit his life?" Clearly, He saw our spiritual standing as incomparably more significant than our material worth.

Jesus said it was better to store up treasure in heaven than on earth (Luke 12:33–34). He also said that real life is not connected to how rich we are (Luke 12:15).

If we ever reach the point of truly grasping all of what Jesus said, the din and babble about prosperity in this present age will seem relatively trivial. I do believe that Jesus wants to prosper us within the parameters I defined in the last chapter (i.e. to provide us with enough so we can meet our needs, fulfil good desires, responsibly support our families now and in the future, and give generously to God and others), but *above all*, Jesus wants men and women to see how relatively insignificant money and material goods are in the grand scheme of things and how much they can distract us from what is most important.

Bottom line: Jesus lifts our eyes to matters higher, nobler, more meaningful, and more eternally enduring than material prosperity. He said that the two most important commandments are to love God and to love others as we love ourselves. In the eyes of Jesus, the material realm is secondary to what life is really all about.

## The Perspective of Paul

After Jesus left this earth, His followers wrote the New Testament. The apostle Paul wrote a vast portion of it. Does he have anything to add to the discussion about material prosperity?

We know that some Christians in later New Testament times were rich. The apostle Paul commented that while *most* followers of Christ were not wealthy or powerful, some were (1 Corinthians 1:26). He did not rebuke them for being rich.

The apostle Paul declared that the Lord "richly provides us with *everything* for our enjoyment" (1 Timothy 6:17 NIV). According to Paul, God does not poorly provide. He "richly" provides "everything" for our "enjoyment." Meditate for a moment on the words "richly" and "everything" and "enjoyment" and try to figure out in your own mind what you think Paul means in that verse. Consider its context. Given that the verse is located within a chapter that focuses primarily on the topic of money, we can assume that Paul was not talking about rich provision in only the spiritual sense.

As Christians, we know that we will sometimes suffer in this life, but God also wants us to have times of enjoying our lives. Pastors usually preach on all the sufferings that Paul went through—and it is true that he suffered much. Yet it was Paul who penned those words about God richly providing us with everything for our enjoyment. We can venture to guess that Paul must have also personally enjoyed times of rich provision. This assumption is supported by Paul's statements in Philippians 4:12 (that he knew how to live with little or with plenty, to be hungry and well-fed), and in Philippians 4:18b (where he reported: "I am well supplied...").

In 1 Timothy 6:6–10, Paul warned Christians about the consequences of loving money and desiring to be rich. He encouraged Christians to be content with basics such as food and clothing. He again acknowledged, however, that some Christians *were* rich. Paul did not tell them to give away all of their wealth. Instead, he provided these instructions: "As for the rich in this present age, charge them not to be haughty, nor to set their hopes on the uncertainty of riches, but on God, who richly provides us with everything to enjoy. They are to do good, to be rich in good works, to be generous and ready to share, thus storing up treasure for themselves as a good foundation for the future, so that they may take hold of that which is truly life" (1 Timothy 6:17–19).

Those last dozen words help to put material prosperity into proper perspective, echoing what Jesus had emphasized—our *real* lives are *not* related to our riches.

## Conclusion

It is my personal belief that what God told His people in the Old Testament about material prosperity still stands. If His people obey all His commands, then He will prosper them. I don't believe Jesus overrode that general principle by anything He said in the New Testament.

Jesus reminded us, however, of many Old Testament commands (not being covetous or greedy, not loving or serving money, putting

God first, giving, helping the poor, etc.). I posit that obedience to *all* those commands is still a prerequisite to material blessing. Given the great weight that Jesus attached to those other money-related principles, we need to be very careful about prosperity teaching that is too narrow and simplistic or which conveys the notion that all prosperity is a sign of God's blessing.

Today, more than ever, we need to balance and counterbalance *all* of the biblical principles about money. I believe that God wants to prosper us materially to the extent I've defined, but only so long as we pay thoughtful heed to *all* of the other money-related themes that the Bible addresses. If we can learn to care as much about what the Bible says about greed and giving as we care about prosperity, we will be travelling the road that leads to balanced truth. Above all, we must care about our relationships with God and others far more than we care about money.

I love what Billy Graham recently wrote on this subject. He said that "material abundance" should not be the ultimate goal of our society but, instead, simply the product of a "strong work ethic, ingenuity, love of others, and abiding by the principles of Almighty God."[67]

*I spoke to you in your prosperity,*
*but you said, "I will not listen."*

Jeremiah 22:21a

*Let the Lord be magnified, who has pleasure in the*
*prosperity of his servant.*

Psalm 35:27b (NKJV)

*…we went through fire and water, but you*
*brought us to a place of abundance.*

Psalm 66:12 (NIV)

---

[67] Graham book, pp. 23–24.

# 15

---

## A WORLD OF DIFFERENCE

*The rich and the poor meet together;*
*the Lord is the maker of them all.*

Proverbs 22:2

Having discussed material prosperity in the biblical context, let's talk more about our lives in *this* day and age. Does God prosper Christians today in material things, and to what extent?

Harvard Professor Niall Ferguson wryly commented that in this present world there are the Haves, the Have-Nots, and the Have-Yachts. This diversity exists in Christian circles too, rightly or wrongly.

### Today's Have-Nots

Some Christians willingly live among the poor and needy. Mother Teresa was an example of this. She freely chose to have few material possessions.

Other Christians are caught up in the tides of history that wash through a fallen world. My maternal grandparents lived in Russia after the Revolution and then in Germany between the world wars, at times when each nation faced great economic challenges. They finally moved to the prairies of Canada just as the Depression was sweeping across the land. For decades, they did not have much money. In many historical epochs, countless Christians have had to trust God to provide their next meal. This remains true for Christians in many nations today.

Still other Christians face financial challenges because of such issues as disability, physical or mental health issues, abandonment by a spouse, lack of education, or loss of a job.

We must be careful not to judge anyone's spiritual maturity, faith, or character by their material wealth or lack of it. Only God knows each person's heart, and only God understands why each person is in the financial situation they are in. Many live impoverished lives through no fault of their own.

A combination of prayer, faith, hard work, consistent application of the many other biblical principles discussed in this book, *and* a helping hand from others can move today's have-nots to the level of material prosperity I defined in this book. My grandparents survived the Depression and moved on to much better financial circumstances. Many Christians, even in the poorest of Third World countries, can bear witness to God and His people helping them to improve their financial circumstances too. In a later chapter on poverty, we will discuss how individuals, churches, communities, businesses, Christian organizations, and governments can collectively help this world's have-nots to have enough.

## Having Enough

A large number of Christians in North America can be considered middle class. For many (though not necessarily all), this is exactly where they want to be. Some identify with these words from Proverbs 30:8–9: "…give me neither poverty nor riches; feed me with the food that is needful for me, lest I be full and deny you and say, 'Who is the Lord?' or lest I be poor and steal and profane the name of my God."

Some do not want to handle great wealth. They are concerned that if they become too rich they might either forget about God or become distracted and double-minded. They do not want to take that risk. Their relationship with God is that important to them.

I recently read about the life of famed evangelist R. A. Torrey. He was the son of a wealthy banker. Not long before his parents died, though, most of their money was lost in an economic downturn. Torrey later said that he was happy that circumstances prevented him from inheriting his parents' fortune. He believed that their fortune would have ruined him.[68]

A middle-class income can usually meet a person's needs, fulfil many good desires, and permit investment for the future, with room for giving. Many middle-class jobs also offer reasonable work hours so that those workers have quality time and energy left over to spend in their relationships with God and others. Many middle-class earners have their life priorities solidly in the right place in that regard.

Notwithstanding all of that, many Christians seem understandably frustrated in the middle class. Over the past few decades, the rich have been getting richer while the middle class has been spinning its wheels and getting nowhere. Average incomes in the middle class have stayed relatively stagnant while the prices of homes, food, cars, gas, and many other items have been rising.

Even the good economic years of the 1990s did not benefit the middle class much. It used to be said that a rising tide (i.e. a growing economy) lifts all the boats. That expression has changed: a rising tide no longer lifts all the boats, just the yachts.

If you are a Christian in the middle class, I encourage you to honestly consider whether you do, in fact, have enough to meet your needs, fulfil good desires, take care of your family, responsibly invest for your family's future, and give generously. If you do not have enough, then perhaps God wants to help you to prosper more. I'm not talking about becoming mega-rich—just prosperous enough to live as the Bible instructs us to live. God is the ultimate angel investor, wanting to invest in each one of us so that we can become all that He wants us to become and do all that He wants us to do.

---

[68] Wiersbe book, pp. 74–75.

## Today's Have-Lots

Many Christians live with substantial material wealth. According to 2005 statistics, about 170 of the Fortune 500 CEOs at that time were Christians. It's quite astonishing that about one third of the world's very top executives that year were men and women of faith.

For a fascinating look at wealthy Christians who are movers and shakers in modern American society, I invite you to read Michael Lindsay's book, *Faith in the Halls of Power*. The author interviewed over one hundred Board Chairmen, CEOs, Presidents, and other senior executives from more than forty Fortune 500 companies.

It seems to me that wealthy Christians either fall into one of two camps—*or* think that they can handily keep one foot in each of those camps.

The first camp is populated by wealthy Christians who have *not* overcome their love of money. This manifests itself in various ways. They work way too hard, then they self-indulgently play even harder. Some spend extravagantly and never question whether they are being greedy. Many take great pride in their possessions, readily flaunting their latest acquisitions. Some don't tithe and rarely give. We can expect their numbers to increase as history marches on, for we are warned in 2 Timothy 3:2 that the end age will be marked by insincere men and women who are boastful and arrogant lovers of money, lovers of self, and lovers of pleasure.

Some wealthy Christians don't live this way all the time but have occasional lapses into one or more such behaviours. These are the individuals who try to keep one foot in each camp or travel back and forth between camps.

In the other camp are those wealthy Christians who have substantially overcome their love of money. They may *have* lots of money, but they don't unduly value it. They work hard but not too hard. They take time to play and rest but are not hedonists. They spend within reason and regularly ask themselves whether they are being greedy. They tithe faithfully and give generously.

God is mightily using wealthy Christians from that second camp. Many of them presently wield great influence in the business, professional, and political worlds. They bring their Christian faith into the highest, most elite corridors of power. Like the apostle Paul, they are able to articulately reason about their faith with non-believers in the marketplace (see Acts 17:17). Some influential Christians are able to visit nations where traditional missionaries and Christian charities are not welcome or even tolerated; they are able to share their faith behind closed doors in foreign palaces and corporate offices.

Many are using their money and power to help churches and parachurch ministries, financially *and* otherwise; they recognize the importance of being not only good stewards of their finances, but also good stewards of their positions of power. In researching this book, I came across many great examples of wealthy Christians who have demonstrated this. Tom Phillips, for example, was the CEO of Raytheon Company, an electronics company that was, during his tenure, the largest employer in all of New England. Phillips is the man credited by Charles Colson with leading Colson to the Lord soon after a disgraced Colson left his position in President Nixon's White House. Colson later became the founder of Prison Fellowship and a renowned author and speaker. According to Colson, he is where he is today because a businessman named Tom Phillips used his influential position for God's purposes.

A friend of mine comes to mind as another great example of this. She has been a senior executive in the oil industry for many years. At one point, the opportunity arose for her to lead her boss to Christ. She recognized that God had placed her in her position to do more than just make money.

I do not believe we can easily separate financial stewardship from positional stewardship. They are intertwined. We should not criticize wealthy Christians just because they have a lot of money. It may very well be that God Himself has strategically placed them where they are. He is counting on them to invest their treasure *and* their time and talent in His purposes.

Bearing strong Christian values, many business leaders are, in fact, powerfully and positively impacting current culture within their sphere of influence. S. Truett Cathy, founder of the huge American chain of restaurants called Chick-fil-A, never lets his outlets open on Sundays. Despite this limitation, his 1,200 fast-food outlets have recently generated more than $1 billion in annual revenue.[69] He sets a compelling example for the rest of us in an era when Sunday is becoming just another day to make (or spend) a dollar.

Other wealthy Christians, such as American billionaire Phil Anschutz, care about current media culture. Philip Anschutz made a fortune in oil, railroads, and fibre-optic cables and rose to become one of the top one hundred wealthiest Americans. He decided to invest a significant amount of money in the American movie business. As the owner of two film production companies, Anschutz has recently financed many family-friendly movies (some with distinctly Christian content) such as *The Lion, The Witch, and The Wardrobe; The Chronicles of Narnia; Because of Winn-Dixie;* and *Amazing Grace* (which told the story of William Wilberforce, the Christian who fought to end the slave trade in the 18th century). Those movies have made billions while powerfully impacting Hollywood and global audiences. Anschutz also owns the largest theatre chain in America (with over 6,000 screens) so that his family-friendly films are assured a certain level of distribution.[70]

Many Christian corporate leaders are buying more and more into the concept of "business as mission." It is estimated that at least 2,000 current books espouse marketplace ministry.

I recently read about a company called Galtronics Inc. Hundreds of Arabs, Jews, and Christians work together in a Galtronics plant in Israel, and further hundreds work in plants in China and South Korea. These plants produce wireless technology products for companies such as Motorola and Samsung. Galtronics has openly maintained a Christian witness to its diverse employees. In Israel, Galtronics has built a church in its community. Companies such as Galtronics make

---

[69] Maxwell article.
[70] Moring article.

significant profits but also seek to spread the gospel in nations around the globe, sometimes in places where there is little Christian witness otherwise. Such companies, funded by investors not donors, create jobs and help their employees both spiritually and financially.[71]

Yeager Kenya Group, Inc. is another great example of "business as mission." The company, which started with the personal funds of the owner of an American software company, has trained more than 1,200 farmers in Kenya to grow onions for Western markets. The farmers' annual incomes have jumped from $500 to $10,000, vastly improving the lives of those employees. Because the company also nurtures their spiritual lives, most farmers eventually become Christians and regularly attend church. A few dozen Kenyan churches have flourished as a result.[72]

To the extent that any of us know wealthy Christians who fall into the God-honouring and Kingdom-building camp, we should encourage them and respect them. We should pray that they maintain right attitudes in their hearts towards their money. We should pray that they will use their unique opportunities to minister well.

I personally know many wealthy Christians who clearly fit into the God-honouring camp. They are impacting our world in ways that bring much glory to God. They work in offices up and down Bay Street and in all kinds of businesses and professions across Canada and beyond. Some rich camels keep skinny enough that they will likely pass through the proverbial eye of the needle into heaven; Jesus Himself conceded that some will.

You have probably heard the saying that for every ten people that God can trust with adversity, He can trust only one with great prosperity. It seems to me that there is some truth to that saying. Has God, in fact, trusted some men and women with a high level of prosperity? By the time you finish reading this book, you might agree with me that He has entrusted many men and women with enormous prosperity and a large number of them have proven themselves worthy of this sacred trust.

---

[71]   Maxwell article.

[72]   Ibid.

Sadly, some wealthy Christians have found their local church parishioners and pastors hostile to them and highly critical of the world in which they are movers and shakers.[73] Some wealthy Christians feel unfairly judged and condemned, perhaps automatically branded as "materialistic" and "carnal" just because they have money. Others feel that their wallets or their leadership skills are always being targeted but that no one really cares about them. It is not uncommon for the very wealthy to have difficulty finding compassionate pastoral support and warm church fellowship.

I once mentored a lawyer who talked to her pastor about the stresses of balancing her career with her family life. When she came to the part about her struggle to find a suitable live-in nanny, the pastor sarcastically commented that he wished that was his biggest problem. His complete lack of caring compassion stunned her.

A few years ago, I heard Henry Blackaby speak on this very issue. He passionately implored pastors to give better support to the business and professional leaders in their churches. He encouraged the pastors to find out how they can help those leaders instead of single-mindedly focusing on how their wealthy parishioners can help the church.[74] Many business and professional leaders have influential marketplace ministries (formal or informal) and need all the spiritual support they can get, even if (because of their extensive work/travel schedules) they cannot be in church every Sunday or commit to mid-week responsibilities.

Those business and professional people who do not connect closely with a local church often seek fellowship in Bible study groups run by business peers, parachurch ministries, and invitation-only gatherings of fellow Christian business leaders, creating what Michael Lindsay has dubbed "a gated community of the soul."[75] Let's cut out the judgment and criticism and welcome them back into our churches.

---

73  Stafford article.
74  From a talk by Henry Blackaby at MissionFest, Toronto, Canada, in March 2007.
75  Stafford article.

## Rich Mega-churches and Mega-ministries

Before leaving this section on prosperity, I want to comment briefly on some of the large mega-churches and mega-ministries in the world today. In America, some have come under recent attack because of the alleged lifestyles of their leaders. In recent years, American Senator Chuck Grassley (a member of the Senate Committee on Finance) undertook an official inquiry into a number of well-known ministries whose leaders live in large homes, fly in private planes, and travel on expense accounts to exotic locations.[76] As a lawyer, I know the importance of assuming innocence until guilt is proven, so I will not name names or pronounce judgment. It is not necessarily a bad thing, however, for *any* church or ministry to be put under scrutiny in this regard. Ministry leaders must be fully accountable for how donations are spent, how much is given to them for personal use, and how luxurious they allow their headquarters, travel amenities, and ministry lifestyles to be.

I admire the leaders of some mega-ministries for particular steps they have taken to avoid falling into disrepute. Rick Warren, pastor of Saddleback Church, wrote the mega-bestseller *The Purpose Driven Life*. Long before he sold more than twenty million copies of this book, Warren resolved that he would not use the royalties to change his lifestyle. Celebrity televangelist Joel Osteen has also written a few mega-bestsellers. Both Osteen and Warren have stopped taking any pastor's salary from their churches; they instead support themselves out of whatever they choose to keep from the proceeds of their books. Tending to their large flocks must take up a lot of their time and energy, yet they are both willing to serve as pastors for free.

Not every Christian ministry leader lives by those standards. Church history is littered with too many examples of how churches and church leaders have been derailed in their quest for excessive prosperity. Let's travel back to the 16th-century Catholic Church. While visiting the Vatican in Rome in that century, Martin Luther was shocked by the unbridled quest for wealth that he observed. Later serving as a

---

[76]  Van Biema article.

priest, Luther was further disturbed by the common practice of selling indulgences. The Church told its adherents that an indulgence would prevent them from being punished after death for their earthly sins—as if forgiveness for sins could be purchased with mere money. A person could buy an indulgence for themselves or for a deceased loved one. To finance such indulgences, parishioners often used money they should have spent on basic needs. The sale of indulgences was stepped up by the Pope when he started building the mammoth St. Peter's Basilica in Rome. The marketing slogan for indulgences was: "When the coin in the coffer rings, the soul from purgatory springs."

Luther's famous 95 Theses, which he nailed to the church door in Wittenberg in 1517, included criticisms about not only the sale of indulgences, but also the overarching greed and worldliness prevalent in the Church's ranks of power in those days.

I do not intend to single out the Catholic Church. Churches of whatever denomination, especially those which preach a lot about prosperity, need to learn some lessons from past mistakes of the Church through the ages. An unbalanced focus on prosperity and material wealth can too easily lead any church, its leaders, and its members down the path of greed, error, and excess.

## Our Changing World

It will be interesting to see how the prosperity debate changes over the next decade. It has been easy up until now for many North American Christians to scoff at the concept of God wanting us to prosper—all the while enjoying a great deal of material prosperity and comfort compared to the rest of the world. But the world is very rapidly changing. For some time, President Obama has kept his eye on the trillions of dollars roaming the globe as capital, waiting to be invested. A lot of this money is not landing in North America as much as it once did. Countries such as China and India have economies that are presently expanding at a much better clip. Heads up, Obama has warned—the material prosperity of tomorrow may not be in North

America.[77] Even in my own country of Canada, I have seen interesting changes. Provinces that for decades were labelled "have" or "have not" are switching places. The playing fields of provinces, nations, and continents are being levelled by the evolving challenges of the modern global economy.

In coming years, both those North Americans who have either focused too singularly on prosperity *and* those who have snubbed their nose at the topic may want to take a closer look at what the Bible as a whole says about it, especially if and when significant economic prosperity packs up and moves to other continents.

I conclude these three chapters on the topic of prosperity by repeating my own personal conviction. Although Christians will likely continue to live across a wide spectrum of incomes, I personally believe that God wants all of us to have enough material resources to: meet our needs, fulfil good desires, take care of our families, invest responsibly for our futures, and give generously back to God and to others. I trust that I will continue to lay sufficient biblical grounding throughout this book to support my case for that level of material prosperity for all. I will suggest ways that those of us who have enough, or more than enough, can help the billions of have-nots who still struggle to survive from one day to the next.

*May the Lord give you increase, you and your children!*

Psalm 115:14

---

# GIVING BACK TO GOD

# 16

————

## THE FIRST TEN

*Honor the Lord with your wealth and with the firstfruits of
all your produce; then your barns will be filled with plenty,
and your vats will be bursting with wine.*

Proverbs 3:9–10

*You shall not delay to offer from the fullness of your harvest
and from the outflow of your presses.*

Exodus 22:29a

*…the righteous gives and does not hold back.*

Proverbs 21:26

I thought and prayed about how to order my chapters and came to
the conclusion that this section on giving back to God had to be placed
immediately following the section on acquiring money. Why? Because
the *very first* and the *very best* action that we can take with the money
we receive is to give a suitable portion of it back to the One who has so
generously provided it.

Martin Luther once observed that a man's pocketbook is usually the last part of him that is converted. We have not truly, sincerely, and wholly committed our lives to God until we are prepared to submit our finances to Him. One of the ways we can demonstrate that is by honouring Him with a share of our incoming wealth before using any of it for ourselves.

God has given us our very lives. He has given us this day. He has offered us the incomparable opportunity to be in intimate relationship with Him. He sustains us and provides whatever measure of health, strength, and energy we presently enjoy. He has given us family, friends, and brothers and sisters in Christ. He has promised us eternal life. We are not nearly able to reciprocate with gifts of that calibre.

God has also given each one of us a measure of material blessing. Offering a material gift back to Him—we *can* do that. Is that humble reciprocity too much to ask of us?

God is not a tangible being on this earth. We cannot physically give to Him in the same way we can give a wrapped present to another person. We can, however, give to Him by giving to His church, to ministries that advance His purposes, and to individuals on His radar. We can thereby demonstrate our love, respect, gratitude, and worship.

In the next three chapters, we will briefly examine the Old Testament foundation for giving back to God from our material possessions, touch on whether the Old Testament practice of giving tithes and offerings carries over into the New Testament, focus on the key concepts about financial giving most prominently emphasized in the New Testament, and discuss some potential objects of our giving.

You might be tempted to flip past these three chapters. Please don't! Giving is an *integral* and *imperative* element of biblically-based financial management. The other biblical principles about money don't operate properly if we ignore God's instructions about giving.

## Tithes and Offerings in Old Testament Times

Genesis 14:20 introduces the concept of giving a portion of our material wealth back to God. This verse records how, on one occasion, Abram (later called Abraham) gave one-tenth of his spoils of war to the priest-king Melchizedek. There is no later record of Abram giving one-tenth of his regular income to any priest. We do not know, one way or the other, if giving God one-tenth of what he received was a routine habit of Abraham's.

A similar example of giving ten percent back to God can be found in Genesis 28:22b. That verse records Jacob's promise to God: **"...of all that you give me I will give a full tenth to you."** If you read the surrounding text, you will see that Jacob volunteered to give one-tenth of his material blessing back to God *if* God watched over him on his journey.

Both of those examples of giving ten percent predated the Mosaic Law.

After Moses arrived on the scene, some centuries after Abraham and Jacob, routine tithes and offerings became a religious requirement. I suspect that most people, unlike Abraham and Jacob, lacked the personal initiative to freely give back to God. As a result, the people had to be told to give to God.

In Exodus 22:29a–30, Moses instructed the Israelites: "You shall not delay to offer from the fullness of your harvest and from the outflow of your presses....You shall do the same with [the firstborn of] your oxen and your sheep..." The Israelites were further told: "The *best* of the *first* fruits of your ground you shall bring to the house of the Lord your God" (Exodus 34:26a). Giving some of the very first and best fruits of their material harvest probably served to mitigate any tendency the Israelites might have had to love their material blessings and to hoard them for themselves.

Moses also wrote: "Every tithe of the land, whether of the seed of the land or of the fruit of the trees, is the Lord's; it is holy to the Lord" (Leviticus 27:30). This is the place in Scripture where the concept of the tithe first formally appears. In ancient Hebrew, "tithe" meant "one-tenth." At this point in time, the fraction of wealth payable to God was very specific; it was not an optional amount.

In practical terms, what did God want the people to do with the tithe they owed Him? Deuteronomy 14:22–28 provides the answer:

> "You shall tithe all the yield of your seed that comes from the field year by year. And before the Lord your God...you shall eat the tithe of your grain, of your wine, and of your oil, and the firstborn of your herd and flock, that you may learn to fear the Lord your God always. And if the way is too long for you, so that you are not able to carry the tithe, when the Lord your God blesses you...then you shall turn it into money...and go to the place that the Lord your God chooses and spend the money for whatever you desire—oxen or sheep or wine or strong drink, whatever your appetite craves. And you shall eat there before the Lord your God and rejoice, you and your household. And you shall not neglect the Levite [the priest] who is within your towns, for he has no portion or inheritance with you.
>
> At the end of every three years you shall bring out all the tithe of your produce in the same year and lay it up within your towns. And the Levite, because he has no portion or inheritance with you, and the sojourner, the fatherless, and the widow, who are within your towns, shall come and eat and be filled, that the Lord your God may bless you in all the work of your hands...."

Let's note a few things in this passage. On an annual basis, people were to set aside their tithe and to feast on it with their own families, along with their local priest (who could not own land). If a family had to travel too far to the place chosen, they could turn their agricultural products into money and then later buy whatever food and drink they wanted. Imagine a grand picnic being held every year. The tithe was celebrated and enjoyed.

Every *third* year, the tithe was to benefit the Levites (the priests) *and* the foreigners, widows, and orphans who lived in each community. God promised to bless the ongoing work of those who gave this tithe.

The concept of giving the tithe to the Levite priests *and* to foreigners, orphans, and widows every third year is repeated in Deuteronomy 12:12 and 26:12. Presumably, individuals were on different tithing cycles. For example, a person's first year would begin at whatever year in adulthood they inherited their land and flocks. At any point in time, statistically-speaking, roughly a third of the adult population would be in one particular year of the three-year tithing cycle. As a result, every year the priests, foreigners, widows, and orphans would receive provisions from roughly a third of the population. The year's bounty was systematically shared.

Numbers 18:23–32 suggests that, besides the above tithe, a separate tithe had to be given to the Levites, solely for their ongoing support. Some scholars believe that, in effect, the Israelites had to pay two tithes (or a total of twenty percent of their income each year). The Levite priests in turn had to tithe one-tenth of what they received to the high priest, Aaron (Numbers 18:26–27).

In addition, the Old Testament talks about other kinds of *offerings*. At each of three prescribed annual feasts, everyone was to give something. Deuteronomy 16:16b–17 records this standard: "They shall not appear before the Lord empty-handed. Every man shall give as he is able, according to the blessing of the Lord your God that he has given you." We see the concept of giving according to one's ability being introduced. These offerings were above and beyond the tithe requirements.

Exodus 35:5–9 describes how all the people were asked to also make a *contribution* of some valuable item for the building of the sacred tabernacle (the Tent of Meeting that pre-dated the Temple). Exodus 35:29 refers to the requested contribution as a "freewill offering." People were to give as the Spirit "moved" and "stirred" their hearts (v.21). Although this contribution was also above and beyond the required tithes and offerings, the people responded by giving so much that they had to be "restrained" from giving more (Exodus 36:6).

Even beyond giving tithes, offerings, and contributions, the people in Old Testament times were encouraged and directed to give to the poor in general (not just the widows, orphans, and foreigners in their midst). We will talk more about this later.

God withheld His blessings when the people neglected their tithes, offerings, and gifts. In contrast, He offered great blessing when they were faithful in their giving. Consider Malachi 3:8–12:

> "Will man rob God? Yet you are robbing me. But you say, 'How have we robbed you?' In your tithes and contributions. You are cursed with a curse, for you are robbing me, the whole nation of you. Bring the full tithes into the storehouse, that there may be food in my house. And thereby put me to the test, says the Lord of hosts, if I will not open the windows of heaven for you and pour down for you a blessing until there is no more need. I will rebuke the devourer for you, so that it will not destroy the fruits of your soil, and your vine in the field shall not fail to bear, says the Lord of hosts. Then all nations will call you blessed, for you will be a land of delight, says the Lord of hosts."

### The Tithe in the New Testament

Many people today believe that the requirement to tithe ceased once the New Testament came into effect. As a result, they do not believe they have to give a prescribed amount of their income back to God. Is that accurate? Is the tithing principle simply a relic buried in the Old Testament?

Nowhere did Jesus specifically say that the days of giving tithes were over. In fact, as an aside to another topic He was addressing, Jesus specifically *affirmed* the practice of tithing. Matthew 23:23 records these words of Jesus: "What sorrow awaits you teachers of religious law and you Pharisees. Hypocrites! For you are careful to tithe even the tiniest income from your herb garden, but you ignore the more important aspects of the law—justice, mercy, and faith. *You should tithe, yes,* but do not neglect the more important things" (NLT).

True, this is the only time that Jesus specifically mentioned the concept of tithing.[78] On all other occasions, instead of talking about tithing, He chose to talk about the broader concept of giving. Let's not too readily forget, however, that He *did* mention tithing on that one occasion and He *did* endorse the practice. I imagine that He tithed.

Tithing is mentioned on only one other occasion in the New Testament, in Hebrews 7. This chapter refers back to the time Abraham gave one-tenth of his plunder to the priest-king Melchizedek. Hebrews 7 also describes later times, after the Mosaic Law had come into effect, when all of the Israelites had to give one-tenth of their income. The chapter then describes Jesus (who was not a Levite but had instead descended from the tribe of Judah) as a priest in the order of Melchizedek (v.17).

Jesus became a permanent priest (v.24) for all of us. Jesus made an absolute sacrifice for our sins, once and for all, when he offered Himself on the Cross (v. 27). Jesus now rules as the High Priest of a new covenant between God and humankind. Under this new covenant, we are no longer required to have Levite priests offer material sacrifices to atone for our sins.

I invite you to read chapters 7 and 8 of Hebrews. While these chapters make it clear that we cannot *earn* our way to Heaven by offering material sacrifices to God, I do not personally believe that they abolish the concept of the tithe. Instead, I see a shift from tithing to mere mortal priests to tithing to our indestructible, immortal, eternal Priest. Abraham's gift to Melchizedek foreshadowed this shift.

In Matthew 5:17, Jesus stated that He had not come to destroy the Law but to fulfill it. I am personally of the view that today we live primarily under grace, not under the strict requirements of every regulation in the Mosaic Law. Clearly, *some* of the Mosaic commands and

---

[78]  A parallel passage can be found in Luke 11:42.

regulations no longer apply. For example, the numerous rules surrounding food no longer apply because Jesus said that it is lawful to
eat all kinds of food. Yet some other aspects of the Mosaic Law remain
in effect. Aren't we still, for example, required to follow the Ten Commandments?

There is much controversy over which concepts from the Mosaic
Law survive the Cross and the establishment of the new covenant
between God and humankind. I am not in a position to resolve that
complex debate in this short chapter. When it comes to the narrow
issue of the present-day application of the tithing requirement, I have
heard arguments on both sides of the matter and recognize that sometimes there is no simple answer.

## A Rationale for Present-Day Tithing

Even if it were irrefutably arguable that all of the Mosaic Law has
been abolished, including the tithing commands, I personally do not
want to throw out the ten percent benchmark for giving. Sam and I
subscribe to the practice of giving at least ten percent of our income
back to God. We are not trying legalistically to follow a rigid requirement of Old Testament Law. Rather, we think that Abraham, Jacob,
and the Israelites set excellent examples for us to follow. If they could
give back to God at least ten percent of what they received, why can't
we?

Given that Jesus is described in Hebrews 7:17 as a priest in the order
of Melchizedek, the example of Abraham freely giving ten percent to
the priest-king Melchizedek takes on special prominence. Perhaps
Jesus wants us to imitate Abraham by giving ten percent because we
*want* to, not because we have to.

I imagine that the base-line amount of ten percent pleases God. He
created the tithe. If that amount was acceptable to Him in the days of
the Israelites, we can assume He is still pleased with it today.

Because the Israelites gave their tithes *and* also gave offerings
*and* other kinds of gifts and contributions, the ten percent amount is
arguably the minimum that any of us should give to honour God. You

may have heard the common expression that ten percent should be the floor, not the ceiling, of one's giving.

Ten percent is not unduly formidable. Although it is not a crippling amount, it *is* enough for most people to feel at least a little pinch in the comfort level of their lifestyle. No one tosses one-tenth of their income into the offering plate without consciously and wilfully doing so. We can reach into our pocket or purse and flippantly pull out a quarter without giving it much thought, but writing a cheque for at least one-tenth of our income is likely to get our full attention.

Regularly giving ten percent properly positions our hearts regarding the remaining ninety percent. Ten percent is a large enough amount to remind us that God is the giver and the rightful owner of *all* of our material assets. By routinely giving at least ten percent, we are more inclined, just as regularly and routinely, to hold ourselves accountable to God regarding the rest of our financial affairs.

Earlier, I expressed my opinion that Jesus wants each one of us to have a heart *willing* to give *all* to Him. Even if we don't *actually* give everything away at one point in time, in theory we must be *ready* to do so if God requires it of us. In our hearts, we must continually hand over to Him the totality of all we own and then wait for His ongoing instructions regarding when and what to give. Regularly giving at least ten percent demonstrates to God and to our own selves that we are *serious* and *sincere* about this willingness of heart, this inner readiness to give. Like putting a down payment on something, giving at least ten percent demonstrates clear and honest intent to make God fully sovereign in the financial domain. When God sees any of us giving that kind of percentage, God knows we mean business when we say to Him in prayer that we are prepared to lay our whole treasure at His feet.

I figure that if my husband and I can't freely and regularly give at least ten percent of our income to God, perhaps we are not holding onto our money with a light enough touch. Any inner struggle that I ever encounter over systematically giving that ten percent makes me question whether I have developed an underlying problem with greed or self-indulgence or anxieties relating to money. Any reticence raises the inner suspicion that I love my money more than I am willing to admit. I don't think you or I can routinely give ten percent of our income away unless and until we have (at least to *some* degree) subdued such natural tendencies as greed, selfishness, and fear of what the future holds. Of course, subduing those human tendencies is an ongoing, never-ending process.

Here's what Sam and I have learned by giving at least ten percent of our income back to God and from talking to others who have also faithfully done the same for a long period of time. The remaining ninety percent stretches much further. Week after week, so many items on my grocery list happen to be on sale. Sam and I regularly find ourselves in the right place at the right time to get a good deal on some purchase. Unexpected expenses don't crop up as often as they seem to for those who don't give regularly (although no one is exempt from occasionally having to pay *some* surprise expenses such as repair bills). Our experiences in this regard are not unique.

God blesses and guards the remaining ninety percent in ways that are often unmistakable. The very day I was writing this paragraph, Sam had a series of conversations with the dealer who was repairing my car. At first, Sam was told that the repairs would cost a few thousand dollars. Later, the dealer called back to say that he was reducing the repair bill by more than a thousand dollars.

Another example of God's protection over the remaining ninety percent occurred when my husband and I were travelling on a night train in Algeria. We learned in the morning that the passengers in every other sleeping compartment had been robbed during the night. Only our compartment had been passed by. I do not believe that was a coincidence. As foreign travellers, we should have been the biggest targets, yet we were the only ones spared.

God's provision and protection in this regard has a biblical foundation. Malachi 3:10–11 records this promise from God: "Bring the full tithes into the storehouse, that there may be food in my house. And thereby put me to the test, says the Lord of hosts, if I will not open the windows of heaven for you and pour down for you a blessing until there is no more need. I will rebuke the devourer for you, so that it will not destroy the fruits of your soil, and your vine in the field shall not fail to bear, say the Lord of hosts." It's awesome that when any of us give ten percent of our income, God promises to protect the rest of our material assets from being devoured.

In my life, I have yet to meet a faithful tither who has not eventually prospered by the definition I gave a few chapters ago. Even after giving, the faithful tithers I have known and read about have had more than enough left over to: meet all of their needs; fulfill their good desires; take responsible care of their families; and give even beyond their tithe.

We should be careful, however, not to give based on selfish motives. We should not give just to get blessing and protection or because we think we have discovered a fool-proof divine recipe for material success. We should give primarily because we are grateful to God and we want to honour Him by giving back a portion of what He has so generously given us.

If we give with right motives, Malachi 3:10 promises us that God *will* "open the windows of heaven" and "pour down…a blessing until there is no more need." God challenges us to put Him to the test.

## Developing the Habit of Giving Regularly

Giving back to God can become a deeply entrenched practice. Even children and teens can be taught to give back a portion of what they make as allowance or from part-time jobs.

Starting in adult life, however, the temptation we all face is to think about our other life expenses and to postpone giving back to God. It's only human to ask ourselves: "Can I afford to give *this* week when I have to pay for…." It's way too easy to prioritize the broken dishwasher, the fence in need of paint, the dentist's bill, and other pressing expenses. The problem with this kind of thinking is that we will *always* have bills to pay. If we wait to give until a time when we have no ordinary or extraordinary expenses, we will wait forever.

One way to circumvent this kind of procrastination is to open up a special bank account. Monies designated for giving (ten percent or otherwise) can be deposited each pay period. Some years ago, Sam and I decided to open a separate account for that purpose. Once we had that account, we no longer thought of other immediate expenses whenever we considered giving to our church, Christian ministries, or needy individuals. Instead, we simply looked at the amount we had in that special account *regardless* of whether the washing machine had to be replaced or the car needed repairs or the kids' university tuition was due. Giving no longer competed with life expenses.

One immediate result of this practice was that I felt so much more joyful about giving. I felt a sense of freedom. Choices regarding giving became totally separated from all other spending choices. Once the money went into that special account, it no longer belonged to Sam and I. It was much easier to see ourselves as trustees of God's money, charged with prayerfully considering how best to spend His money. Giving became much more interesting and sometimes even exhilarating. I encourage you to consider opening your own special giving account.

## The Broader New Testament Approach to Giving

Even if a person believes that the practice of tithing has been rendered obsolete in the New Testament, they must surely concede that the *general* concept of giving is very strongly reinforced throughout the New Testament.

Jesus cared about what people chose to put into the Temple offering box. In Mark 12:41, we can read about Jesus sitting in the Temple, observing what people gave. Why would Jesus bother to sit and watch what people were putting into the offering box if it didn't matter to Him? Jesus valued the practice of giving very highly.

In the next chapter, we will focus in more depth on the three key kinds of giving most commended by Jesus and various New Testament authors.

## Final Comments

Giving back to God is a foundational and integral dimension of biblical financial management, stability, and prosperity. It is at the critical core of what the Bible teaches about money. If we routinely ignore giving back to God a portion of what He has so generously given to us, we do so at our peril. We do more than short-change God—we short-change ourselves. We cannot expect God to bless any other aspect of our financial affairs (or our lives as a whole) if we neglect giving Him some of the first and best of our material profits.

Giving back to God need not be burdensome. I have learned that giving back to God somehow releases us from the tight and tyrannical grip that money can too easily have on our souls. Beyond being liberating, giving back to God enriches our souls. Remember, Jesus said that where our treasure is our heart will be also. We will find our hearts rejoicing in all that is happening in the advance of God's Kingdom, especially in those matters and those people in whom we have invested. It will all become much more real, exciting, and meaningful to us.

*Isn't it strange that $20 seems like such a large amount when we put it in the offering plate but such a small amount when we go shopping?*

Author unknown

*...give to God what belongs to God.*

Luke 20:25 (NLT)

*With a freewill offering I will sacrifice to you; I will give thanks to your name, O Lord, for it is good.*

Psalm 54:6

# 17

---

# CHEERFUL, GENEROUS, AND SACRIFICIAL GIVING

*…God loves a cheerful giver.*

2 Corinthians 9:7

*…give, and it will be given to you. Good measure, pressed down, shaken together, running over, will be put into your lap. For with the measure you use it will be measured back to you.*

Luke 6:38

*Give as freely as you have received!*

Matthew 10:8b (NLT)

I learned some valuable lessons about giving during my teen years. At that time, both of my parents were working hard and still paying off considerable debt. Even in the toughest financial times, however, they insisted on giving money away. They routinely modelled cheerful, generous, and sacrificial giving.

Some days, as I watched, my mom would place money in an envelope and address it to one of her favourite Christian ministries. Sometimes her donation only consisted of a five- or ten-dollar bill. Even that amount seemed wildly extravagant to me at the time, maybe even foolhardy. After all, I thought, who gives money away while they have pressing debts to pay? With a chipper smile, Mom told me to watch what God would do in response. Watching money get mailed away while it was such a scarce commodity scared me a little, but I also felt a thrill of excitement. What, I wondered, *would* God do in response?

Soon after my parents, by their example, began to teach my siblings and me about the importance of giving, their financial trajectory inclined remarkably. My dad found the best job of his life and quickly worked his way up from a sales position to a managerial position. He was then given some equity in his company and began receiving dividends. My mom was able to quit work. Debts were paid off. Investments could be made. The giving escalated. Dad eventually became the Chairman of the Board. Now, many years later, my parents have significant net worth. They both continue to give more generously than ever.

One cannot draw precise linear conclusions from what happened to my parents' finances. When it comes to material success, none of us are in a position to truly evaluate what amount results from God's blessing (perhaps as a response to faith and/or as a reward for giving) and what naturally results from diligent hard work and good economic times. We cannot look at one couple's story and draw any simple conclusions.

Having watched my parents' lives over many decades, however, I am convinced that their faithful years of cheerful, generous, and sacrificial giving have played just as important a role in their financial health as their hard work, business acumen, and human ability. Even back in the lean years, Mom expressed resolute faith that God would meet all of our family needs *and* that somehow there would always be enough money to keep on giving. My parents have been outstanding examples of the New Testament principles of giving that we will examine in this chapter.

## Cheerfully Giving

The New Testament does not focus on giving a strictly stipulated percentage of our income. Instead, we are encouraged to give cheerfully, because we *want* to, with sincere motivation of heart. The emphasis is on our attitude, not the amount we are giving. We are to give because we love God, His purposes, and His people. Giving is not meant to be a duty or a burden.

The classic verse on giving cheerfully is 2 Corinthians 9:7: "Each one must give as he has made up his mind, not reluctantly or under compulsion, for God loves a cheerful giver."

This verse should not be used as an excuse for those who don't want to give. Imagine someone thinking: "I can't give cheerfully this week, so I can be excused from giving." Someone else might rationalize: "I can only cheerfully give $10, so I don't need to consider giving more than that." We must be careful that we are not using this verse to mask our selfishness, greed, desire to hoard, or reluctance to share.

Great blessings flow to those who give cheerfully. Notice what Paul says in 2 Corinthians 9:8, the verse immediately following his comment about giving cheerfully: "And God is able to make all grace abound to you, so that having all sufficiency in all things at all times, you may abound in every good work." If we want "all sufficiency in all things at all times," we must practice giving cheerfully.

## Giving Generously

In Psalm 37:21, we are told that "the righteous is generous and gives." This theme carries over into the New Testament.

As we consider giving more freely, let's remember that the measure of our spirit of generosity will be inversely proportionate to our spirit of greed. One spirit will squeeze out the other. If we are not generously giving, perhaps we have a greater problem with greed than we have been willing to admit.

I have been inspired (and humbled) by many Christians who have modelled generous giving. One of my uncles started a business back in the 1950s. Although he was a young Christian at the time, he resolved from the outset to give fifty percent of his business profits back to God. My uncle rapidly became one of the pillars of his church, financially and otherwise. Over the years, he was also incredibly generous to many individuals, including my family and myself. As just one example, he paid for me to go to a Christian camp for three summers in a row (pivotal summers in my spiritual journey). Decades later, he became one of the benefactors of my first book, buying many copies to give away to his family and friends. He died in his mid-eighties, still a generous giver. Many talked about his generosity at his funeral. This quality had clearly defined his life.

My uncle esteemed the late Christian businessman R. G. LeTourneau, known to have regularly and generously given ninety percent of his wealth back to God.[79] In our present day, American Pastor Rick Warren also gives ninety percent of what he earns back to God.[80]

Not everyone can give on that scale, but we can still give generously. In doing so, we soon discover that we cannot out-give God. God has shown Himself to be generous to the generous. What has God done for Pastor Rick Warren? The last time I checked, his best-known book, *The Purpose-Driven Life*, had sold tens of millions of copies and now ranks as the second-highest-selling non-fiction Christian book in all of history, next to the Bible.[81]

The apostle Paul said this about generous giving: "Whoever sows sparingly will also reap sparingly, and whoever sows generously will also reap generously. Each man should give what he has decided in his heart to give, not reluctantly or under compulsion, for God loves a cheerful giver. And God is able to make all grace abound to you, so that in all things at all times, having all that you need, you will abound in every good work…Now he who supplies seed to the sower and bread for food will also supply and increase your store of seed…

---

[79] Cunningham book (*Daring…*), p. 110.
[80] Facts from Larry King's television interview of Warren on April 6, 2009, and from Lindsay book.
[81] Lindsay book.

You will be made rich in every way so that you can be generous on every occasion…" (2 Corinthians 9:6–11, NIV).

God invites us to enter into that blessed cycle of giving, receiving, and then giving again.

In recent decades, a few evangelists have been accused of misusing this financial sowing-and-harvesting principle. To maximize donations, they have promised a divine return on any money donated to *their* ministries, sometimes even a *set percentage* of return. They have aggressively solicited money for their own agenda—an agenda which has usually included their own personal financial benefit. In doing so, they have reduced Paul's powerful words to a slick, self-serving marketing formula. Despite this misuse of the financial sowing-and-harvesting principle, we can still believe what Paul wrote in 2 Corinthians 9:6–11.

We *all* need to be careful about the snare of succumbing to the "bless me" mentality that pervades so much of North American Christianity. When we give, let's keep the primary focus on how we can *keep on* being a generous channel of God's blessing instead of shrewdly calculating how we will benefit from our giving. George and Mary Mueller, the couple who helped thousands of orphans in 18th-century Britain, saw themselves as channels of God's blessing. They believed that every time God materially blessed them it was so that they could bless many others. Blessing their own selves was not their primary goal.

I believe that if we give with right motives we will harvest much more than we sow. Genesis 26:12 recorded that Isaac reaped one hundred times the grain he sowed. We will not always reap a hundredfold return every time we give; however, we *will* reap enough to allow us to keep on giving generously. We can believe that God will abundantly replenish the financial seeds that we plant for God's purposes. In Proverbs 11:24, it is written: "One gives freely, yet grows all the richer…"

## Giving Sacrificially

God also loves a sacrificial giver. Mark 12:41–44 records this convicting story: "[Jesus] sat down opposite the treasury and watched the people putting money into the offering box. Many rich people put in large sums. And a poor widow came and put in two small copper coins, which make a penny. And he called his disciples to him and said to them, 'Truly, I say to you, this poor widow has put in more than all those who are contributing to the offering box. For they all contributed out of their abundance, but she out of her poverty has put in everything she had, all she had to live on.'"

The story of the widow giving her two coins reminds me of a little girl Sam and I met while travelling through a hot jungle in Liberia, sharing a bush taxi with her and her mom. Sam and I had not realized how many hours we would be driving in the dense jungle, far from any place where we could buy food or drink. The little girl had a small bag of oranges. Noticing after a while that we had nothing to eat or drink, she sacrificially shared a few of her oranges with us. I was humbled by her example!

In 2 Corinthians 8:1–4, the apostle Paul talked about other poor people who sacrificially gave: "We want you to know, brothers, about the grace of God that has been given among the churches of Macedonia, for in a severe test of affliction, their abundance of joy and *their extreme poverty* have overflowed in a wealth of generosity on their part. For they gave according to their means, as I can testify, *and beyond their means*, of their own free will, begging us earnestly for the favor of taking part in the relief of the saints…"

Many Christians over the centuries have been remarkably sacrificial in their giving. Hudson Taylor, the renowned pioneer missionary in China, at one point sold everything he owned to help feed victims of a famine. Martin Luther developed a reputation as a very sacrificial giver. It got to the point that his wife had to make a practice of hiding some of the money they received or Luther would have given it all away. The Luther home routinely housed orphans, widows, students, and guests alongside their own brood of children.[82]

My sister is a sacrificial giver. Back in our mid-twenties, my sister and I lived together. We became acquainted with a poor woman

---

[82] Petersen book, p. 159.

named Rachel who begged for money in our downtown neighbourhood. Rachel rented a small room in a decrepit building. She slept
on the floor of her room, thankful that she was not sleeping on the
street. I came home from work one day to find out that my sister had
given her own bed to Rachel, planning to sleep thereafter on our sofa.
Years later, it did not surprise me when my sister decided to work
with underprivileged women in Afghanistan. Sacrificing the comforts
of living in North America did not faze her.

To be able to give sacrificially, we need to trust deeply in God's
promise to meet our needs every single day. If we give sacrificially
today, we are promised fresh provision for tomorrow. I pray that God
helps us all to *really believe* that if we give sacrificially today that we
will have enough for tomorrow—and for *all* our tomorrows on this
earth, even if we live until age ninety or beyond. For some of us, the
fear is not about how we will live in our literal tomorrow, but how we
will afford to live farther down the road in our old age.

I am challenged by this statement made by C. S. Lewis: "I do not
believe one can settle [precisely] how much we ought to give. I am
afraid the only safe rule is to give more than we can spare. In other
words, if our expenditures on comforts, luxuries, amusements, etc.,
is up to the standard common among those with the same income as
our own, we are probably giving away too little. If our charities do not
pinch or hamper us, I should say they are too small."[83]

## The Overflow Principle

Many passages in Scripture talk about how God will give His faithful
ones *more* than enough so that we can keep on giving. He will give us
overflow. Moses stated: "You will have such a surplus of crops that you
will need to clear out the old grain to make room for the new harvest!"
(Leviticus 26:10 NLT). The author of 2 Chronicles 31:10 recorded: "…
Since they began to bring the contributions in to the house of the Lord,
we have eaten and had enough and have plenty left, for the Lord has
blessed his people, so that we have this large amount left." King David

---

[83]   Lewis book, p. 78.

exalted: "...my cup overflows" (Psalm 23:5). In Ruth 2:14, we can read about how Boaz blessed the recently impoverished Ruth; Ruth ate the food he gave her until she was satisfied, yet she still had some left over.

Jesus also lived in the realm of overflow.

In each instance where Jesus multiplied loaves and fishes, there was enough for everyone present *and* some left over. In Matthew 14, for example, we learn that twelve surplus baskets of food remained after Jesus fed five thousand people. Mark 8:1–9 describes how Jesus fed a crowd of four thousand, with seven baskets of food to spare.

Do you think God doesn't know how to count? When He multiplied the loaves and fishes, was His math sloppy? I don't think so. I believe that He could have multiplied the loaves and fishes on each occasion to provide the *precise* number of meals needed, just like He so precisely provided manna to Moses and the Israelites. The surplus amount is meant to demonstrate something.

Jesus did not live in the realm of "not enough" or "barely enough." He lived in the realm of "enough, with some left over."

Jesus also *talked* about the overflow principle. He encouraged people to give, promising overflowing return to those who did so. Luke 6:38ab documents these words of Jesus: "...give, and it will be given to you. Good measure, pressed down, shaken together, *running over*, will be put into your lap." This is the amount God wants to give us if we follow His command to give.

Jesus made it clear, however, that the overflow principle will not benefit greedy and selfish people who choose to hoard their riches for their own consumption. In Luke 12:16–21, Jesus gave this warning in a parable: "...The land of a rich man produced plentifully, and he thought to himself, 'What shall I do, for I have nowhere to store my crops?' And he said, 'I will do this: I will tear down my barns and build larger ones, and there I will store all my grain and my goods. And I will say to my soul, Soul, you have ample goods laid up for many years; relax, eat, drink, be merry.' But God said to him, 'Fool! This night your soul is required of you, and the things you have prepared, whose will they be?' So is the one who lays up treasure for himself and is not rich towards God."

In the parable, the greedy and selfish man purposed to keep the whole overflow of his crops and his possessions for himself. He did not intend to give any of it away. His plan quickly backfired. God saw to it that he lost everything, including his very life.

## Giving is Good for Us

The John Templeton Foundation has compiled a 300-page bibliography listing studies in the fields of psychology, sociology, and biology that all conclude that the act of giving benefits the health of the giver.

MRI scans have shown that giving triggers the release of a hormone called dopamine, which creates feelings of pleasure and positively impacts our stress levels. Apparently, generosity also strengthens our immune systems. Givers generally enjoy better physical, mental, emotional and spiritual health than those who don't routinely give.[84] Psalm 112:5 observes: "It is well with the man who deals generously…"

Giving can generate a profound sense of fulfilment, significance, and purpose in life. Winston Churchill once noted that we survive on what we get but make a life by what we give.

Giving will also provide for us eventual eternal gratification, not just present gratification in this world. Time without end, we will get to enjoy the treasure we have stored up in heaven.

Those who don't regularly give should consider this: the words miser and misery come from the same root.

## Deciding to Give

It is crucial in these present days that Christians purpose to give. Since the onset of the global financial crisis in 2008, an increasing number of people have been relying on charities for food, clothing, shelter, and medical aid.

One hundred Canadian CEOs of Canadian charities were polled at the end of 2008. They expected demand for charitable services to increase by 24% in 2009. They also predicted that actual donations would

---

[84]   Renkl article.

decrease by 22%, creating a substantial gap between what would be given and what would be needed. Various reasons were cited for the growing gap, beyond the global financial crisis, including donor fatigue and the perception that many charities lacked both accountability and effectiveness in their performance.[85] A widened gap between giving and need did, in fact, occur and still remains today.

The sad reality is that many Christians don't give much or give only just enough to soothe their consciences. In the United States, more than one out of every four Protestants gives *nothing at all* to church or charity. Those who describe themselves as evangelicals fare somewhat better in surveys—only about 10% of them give nothing. What about those Christians who do give? About 36% of American evangelicals give less than 2% of their income; only 27% practice tithing. The median giving for an American Christian is $200 on an annual basis—an underwhelming statistic, isn't it?[86]

These survey results are surprising, given the wealth of many American Christians. Those who describe themselves as "committed Christians" (who consider that their faith is very important to them and who attend church at least a few times a month) collectively earn about $2.5 trillion every year. If each committed Christian decided to give away 10% of their after-tax income, giving to Christian ministries would increase by $46 million annually.[87]

As I pored over further statistics, I was surprised to learn that the poorer brackets of Christians out-give the wealthier brackets. Among the wealthy who do give, a small percentage of donors give the bulk of what churches and charities receive (skewing the statistics as to what the average believer gives).[88] In Canada, for example, I have often heard that one dozen donors give a large percentage of what is received by Christian parachurch ministries. In the U.S., the top 5% of evangelical donors give 51% of all charitable contributions to Christian causes.[89]

---

[85]  Castaldo article.

[86]  Moll article ("Scrooge…").

[87]  Ibid.

[88]  Ibid.

[89]  Lindsay book, p. 203.

We can contrast all this data about Christian giving with the giving of those who do not publicly profess to be Christians. Take Bill Gates as one stellar example. A brilliant businessman, he created the giant software company Microsoft back in the 1970s. He is widely credited with kick-starting both the personal computer revolution and the global communications revolution. Around the year 2000, he and his wife started the Bill and Melinda Gates Foundation, donating billions of dollars of their own money. Famed investor Warren Buffet was so impressed that in 2006 he contributed a large amount to the Foundation. The last time I checked, the Gates and Warren Buffett had each given over $30 billion of their personal money to the Foundation.

Bill Gates now spends nominal time working at Microsoft, preferring to focus on how he can help the poor and the sick. His Foundation has decided to address Third World medical issues such as malaria, tuberculosis, and acute diarrheal infections (conditions which do not otherwise attract large charitable donations). Did you know that ten times the amount of money is spent seeking a cure for baldness than a cure for malaria, even though malaria takes the life of a child every 30 seconds in Africa alone?

Gates and Buffett have made the most significant philanthropic efforts in modern history. They are living out Matthew 25:35–46 without even claiming to do so, leaving Christians in the dust when it comes to giving. They have managed to out-give renowned philanthropists John D. Rockefeller and Andrew Carnegie, American business titans in the last century who made their fortunes in oil and steel and who later became great benefactors in the realms of health care, education, and the alleviation of poverty. Carnegie gave away most of his money—an amount that would equate in current dollars to about $4 billion.[90]

Almost every day, I read of television and movie stars such as Oprah Winfrey, Angelina Jolie, Matt Damon, and Leonardo DiCaprio modelling generous giving. Some sarcastically label them charity glitterati, making the assumption that they give just to be in the spotlight.

---

[90]   Maich article ("The Gospel...").

Whatever their motives, I say that their giving puts many of us professing Christians to shame.

Let's purpose to give whatever *we* can. We may not be able to rival Buffett or the Gates family, but collectively we Christians should be making a much bigger difference in this world.

## Deciding What Amount to Give

In 2 Corinthians 8:12, Paul wrote that giving should be "according to what a person has, not according to what he does not have." God wants us to give out of what we actually have. Although we are called to give cheerfully, generously, and sometimes even sacrificially, we are *not* to give recklessly, foolishly, or impulsively. We need to give wisely and prayerfully.

In Acts 11:27–30, the story is told of how Christians in Antioch gave to brothers in need in Judea, "…everyone [giving] according to his ability…" (v. 29). We should take our existing ability to give into account.

In coming chapters, we will talk about wise saving, strategic investment, prudent budgeting, appropriate spending, and being careful about debt. We need to integrate our giving decisions with those other vital activities. There's not much point giving away too much money in rash unreasoned response to an emotional appeal, only to find ourselves in a financial mess the next day. There's also no point in giving cheerfully, generously, and sacrificially if the end result is that we become a burden to others.

In my personal view, it is best to premeditate what specific percentage of our income we can routinely and systematically afford to give, thoughtfully taking into account life expenses, our debt load, and some reasonable provision for future needs such as our children's education and our retirement. We don't have to wait until all debt is paid or all future needs prepared for. We should, however, have a rational plan regarding how much we can allocate to giving from month to month in proportion to what we are contributing to those other important dimensions of our unfolding lives. Sometimes we can give spontaneously in the unplanned spur of the moment, but such times should be the exception, not the rule.

If you want nuts-and-bolts help in figuring out how much you should save, how much you will need to retire, and how much you can reasonably give at *this* point, I highly recommend a book called *The Eternity Portfolio*. That book practically lays out how to give regularly and generously while still wisely taking into account current and future financial health. Giving requires dollars and sense.

Once we have decided what we will give, we need to follow through. Proverbs 25:14 observes: "Like clouds and wind without rain is a man who boasts of a gift he does not give." Let's faithfully deliver what we have purposed and promised.

> *Everyone to whom much was given, of him*
> *much will be required...*

Luke 12:48b

> *It is more blessed to give than to receive.*

Acts 20:35b

# 18

———

# WHERE TO INVEST OUR GIVING

*…use your worldly resources to benefit others…*

Luke 16:9 (NLT)

*Do all the good you can, by all the means you can, in all the ways you can, in all the places you can, at all the times you can, to all the people you can, as long as ever you can.*

John Wesley

Prayer alone cannot fully accomplish God's great purposes on this earth. When God touches our heart about something or someone, He may also want to reach for our pocketbook. I admire the example set by the well-known prayer warrior Rees Howells. At one point in his remarkable life, he resolved that he would never again ask God to answer a prayer through others if God could answer it through him. Whenever his prayers involved financial need, he determined he would be the first person to give something, however modest.[91] We can similarly resolve to put a financial stake in the situations we are praying about. Giving leverages prayer.

---

[91] Grubb book, pp. 41, 72.

## Giving to Our Church

Our churches embody Christian community. They offer evangelism, teaching, discipleship, communal prayer, communal worship, fellowship, sacraments such as baptism and communion, ceremonies such as weddings and funerals, and the operation of the promised spiritual gifts. Every Christian is meant to belong to a local body of believers.

It takes money to run our local churches.

God highly values His Church. In His eyes, it is a serious matter to neglect the finances of His house. I invite you to consider Haggai 1:3–6: "Then the word of the Lord came by the hand of Haggai the prophet, 'Is it a time for you yourselves to dwell in your paneled houses, while this house [the house of the Lord] lies in ruins?...Consider your ways. You have sown much, and harvested little. You eat, but you never have enough; you drink, but you never have your fill. You clothe yourselves, but no one is warm. And he who earns wages does so to put them into a bag with holes." (The NIV and the NLT translations refer to a "purse" or a "pocket" full of holes.)

A few verses later, God becomes even sterner: "You looked for much, and behold, it came to little. And when you brought it home, I blew it away. Why? declares the Lord of hosts. Because of my house that lies in ruins, while each of you busies himself with his own house. Therefore the heavens above you have withheld the dew, and the earth has withheld its produce. And I have called for a drought on the land and the hills, on the grain, the new wine, the oil, on what the ground brings forth, on man and beast, and on all their labors" (vv. 9–11).

After discussing the evil and selfish hearts of the people who lived at the time of Haggai, the words continue in sober vein: "...I struck you and all the products of your toil with blight and with mildew and with hail, yet you did not return to me, declares the Lord" (Haggai 2:17).

After the people once again laid the foundation of God's house, the Lord said He would henceforth bless them (v. 19). God's blessing on His people in the material realm was clearly linked to the attention they paid to maintaining His house. In an earlier chapter, I quoted a similar passage from Malachi 3. God was not just concerned about the physical Temple. He was more concerned about the states of the Israelites' hearts; they were spending their money on themselves and ignoring Him and His people.

## Giving Beyond Our Local Churches

The Temple in Jerusalem was destroyed in 70 A.D. and has never been rebuilt. The apostle Paul declared that *we* as individuals are now the Temple of God, indwelt by the Holy Spirit (1 Corinthians 3:16). Peter told his fellow Christians that they had all become "royal priests" (1 Peter 2:9).

Joined together as the Body of Christ, Christians now span the globe, networking and working together in both church and parachurch ministries. On the local level, Christians gather together for "church" in a brick-and-mortar sanctuary, or in a home, or perhaps even in a modern movie complex. God's Kingdom continues to operate through such local churches, whatever they look like, but also through countless parachurch ministries, and through the royal priesthood of a few billion individuals.

Because of all the important functions taking place in our local churches, we should still financially support those churches, but the great work of various parachurch ministries and individuals (especially in the areas of evangelism, discipleship, teaching, and helping the needy) also merits our monetary support.

Perhaps, when the pews get a little too plush, it might be time to prayerfully consider giving beyond our local church. Throughout history, one can find examples of churches hoarding too many treasures within while the poor, the needy, and the unsaved died on the streets outside.

I will comment below on a few significant causes that are dear to God's heart and my own heart. I will reference a few credible organizations that advance those causes and which, at the present time, remain officially registered as charities or non-profit organizations in Canada. Many are also registered charities in the United States and other countries. For every organization I mention, I will provide a website address in the bibliography. I encourage you to explore what these organizations do if you are not familiar with them.

I am referencing a few ministries because I know that many Christians want to give to ministries beyond their local church, but in some cases they don't know which organizations are trustworthy and effective in what they do. As of the date I send this book to print, I can vouch for the organizations mentioned here. In the future, you can keep an eye on them yourself.

## Supporting Evangelism and Discipleship

Luke 8:1–3 lists some of the earliest supporters of evangelism and discipleship: "Soon afterward he [Jesus] went on through cities and villages, proclaiming and bringing the good news of the kingdom of God. And the twelve [disciples] were with him, and also some women...Mary, called Magdalene...and Joanna...and Susanna, and many others, who provided for [Jesus and His disciples] out of their means." What an awesome privilege it must have been for Mary, Joanna, Susanna, and others to support Jesus and His aides with their finances!

Many Canadians will not darken the door of a church. But they will explore Christian faith in a friend's home, in a university club, or in an office boardroom. Organizations such as Alpha Canada and Power to Change facilitate such exploration.

Acts 1 records how God's witnesses were commissioned to go, not just to Jerusalem and then nearby Samaria, but also to the ends of the earth. This is still our mandate today. In addition to supporting organizations that offer evangelism and discipleship opportunities in our own country, we can support such endeavours abroad. We can support the missionaries sponsored by our local church or denominational body; we can also consider supporting missionaries and evangelists sent by parachurch organizations. Some of the greatest missionaries and evangelists in history have not been sent by a local church. Hudson Taylor, for example, was supported by the China Inland Mission. Billy Graham was financed by the parachurch organization he founded.

## Sending the Word

God loves His Word and wants us to take it to the ends of the earth. Many good organizations, such as The Bible League of Canada and Open Doors, distribute Bibles around the globe. Many also organize Bible studies and develop house churches in other countries. Effective evangelism, discipleship, and church planting ultimately require access to Bibles.

I have particularly loved supporting Bible-related ministries and consider them one of the best ways to invest donated dollars. God first captured my interest with this thought. If I donated enough money to provide Bibles for twelve believers in a particular country, then I was, in effect, equipping a dozen disciples with the important resource of the Word of God. If the twelve disciples appointed by Jesus could accomplish so much without the benefit of the entire written Word, how much more can a dozen disciples in *our* day accomplish *with* access to the completed Bible? In many nations, Christians can wait for years before owning a personal Bible. I became determined to send Bibles, twelve at a time, to every country I could.

Do you know how much it presently costs to equip one dozen disciples in another country with their own Bible? The answer is, on average, about $50 or less. Sending New Testaments is even cheaper. To equip twelve men and women with a New Testament costs less than a Friday evening movie date with our spouse.

Loren Cunningham once observed that if every Bible-believing person gave less than $10, Bibles could be provided for every home in the world.[92]

## Reaching and Training Our Youth

Matthew 10:42 promises: "whoever gives one of these little ones even a cup of cold water…truly, I say to you, he will by no means lose his reward." We can offer our youth so much more than a cup of water. We can offer them *living* water.

---

92  Cunningham book (*The Book…*), p. 193.

Studies have shown that most people make their commitment to Christ by the time they reach their mid-to-late teens. Kids raised in church have ample opportunity to make such a decision. What about all the kids who grow up in families that don't attend church? To reach those kids, we can invest in organizations such as Youth Unlimited, Urban Promise, and the Muskoka Woods Youth Foundation. Over many years, I have seen the deep impact such organizations have had on countless youth in our nation, many of whom come from un-churched backgrounds.

## Helping the Poor

This category of giving is so significant that we will examine it in much greater depth later. Hundreds of verses instruct us to help the poor. We may not personally know many poor people, but we can still help the poor by donating to such excellent charities as World Vision and Samaritan's Purse.

## Advancing Justice

I believe God cares about advancing justice. We are told many times in Scripture how much God loves justice. If issues of justice resonate with you, perhaps you might consider giving to a ministry such as the Christian Legal Fellowship. Among other activities, this organization intervenes in court cases to present a Christian position on pertinent societal issues.

## Finding Meaningful Causes

I wish I had the space to present many other significant causes and their corresponding charities. The above organizations represent just a few of the great Christian organizations that minister in Canada and, in some cases, further afield. It is my prayer that all of the organizations I have mentioned remain worthy of endorsement.

I imagine that most of you have your own list of ministries that you endorse and support. I encourage you to keep giving to them. It is important to give to organizations and causes that we can be personally passionate about. Let's get excited about our giving and move from being half-hearted donors to becoming true philanthropists. Charitable giving involves donating (maybe even just once) to a particular cause; philanthropy involves a higher level of planned, strategic, systematic, engaged giving.

I went through a period earlier in my life when I gave somewhat randomly and erratically to organizations that sent an unsolicited appeal in the mail or which happened to be visiting my church one Sunday. I sometimes gave impulsively, perhaps because I had been emotionally moved in the moment. Over the years, I have become much more deliberate and premeditated. I now give my largest donations to organizations I am excited to read about and am willing to regularly support in prayer. Some interest me to the point that I am also prepared to volunteer my time and/or talents. I want to attend events they host and to meet their senior executives and key staff. I want to stay informed and connected. If I am not, at a bare minimum, interested in reading whatever material an organization sends me, I eventually reconsider whether or not I should be sending them any money at all.

Choose to find substantial personal purpose in your giving.

## Giving Carefully

Wisdom dictates that we spend time researching the organizations we want to give to unless we are already well-acquainted with them. We can explore their websites. We can note whether they belong to a Christian financial accountability organization such as the Canadian Council of Christian Charities (the CCCC) or, in the United States, the Evangelical Council for Financial Accountability (the ECFA). In Canada, we can search for basic information about a charity on the government website www.cra-arc.gc.ca, in the section titled "Charities and Giving."

An American organization, known as MinistryWatch.com, publishes a database containing information about more than five hundred Christian organizations. It provides financial efficiency ratings for most of those entities. The founder of that organization has urged donors to be cautious. After he examined the organizations on which Ministry-Watch had financial information in 2008, he formed the opinion that about $1 billion of the $14 billion in donations given that year had been given to financially unaccountable ministries.[93]

A 2009 *Wall Street Journal* article recommended these additional watchdog websites: Charitynavigator.org, GiveWell.net, and Guide-Star.org.[94] These sites offer details such as executive compensation, administrative and fund-raising expenses, and program impacts.

It is prudent to regularly monitor the organizations we give to. We should exercise the same due diligence regarding investing in charities as we exercise regarding investing in a home, a business, or a stock market share. I love these words penned by Reverend Samuel Harris in the 19th century: "And what shall we say of those professors of Christ's religion who show so thorough an understanding of the necessity of system in worldly business, so utter a neglect of it in their contributions to benevolence: who are full of forethought and anxious calculation to realize the utmost of worldly acquisition; deliberate and farsighted in planning, cautious in executing, lynx-eyed to discern an opportunity to gain, exact to the last fraction of their accounts, but heedless and planless in all they do for charity?"[95]

Exercising due diligence in our giving decisions can be overwhelming if we give to many organizations. I confess that I went through a stage of being annoyed at all the marketing mail I received from organizations we had given to in the past; I used to toss it all into the recycling bin. I realized that this was wrong. I decided to request that our names be removed from the mailing lists of some organizations. Once I had whittled our list of favourite charities down to a manageable number, I resolved to read all the literature they sent and to keep on top of their activities and their prayer requests. I do not lightly give a one-time donation to a new organization because I don't want to be swamped again with too much mail.

---

[93]   Moll article ("Overturning…").
[94]   Banjo article.
[95]   Harris booklet, p. 25.

## Giving to Individuals

We can, of course, also give directly to individuals. Many of us already routinely do this, but so much of our giving revolves around Valentine's Day, Christmas, birthdays, weddings, anniversaries, new babies, and new homes. I am not saying that we should stop giving these kinds of material gifts. They can, of course, be meaningful expressions of our love.

Giving can also be an *investment* in others, helping to meet their needs and, on yet a higher level, helping them to become the very best people they can be. This kind of giving trumps the usual kind of token gift-giving our culture encourages.

William Bryan and his wife, Mary, provide excellent examples in this regard. (Bryan achieved fame decades ago as the Christian lawyer who argued against Clarence Darrow in The Monkey Trial; unfortunately, Bryan's client lost that case, resulting in evolution being taught routinely in American public schools.) Bryan and his wife were known for their incredible generosity. One day, a Japanese boy knocked on the door of their home. The Bryans asked the young stranger what he wanted. He replied that he would like to get an education. Without hesitation, the Bryans took this young man into their home and for five years they provided him with room, board, and tuition until he graduated from university.[96]

This reminds me of the true story, portrayed in the 2009 movie *The Blindside*, about another American family who took in a less fortunate youth and helped him with his education and his athletic development. He eventually played professional football.

It also reminds me of some stories I have read about Earl Carter, the father of former U.S. President Jimmy Carter. Earl financed several college educations for students not related to him. He gave some of his land away so that others in his community could farm. He gave much money to supplement the income of yet others who were trying to develop their careers or businesses. At a time in the Deep South when not all of his neighbours would have approved, he gave generously

---

[96] Petersen book, p. 115.

to both blacks and whites, telling the recipients of his largesse to keep the gifts a secret. President Carter did not know about the extent of his father's generosity until after Earl's death, when cards and letters started pouring in, gratefully commenting on Earl's kindness.[97]

Internationally renowned apologist Ravi Zacharias began an outreach ministry in 1983, aimed at well-educated intellectuals, especially those of agnostic or atheistic mindsets. Around the time that the ministry was just getting off the ground, a wealthy businessman unexpectedly approached Ravi in a hotel lobby and gave him $50,000. Ravi had never met him before. This investment in his dream encouraged Ravi, who thereafter built a remarkable and unique ministry over the following decades.[98]

Most of us will not be benefactors of the magnitude I have described in the examples above, but we can look for opportunities to invest in others.

We can especially give to those in need within our own faith community. Referring to the thousands of believers who joined the early church in Jerusalem, Luke wrote: "…they were selling their possessions and belongings and distributing the proceeds to all, as any had need" (Acts 2:45). He described similar radical giving in Acts 4:32, 34–35: "…no one said that any of the things that belonged to him was his own, but they had everything in common….There was not a needy person among them, for as many as were owners of lands or houses sold them and brought the proceeds of what was sold and laid it at the apostles' feet, and it was distributed to each as any had need." By this point, what was being given to help those in need was pooled in what a modern church might call a benevolence fund. While many churches still have such funds, I imagine it would be difficult to find a church today whose members pool everything to meet the needs of all!

The example of the Acts church certainly puts into perspective the debate as to whether every Christian should give at least ten percent of their income back to God. It hammers home why ten percent should

---

[97]   Norton and Slosser book, p. 18.
[98]   Zacharias book, p. 197.

be considered the floor and not the ceiling of our giving. How paltry ten percent appears in the shadow of the remarkable giving demonstrated by the first-century church!

## Comments About Giving at Christmas

Retail Christmas spending in the U.S. reached $66 billion in 2007. A Deloitte and Touche study that year indicated that the average American planned to buy twenty-three Christmas gifts. World-wide, Christmas retail spending now tops $145 billion.[99]

We have likely all given and received some meaningful gifts at Christmas. I suspect that most of us have also given and received some pretty useless gifts. If every American spent just $10 on a junk gift each year, the total spent would exceed $3 billion. Joel Waldfogel, an economics professor from Wharton University, has studied Christmas economics for decades. In 2009, he wrote a fascinating book on the subject called *Scroogenomics: Why You Shouldn't Buy Presents for the Holidays*. He estimates that about $25 billion is spent each year on wasteful gifts that are neither used nor appreciated. Gift cards are not the perfect solution to this because about ten percent of the aggregate value of purchased gift cards is never redeemed by recipients.

Perhaps it's time to pare down our Christmas lists, lighten our gift budgets, and otherwise tone down our participation in the rampant consumerism of the holiday season. The great challenge is finding consensus on how to handle this within Christian marriages, families, and extended families. Childhood memories and family traditions carry weighty sentiment. No one wants to be called a Scrooge…

## Giving through Generous Hospitality

We can lovingly give to individuals by inviting them into our homes, even if it's just for a meal. Biblical references to hospitality are numerous. I love the story told in 2 Kings 4:8–17 about a wealthy woman who kept inviting Elisha for meals whenever he came to her

---

[99] Timm article ("Why…").

town. Eventually, she talked her husband into making a small room for Elisha. She furnished it with a bed, table, chair, and lamp, so Elisha could stay overnight when he passed their way.

Peter urged the Christians of his day: "Cheerfully share your home with those who need a meal or a place to stay" (1 Peter 4:9, NLT).

Maybe you don't have much cash to give away, but you can offer someone a cup of tea.

## Full Circle

We began this chapter by talking about prayer. Let's finish on that same note. We can pray about our giving, asking God where we should give. As we pray about a host of other matters, we can find clues as to where God wants us to give (beyond our responsibility to help support our local church). Giving can follow praying. Praying can follow giving.

*…I will counsel you…*

Psalm 32:8

*…all things come from you, and of
your own have we given you.*

1 Chronicles 29:14b

*What shall I render to the Lord for all his benefits to me?*

Psalm 116:12

SAVING AND INVESTING

# 19

———

## COLLECTING AND COMPOUNDING

*…for seven years the land produced bumper crops. During those years, Joseph gathered all the crops grown in Egypt and stored the grain….He piled up huge amounts of grain like sand on the seashore.*

Genesis 41:47–49a (NLT)

The concept of saving and storing material goods can be found throughout the Bible. Genesis 41 describes, for example, how Joseph wisely saved and stored grain for a period of seven years while serving as second-in-command to Pharaoh. This stored grain kept the people of Egypt alive during the years of famine that followed. All of us would be wise to save some of our present harvest so that we, too, are responsibly prepared for whatever the future brings. The practice of saving is a fundamental aspect of financial health.

Have you ever noticed that, after He fed the five thousand, Jesus instructed His disciples: "…Gather the pieces that are left over. Let nothing be wasted" (John 6:12 NIV)? Ponder for a moment that Jesus bothered to save leftovers.

On behalf of Jesus and His disciples, Judas carried a purse with some money in it. There was enough money saved in that purse for Judas to—dishonestly—dip into it from time to time without anyone other than Jesus noticing (John 12:6). In fact, Mark 6:37 suggests that the purse contained funds equivalent to at least eight months' wages. Even Jesus and His disciples saved some money for future needs.

### Five Reasons to Save

Author Phil Callaway once cracked that he had saved up enough money to last him the rest of his life...unless he lived past Wednesday. Joking aside, it is worthwhile giving some thought to how much money we reasonably and responsibly ought to save. Most people save for the following five reasons.

Once a person begins living independently, their first savings often go toward building an emergency fund they can rely on to support themselves in times of unemployment or to pay for unanticipated expenses. Common wisdom holds that, at a minimum, the fund should have enough money in it to cover living expenses for at least three to six months. The fund needs to remain liquid enough so that it can be accessed at any time.

Many people next begin saving for the purchase of a home. Home ownership becomes, in essence, a forced savings plan; the mortgage *has* to be paid every month. If the value of the home remains stable or increases, the home-owner's equity systematically increases.

After starting a family, most parents eventually consider their children's future post-secondary education. (Post-secondary education costs money—lots of it! Perhaps you have heard the old joke circulating amongst parents of college students: Q: What is your son/daughter taking at college? A: My money.) Canadians can regularly save money in a Registered Education Savings Plan (RESP). For each year of contribution, the federal government offers grants proportionate to the amount of the parents' contribution. Yearly appreciation of the investments inside the RESP remains tax-sheltered until the money is withdrawn. When funds are taken out to pay for educational expenses, the accumulated appreciation on the contributions made can be taxed in the hands of the student, not the parents. The student is usually in a much lower tax bracket.

Along the way, most of us also consider starting a retirement fund. We can prudently plan for our own later years so that we do not become a financial burden to others. In 1 Thessalonians 4:11–12, Paul instructed us to: "…aspire to…mind your own affairs, and to work with your hands…so that you may live properly before outsiders and be dependent on no one." He reaffirmed this principle in 2 Thessalonians 3:10–12: "…If anyone is not willing to work, let him not eat. For we hear that some among you walk in idleness, not busy at work, but busybodies. Now such persons we command and encourage in the Lord Jesus Christ to do their work quietly and to earn their own living." In 1 Timothy 5:8, Paul even went so far as to say that a person who does not provide for their own self and their own household has denied their faith.

A Canadian can systematically save for their retirement by means of a Registered Retirement Savings Plan (RRSP). Each working person can deposit into their RRSP a certain amount of tax-free retirement savings each year. The exact amount depends on the individual's income. These funds (and their growth) only get taxed when they are taken out of the RRSP account years later, presumably after retirement.

Here's an example of how that money can grow. Assuming a 6% annual rate of growth and a $1,000 contribution to the RRSP each year, $42,199.86 will accumulate over twenty years. Those able to contribute $10,000.00 each year would amass $421,998.60 at the end of the same twenty years. Imagine how much more will accumulate by the end of thirty or forty years of contribution! I've been told countless times that contributing to an RRSP is one of the smartest tax moves a wage-earning Canadian can make. Bear in mind, however, that no one is guaranteed a 6% annual rate of growth.

How much will any of us need in our retirement? If we want to maintain a somewhat similar lifestyle, standard advice holds that we will need about 70% of our current annual working income for each year of retirement. If we live into our eighties or nineties, we will need a pretty big retirement fund to draw from. I encourage you to find an advisor who can help you work out the total amount you will likely need, based on your intended lifestyle, the age you plan to retire at, the age your spouse will retire at, any debts (such as a mortgage) that will not be fully paid off at the time of retirement, your life expectancy, etc.

Numerous studies show that not enough Canadians are saving sufficiently for their retirement. Most people do not have a company pension they can draw from. At the end of 2009, only one-fifth of Canadians were enrolled in an employer pension plan. Another one-third of Canadians were independently saving enough in their RRSPs to be on track to provide for basic expenses in their retirement years. Almost *half* of working Canadians did not have either a pension plan or an RRSP.[100]

Americans have been almost as lax. While six in ten have been saving something for retirement, only four in ten have actually calculated and started to save the amount of money they will realistically need to support themselves.[101]

Government old-age payments will not be sufficient, on their own, to carry us in our retirement years. Government payments are meant to *supplement* our own pensions and/or retirement savings. As the boomer generation ages in both Canada and the United States, the societal safety net will become shakier because of the sheer number of people who will soon be retiring.

Beyond building an emergency fund, buying a home, getting our kids through college, and financing our retirement, many of us want, eventually, to leave an inheritance for our children. The concept of passing an inheritance to our sons and daughters is deeply rooted in the Bible.

In recent years, I have heard many boomers discuss how much money they should leave for their children. The wealthy, in particular, are debating this. Instead of bequeathing most of their money to their

---

[100] Moist article.

[101] Ferguson book, p. 221.

children, Bill and Melinda Gates decided to give tens of billions of dollars to their Foundation to help the poor and the sick. Before starting the Foundation, Bill Gates had apparently read a 1986 article in *Fortune* magazine, which talked about the dangers of leaving too much wealth for our children. When children know they will inherit a certain amount of money, they often lose motivation to do anything with their lives, thus affecting their educational aspirations and work ethic. Billionaire Warren Buffett agreed with Gates' approach. In his will, Buffett has bequeathed enough money to his children so that they will not have financial worries in life, but not so much that they lose their drive to work or their desire to make their own contribution to the world.[102]

Here's more food for thought regarding passing on an inheritance to our children. Why should our children wait until we die and our will is probated? Assuming we have set aside enough for our own retirement needs, we can give to our adult children while we are still alive, at a point in time when that money can really matter (e.g. when they are buying their first home, growing a business, or helping their kids through college). I am very thankful that my parents have generously given my siblings and I some money while they are still living. Their gifts have blessed us all tremendously.

## Can We Save Too Much?

Can a Christian save too much? Should there be a limit to what we save? At what point does reasonable and responsible saving cross the line to become selfish hoarding?

Let's consider the parable (told in Luke 12:16–21) of the man who already had a big barn in which to store his crops but wanted to build further, bigger barns to store up even more. He was not condemned by Jesus for having *one* full barn. Jesus condemned him for his *excess* — wanting to build more and more, bigger and bigger, with no limit. A line has to be drawn between what is wise and reasonable on the one side and what is excessive and greedy on the other. While we should plan wisely for matters such as retirement, we need to give thought

---

[102] Gibbs article ("Persons…").

to when we have accumulated enough. No exact dollar amount can be placed on this. Each person has to prayerfully think this through.

The man Jesus criticized in the above parable planned to live a future life of pure ease, eating and drinking and being merry, all the while ignoring God. That was the part that Jesus was most upset about—that the man in the parable was not rich toward God. We have already talked about how God wants us to work hard, to enjoy our work, and to enjoy the fruit of our labours—but the *end* goal cannot be to accumulate money purely for our own self-indulgence and excessive consumption.

I encourage you to develop a reasonable saving plan. Calculate how much you need to save towards a realistic emergency fund. Consider whether or not you want to save up to purchase your own home. When you start to raise a family, calculate how much you will need to save for your children's later education. As early as your twenties or thirties, begin calculating how much you will reasonably need to save for retirement. In your later years, decide what kind of inheritance you want to give to your children during your lifetime and/or upon your death.

On an annual basis, we can figure out how much we will need to save in the current year to execute the various aspects of our overall saving plan. When we make spending or giving decisions, we can keep our long-range saving plan in mind. We don't want to spend and/or give away so much each year that we sabotage our saving plan. But neither do we want to build too many barns. Saving, spending, and giving need to be balanced and coordinated.

## The Investment Imperative

God expects us to do more than simply save our money in a porcelain piggy bank or a minimal interest savings account. The Bible sets out a clear investment imperative.

Matthew 25:14–30 records the parable of the talents. Talents were a kind of monetary unit. Far from being small change, each talent was worth about twenty years of wages. Five talents would have been worth one-hundred years of wages.

In this parable, a man entrusted some of his money to three servants. The man gave five talents to one servant, to another he gave two, and to the last, he gave only one. The servant with the five talents invested the money and doubled it. The servant with the two talents did the same thing. The servant with the one talent dug a hole in the ground and buried it. When the master returned, he commended his two faithful servants who had earned profits; he put them in charge of even more of his wealth. In sharp contrast, the master had harsh words for the third servant, calling him lazy and wicked, telling him he should have at least deposited the money in the bank to gain some interest on it. The master took the one talent from the lazy servant and gave it to the first servant, who had productively doubled his five talents.

Notice the *point* of the trust arrangement. The money was not to be spent or given away or squirreled away; the recipients of the money were to invest the money so that it increased. Those who did so could and would be entrusted with more. In Matthew 25:29, Jesus expressed the moral of the parable this way: "To those who use well what they are given, even more will be given, and they will have an abundance" (NLT).

In Luke 19:11–27, Jesus unfurled a similar parable. In this second parable, a rich nobleman who planned to travel abroad gave the same sum of money to three servants (to each, the equivalent of three months wages). His simple instructions were: "Engage in business until I come" (v. 13). The NLT translation presents this verse as: "Invest this for me while I am gone."

When the nobleman returned, he found out what the servants had done with his money. The first servant had invested his sum and increased the amount tenfold. By also investing, the second servant had increased his money fivefold. The nobleman, pleased with those men and their investments, promised to entrust them with even more. The third servant came forward, returning the original amount of money; he had let the money stay idle, wrapped up in cloth. The nobleman was upset at this servant for not even depositing the money in the bank so at least he would have some interest to show for it. The nobleman took the unfruitful money from the unfaithful servant and gave it to the man who had earned a tenfold return.

Some Christians judge other Christians who have accumulated a sizable amount of money as a result of their various investments and business pursuits. In light of the two referenced parables, this kind of criticism needs to be addressed. Whom would Jesus commend: the critics on the sidelines *or* the industrious business successes, who have rolled up their sleeves, worked hard, invested their talents, and earned a handsome return? At the end of the day, who is in the best position to take proper care of themselves and their families, to share and to give, and to help finance God's work in this world? Should we most admire the denouncing tongues *or* the working hands, focused minds, and smart stewards? As the years pass, who will God give even more to?

We have all been entrusted by God with some measure of material wealth, however little. We are ultimately answerable to Him regarding what we do with it. We are not to hide our money under a mattress. Nor are we to spend it all or give it all away. In the two parables above, we have, in effect, been clearly instructed to invest *some* of our money. God can help each one of us to sort out how we manage the sacred trust He has granted to us.

Some Christians feel inadequate in the area of financial invest-ment. Thankfully, more and more resources are available to help us learn, in practical terms, how to invest our money.

The late Larry Burkett was once an agnostic, driven, hard-work-ing department head at General Electric, who wanted to make a lot of money. Along the way, he became a Christian and a few years later began working for Campus Crusade for Christ. He developed a keen interest in what the Bible said about finances and soon starting coun-selling, speaking, and writing on the subject. Eventually becoming the founder of Christian Financial Concepts, Larry also started a popular radio talk show called *Money Matters*. His books and radio program have offered lots of advice for Christians who want to steward their money wisely.[103]

---

[103]    Loveless book, pp. 118–121.

In 2000, Larry Burkett blended his successful ministry with another, and the new ministry became known as Crown Financial Ministries. This organization has a very useful website.[104] While I cannot vouch for everything posted on an ever-changing website, the material I perused appeared to be practical and biblically-based. The website offers a variety of materials, including a calculator that can assist you in assessing how much you will need to save for retirement.

Some Christians don't want to spend much time learning how to invest their money. Some hold the view that thinking about their money is tantamount to loving money. I have erred in this way in the past. Over the years, I have slowly learned that it is important to focus deliberately on this aspect of our financial lives. I now firmly believe that God does not want us to put our heads in the sand when it comes to what we do with our savings. On the contrary, God wants us to be diligent to *increase* what we have, instead of squandering it by in-attention. Even money sitting in a bank account can diminish in value over time because the rate of inflation is often higher than bank interest rates.

In the next chapter, we will explore some specific investment pos-sibilities.

> *...to those who use well what they are given, even more will be given. But from those who do nothing, even what little they have will be taken away.*

Luke 19:26 (NLT)

---

[104] www.crown.org.

# 20

## SPECIFIC FINANCIAL INVESTMENTS

*…I am the Lord your God, who teaches you to profit…*

Isaiah 48:17

*…our land will yield its increase.*

Psalm 85:12

I am amazed at the basis upon which some people make their investment decisions. Just this morning, I read in the paper about a lawyer I know in my city. He had paid a woman to contact a dead relative to ask them what he should invest in. This lawyer paid his occult consultant a fee in the six figures for her services before she was exposed as a fraud. I have met several other successful professionals who routinely turn to fortune-tellers for financial advice.

On what do you base your investment decisions?

The book of Proverbs talks extensively about acquiring wisdom, knowledge, good judgment, insight, understanding, prudence, and common sense. When it comes to investing, these qualities are often in short supply. I believe that there is a great connection between godly wisdom and wealth, which we as Christians ignore to our detriment.

Proverbs 8:18–21 claims: "Riches and honor are with me [wisdom personified], enduring wealth and righteousness. My fruit is better than gold, even fine gold, and my yield than choice silver. I [wisdom] walk in the way of righteousness, in the paths of justice, granting an inheritance to those who love me, and filling their treasuries."

Although we acquire foundational wisdom, good judgment, and understanding from God's Word, we can also obtain some practical insight from mature Christians we respect and from licensed financial professionals. Since I don't profess to be an investment expert or a legal expert in the areas of tax or finance, I have spent much time over the years talking to qualified advisors about the world of investments. I have also spent time informally talking with family members and friends who are CEOs, bankers, and accountants. My comments throughout this chapter will blend the best of their helpful advice and insights.

This brief chapter is *not* meant to be a substitute for obtaining up-to-date personal financial advice from your investment professionals, lawyers, or tax experts. My goal is simply to present some investment possibilities you can further explore with the financial advisors you trust. Your life will keep changing; so will the economy, the investment products available, and the legal framework for investment. Over the years, keep communicating with your trusted advisors about your individual financial situation.

## Diversifying Investments

One commonly accepted fundamental principle of investment is this: invest in an asset mix. You have, no doubt, heard the standard advice that we should avoid putting all of our eggs in one basket. The objective of an asset mix is to balance our overall risk and hopefully to reduce drastic fluctuations in our bottom line. When certain kinds of investments are faring poorly, other kinds of investments might be doing well. When interest rates are low, for example, the value of real estate often increases.

The goal of our portfolio of investments should *not* be to get rich quick. A more realistic goal would be to preserve our capital and increase it to the point that it outruns inflation over coming years. Inflation erodes the future purchasing power of each present dollar. For that reason, we might not want to keep *all* of our money in the safest, most conservative fixed-return investments; over the long haul, the safest investments are not likely to beat inflation. On the other hand, we don't want to expose all of our money to higher levels of risk even though the returns can potentially be much greater. Instead of either extreme, we can seek a balance between various levels of risk and various levels of return.

After setting aside some cash in a savings account (or some kind of fairly liquid investment) to be used in the event of an emergency such as losing a job, here are some ways we can invest our further savings.

## Owning a Home

Mark Twain once wise-cracked that everyone should buy land because God is no longer in the business of manufacturing it. The world population is approaching seven billion. Land is in ever-decreasing supply. Even on that simple basis, buying residential real estate can be a good long-term investment *if* we buy wisely, *if* we have the choice as to *when* we eventually sell our home, and *if* we don't have to leverage its purchase too highly.

In Canada, buying real estate for the purpose of home ownership can be an especially good investment. Why? Our principal residence is the only capital investment we can eventually pocket a profit on that will be totally tax-free, no matter how large the gain. If our home increases in value by $100,000, for example, we will pay no tax on that amount when we sell it. If other investments grow by that same amount, there will be a tax bite when we sell them.

The concept of owning land permeates the Old Testament. God gave His people the Promised Land and subdivided it for the twelve tribes of Israel. Each generation inherited land from their fathers. Does the New Testament displace this divinely ordained concept of possessing land? I don't think so. Jesus and His disciples did not own land but they did stay in the homes of those who did. Nowhere is there a biblical prohibition against owning land.

Deciding whether or not to buy a home requires careful thought. In Luke 14:28–30, we are advised to first count the cost before we begin building something. Prospective home-buyers should make sure they can afford the required down payment, mortgage payments, realty taxes, insurance, utility bills, maintenance costs, and other home-related expenses. They should consider the possibility of higher mortgage payments if interest rates go up. It would be wise to sit down with someone who has owned a home for a long time, perhaps a parent or other relative, and talk about all the costs. Let's not forget that the recent global financial meltdown began with a large number of people buying homes they could not really afford—they were subsequently unable to pay their mortgages. Although this was partly the fault of those who gave home-buyers too-easy credit, some portion of the blame must lie with those who bought what they couldn't afford. The lesson is that we shouldn't over leverage ourselves.

Various studies have compared the increase in the value of a home during a given time frame versus the financial increase that could have been achieved if that same amount of money had been invested in the stock market instead. For example, Harvard professor Niall Ferguson compared home appreciation in the U.S. with investment in the S&P 500 during the twenty year period between 1987 and 2007. He found that stocks outperformed home appreciation, before taking into account either the rent saved by living in one's own home or the tax factor; the difference in profitability between the two investments was reduced when those other factors were considered. A British study over the same time period had different results: the increase in home values (up by a factor of 4.5) outperformed stocks (up by a factor of 3.3).[105]

Of course, home values don't always go up. We also need to take that reality into account. Home values have decreased in many places in the years following those two studies. Stock values can also decline.

---

[105]   Ferguson book, pp. 262–264.

To analyze whether it is better for *you* to buy or rent where you live at a particular point in time, you might consider starting with the following preliminary research. After deciding on the price of the home you wish to purchase and finding out the cost of renting something comparable in your community, you can utilize the *New York Times* on-line calculator footnoted below.[106] If you fill in the information requested about your locale (including the previous year's percentage increase or decrease in home prices and rents), you will receive an assessment as to whether it is better for you to rent or buy under prevailing economic circumstances. By using a combination of historical facts and specific current information, the calculator provides a data-based prediction of how relatively beneficial home ownership will be in your unique situation from year one up to year thirty. Keep in mind, this calculator does not pretend to act as a crystal ball. No one can tell you for sure what the future holds for home values. There's no guarantee they will hold steady or increase.

Pure finance aside, buying a home can be an attractive investment for many people because it can be lived in, enjoyed, and shared with others. By investing in hobbies such as gardening, decorating, and carpentry, we can also potentially increase our home's value while exercising our bodies, our minds, and our creative talents.

After buying a home, paying off the mortgage should become a high priority. It's worth taking the time to learn about amortization tables. A large portion of mortgage payments in the early years goes towards paying off interest. In contrast, much further down the road, a larger share of each mortgage payment goes towards paying off the principal amount owed. By making one lump sum payment each year on top of regular mortgage payments, a home-owner can jump much further down the amortization table, thereby skipping a lot of interest payments.

---

[106]   www.nytimes.com/interactive/business/buy-rent-calculator.html# (last accessed on April 19, 2011).

## Other Real Estate

In Canada, investing in real estate beyond one's own home does not have the same tax advantage as investing in a home that is used as a principal residence. Investing in other property might still be profitable over the long haul, if the investor maintains full freedom regarding when they sell the property.

Of course, it is necessary to thoroughly research the market. Some properties are better investments than others. If a purchaser buys property, for example, in a small town where the main factory has just closed down, they will likely lose money. Investing in property in a thriving urban center is a whole different story.

Some choose to invest in a recreational property. My family members invested in a cottage property in the late 1970s. The investment value has quadrupled over the years. The best part is that we have all enjoyed the cottage as a place of extended family togetherness for more than three decades.

I have also known many people who have invested in rental properties (residential or commercial) that have produced a fairly steady stream of revenue. Someone researching the merits of this kind of investment must carefully consider, however, whether they are prepared to deal with the hassles of being a landlord.

One can also buy shares in real estate investment trusts, which invest in a number of commercial buildings such as office complexes and shopping malls in a diversity of locations. This will provide a broader exposure to the commercial real estate market without the burden of property management.

## Securities

Some savings can also be invested in securities such as stocks, bonds, mutual funds, index funds, and exchange traded funds. (The term "securities" is a misnomer. As we discussed earlier, *no* material investment is truly secure in this world!)

To aid this process, it is worth finding a good investment advisor or two. Even sophisticated, knowledgeable investors often rely on investment advisors. Advisors can tailor-design an investment strategy and portfolio custom-suited to a client's income level, risk tolerance, financial goals, liquidity needs, and time horizon. Recognizing that we need ongoing investment assistance, Sam and I regularly consult with a few financial advisors.

When interviewing a potential advisor, we should not be afraid to ask about their training and experience. Preferably, they will have had at least five years of experience and ideally will have weathered at least one recessionary cycle. Before engaging an advisor, it's worth asking them upfront how they will be compensated beyond any salary they earn: by sales fees and commissions (paid by you and/or the company invested in) or a flat fee (paid by you) based on the monetary value of the assets being managed. Unless you have a lot of money to invest and are prepared to pay an annual premium fee, your advisor is likely to fall into the first category. If they do, recognize that their advice will never be fully objective; they will encourage you to consider investments that maximize their own profits.

As you develop your relationship with your advisor, I encourage you to notice if they are "churning and burning" your account. If they are constantly suggesting you sell this and buy that, they are likely trying to earn fees and commissions. Investment portfolios should be adjusted (re-balanced) to some extent once a year. A few changes can be made during the year, but too much activity (unless we are requesting it) is generally a sign that our advisor is thinking more of their own profits than ours. The discipline of annual re-balancing involves making sure that the relative percentages of our portfolio invested in fixed-income securities and in equities remain on target. We will discuss this more in a moment.

At a certain point, when an investment portfolio has grown large enough, it's worth finding a second advisor at a different financial institution. Because there is a limit as to how much investment accounts are potentially insured (in the event that a financial institution goes bankrupt), it is wise to eventually spread investments between a few institutions. A second source of advice is also helpful. No one consultant has a perfect understanding of the markets.

We can also inform ourselves about financial markets. We can read books about investment. We can follow our newspaper's business section. Even educating ourselves a few minutes a day will make a difference over time. At first, I found those exercises boring, but over time, my interest has grown.

We can also surf trustworthy websites such as www.investored.ca. Funded by the Ontario Securities Commission, this Investor Education site is one of Canada's objective, non-profit sources for tools and information designed to help Canadians make better investment decisions. Exploring sites like this can help us to have informed discussions with our advisor(s).

I especially encourage women to learn more about investing. I read recently that only 5% of Canadian women feel "very confident" about investing. Since most adult women may be single at various points in their lives due to choice, marrying at a later age, divorce, or widowhood, it is important for women to learn about the investment world.

Let's now spend a few moments considering the various kinds of securities we can add to our investment portfolios. If you find the rest of this section on securities either too simple or too technical, you are welcome to flip past it.

### Stocks

Stocks are a form of equity investment. Over several decades, wisely diversified investors usually make a profit on the stock market if they can exit when the stock market is doing well. Increase may occur in saw-tooth fashion, but history suggests that over a long span of time it is likely to happen. It is important to recognize, however, that all stock investments carry some measure of risk. This kind of investment carries no guarantees. Past performance of the stock market as a whole, or of individual stocks, is never a guarantee of future performance.

Ideally, how much of a portfolio should be invested in stocks? This depends on a number of factors. Our age, risk tolerance, and investment time horizon are the most important considerations.

Some suggest that for those under forty years of age, at least sixty percent of their investment (not counting real estate) should be in stocks and up to forty percent in fixed income investments (such as bonds, guaranteed investment certificates, or savings accounts). By the time a person is fifty years old, the ratio between stocks and fixed income investments can be more in the order of fifty-fifty. The percentage in stocks should continue to decrease as a person ages and gets closer to retirement. In retirement, it is risky to put more than twenty percent of investment in stocks, if even that. As the percentage of investments in stocks decreases over the years, the percentage of investments in fixed income vehicles should increase correspondingly.

An even simpler rule of thumb is to subtract our age from the number 100 and take the result as the amount we can consider investing in stocks. For example, if a person is thirty-five years old, they might consider investing 65% of their portfolio in equities.

If watching the upticks and downticks of the stock market makes you really anxious, perhaps you should invest very little in stocks regardless of your age. Harvard professor Niall Ferguson has described financial history as a crazy mix of "ups and downs, bubbles and busts, manias and panics, shocks and crashes."[107] If you do not have the stomach for that kind of volatility, you should stick to fixed income investments. You may not make as much profit over the long haul, but at least you will sleep better.

There are a variety of ways to enter the stock market. Investors can buy a diversified bundle of stocks in investment vehicles such as mutual funds or exchange traded funds. They are all managed, at least to some extent, by investment professionals.

If you are willing to regularly watch the market, read financial analyses, and manage your own stock market account, you can consider investing directly in individual corporate stocks.

---

[107] Ferguson book, p. 344.

The huge advantage of investing directly in corporate stocks is that you, the investor, keep all the profits made from stocks that do well, without losing anything on fund management fees. You will have to pay broker fees, but those are usually small in comparison to fund management fees if you buy stocks with the intention of holding onto most of them for a period of years.

The main disadvantage of self-managing a stock portfolio is the amount of time that needs to be spent. One financial journalist has suggested that a person dedicate an hour per week for every stock holding they self-manage, to keep on top of where it is going.[108] This involves monitoring the individual corporations invested in, the stock market in general, and market-moving events such as political changes and natural disasters around the world.

Diversifying the kinds of stocks we own is as important as diversifying more broadly our investments in categories such as real estate, stocks, and bonds. Standard and Poor's analysts set out ten stock sectors: energy, materials, industrials, consumer discretionary, consumer staples, healthcare, financials, information technology, utilities, and telecommunications services. A sophisticated investor will seek some investment in each sector (or at least most of them), although not necessarily evenly weighted. Here's the underlying theory: while some sectors of the market are up, others will be down, and from time to time they will reverse position.

One financial journalist described this theory by comparing market rotation to a roller coaster ride. He asked his readers to imagine the financial, utility, and consumer sectors riding in the front cars of the roller coaster. The telecommunications, technology, and industrial sectors would follow in the middle cars. The energy and material sectors would ride in the end cars.

He then said to imagine the roller coaster in motion, with the front cars cresting at the peak first, while the middle and end cars were still climbing uphill. Of course, the middle and end cars would eventually have their opportunities to crest while the lead cars were rolling

---

[108]  Roseman article ("Profitable…").

downhill. So on and so forth. It usually takes between ten to fourteen months for the roller coaster to complete its up and down journey.[109]

The recent global downturn challenged sophisticated investors, however, as at times it seemed that all sectors were riding quickly downhill and the usual "rules" were not working. We have to be careful when we apply these kinds of theories because they will not always hold perfectly true.

Besides investing in different sectors of the market, we can also consider investing across the range of small-cap, mid-cap, and large-cap companies. Successful small companies often grow quickly, although the great challenge is to figure out which ones are likely to do that! Larger companies usually grow more slowly but are more likely to be relatively stable and secure.

We can also consider diversifying globally. In recent years, the economies of countries such as Brazil, Russia, India, and China have been rapidly growing. It is worth keeping an eye on foreign markets. Investments in foreign assets can be made through some of the fund vehicles we will discuss below.

As we modify our stock portfolio from time to time, we should not blindly follow the pack. Some of the most successful investors do the opposite of what the crowd is doing (especially when the crowd has been doing it for a while). Renowned investor Warren Buffett, for example (whose net worth is tens of billions of dollars), commented in recent years that we should be fearful when others are greedy, and greedy when others are fearful. We should consider getting more into the market when others are stampeding out; we should consider selling some of our holdings when others are clamouring for bigger stakes. Although we have already opined that Christians should be neither fearful nor greedy, I think you get the drift of Buffett's advice and there's probably some wisdom in it. Along similar lines, Buffett also advised that we should not wait too long when a down market starts to pick up. With his characteristically metaphoric counsel, he cautions that if we wait for the robins to show up, spring will be over.

---

[109]  Carrigan article.

### *Actively Managed Mutual Funds*

Actively managed mutual funds are a diversified mix of stocks and/or bonds granularly managed by top investment experts, across a range of market sectors.

An equity mutual fund is invested in a wide variety of corporate stocks (usually from at least fifty to one hundred companies). The fund's professional managers buy and sell the corporate stocks within the fund as they see fit on the basis of ongoing research and analysis. Investors can purchase Canadian or foreign equity mutual funds (or ideally both). There are also mutual funds that invest in a basket of bonds or a blend of both stocks and bonds.

Mutual funds of any kind are best suited to those whose investment goals have long time horizons (at least five years, preferably a few decades).

The main downside of an actively managed mutual fund is the MER (Management Expense Ratio) that is taken off the investment before the investor makes any profit. In an actively managed mutual fund, the MER can be around 2 or 3% of the portfolio's value.

Think of how the MER can add up year after year. I recently listened to a video by John Heinzl of *The Globe and Mail* Investor's Clinic. He provided an example based on the assumption that the stock market returns an average of 7% annually. If $100,000 was invested directly in the stock market, after thirty years that investment would be worth $761,225. If that same $100,000 was invested in an actively managed mutual fund (comprised of those same stocks) with a MER of 2%, the investor would in effect only make 5% a year. Over thirty years, the $100,000 would only turn into $432,194. The striking difference between the directly-invested stocks' increase in value and the fund-invested stocks' appreciation is $329,031.

It is also worth noting that in tough economic times, when investors often sustain market losses on their actively managed mutual funds, MERs *still* get deducted from the invested funds. Ouch.

Notwithstanding the MER factor, I personally believe it makes sense to invest in a few actively managed mutual funds on the premise that the managers who benefit from the hefty MERs do something for their fees. Investors can invest in/hold onto whatever specific funds perform well enough over time to justify their particular MER.

The dilemma we all face is deciding on *which* mutual fund(s) to invest in. I searched "mutual funds" on Google the other day and found more than eleven million results! That's a bit intimidating, even for seasoned investors. Financial advisors can be helpful in this regard, although bear in mind they might receive greater personal reward from signing you up to one fund instead of another. The advisor should be asked to justify why a particular mutual fund would make a good investment. Once you invest in the fund they recommend, keep an eye on it over later years. Don't keep it if it's not profitable enough to justify the MER. Don't keep it if it's not regularly beating the market benchmarks.

Canadians still invest heavily in mutual funds. In fact, a third of all the financial investments of Canadians are held in mutual funds, to the tune of more than $700 billion. This form of investment vehicle is not disappearing anytime soon.

### Index Funds

Index mutual funds (or what are simply known as index funds) differ from more broadly-based, more actively managed mutual funds. Index funds generally attempt to keep pace with a particular market, either the equity market or the bond market or some narrower market sector. They will not usually rise or drop in value much above or below the benchmarks for that market or sector. Unless the market is going wild in either direction, the investor usually makes an average return—neither a huge gain nor a huge loss.

The great advantage of an index fund is the relatively low MER, sometimes lower than 1%. Contrast this with the 2–3% MER charged by many actively managed mutual funds. Index funds are managed to *some* extent, but the management is considered passive; that's why the MER can be lower.

Index funds are not traded on the stock exchange. In Canada, they do not require a brokerage account. They can be purchased from a bank.

An index fund that tracks a broad index, such as the S&P/TSX composite index or the S&P 500 index or perhaps the top fifty or sixty stocks traded on the TSX, is likely less risky to invest in than an index that tracks a very narrow index, such as precious metals. This relates back to the principle of diversification.

### Exchange Traded Funds

Exchange Traded Funds (ETFs) are a relatively new form of investment vehicle. Like index funds, their main advantage is that they have a relatively low MER, usually lower than 1%, sometimes even lower than 0.5%. Also, like index funds, they are managed passively; their purpose is to track the performance of a market or a sub-sector of a market. Unlike index funds, ETFs are bought and sold like stocks (so you need to have a brokerage account somewhere). An ETF that tracks a broad market, such as the main TSX index or the S&P 500, is more diversified and likely less volatile than a smaller index ETF, such as one that only tracks the TSX financial services index.

ETFs usually don't beat the average market or submarket return, but bear in mind that not many actively managed mutual funds beat the market these days.

A recent study done by a major Canadian bank showed that just 7% of Canadians were aware of ETFs, compared with 92% who were familiar with mutual funds. Yet ETFs now have a combined value of $36 billion on the TSX. They represented 14% of trading on the TSX in 2009.

ETFs are best for investors who want to invest larger sums at one point in time, not for investors who want to make a contribution to their investments weekly or monthly; frequent brokerage fees would defeat the purpose of choosing an investment with a relatively low MER.[110] For the same reason, ETFs are best for those investors who plan to buy and hold for at least five or ten years.

---

[110]  Daw article.

If you do not already have a broker, you can ask your bank which brokerage they are affiliated with. Many discount brokerages now conveniently operate on-line.

### Fixed Income Investments

Fixed income investments include corporate bonds, government bonds, and guaranteed investment certificates (GICs).

Bonds are traditionally considered to be safer investments than many stocks, although they are not totally fail-safe. Companies can go bankrupt and governments can fail. We can ask our advisor about the ratings of any bonds he is suggesting. The higher the rating, the lower the likely risk; correspondingly, the probable return will also be lower.

GICs are safer than bonds, but quality bonds usually offer a few percentage points better return than GICs. Ideally, investors will acquire a mix of bonds of different ratings and some GICs so that they minimize their overall risk but still hopefully get a return above the inflation rate.

Do not expect double-digit returns on bonds. Sometimes you may wonder if they will beat inflation. Over the long haul, their returns will not likely be as high as equity returns. In the seventy-year stretch between the 1920s and the 1990s, stocks generally outperformed bonds.[111] It is quite interesting to note, however, that in a shorter, more recent time frame (from 1995 to 2009) bonds produced an average annual rate of return of 6.24 % compared to the almost identical S&P 500 Index return of 6.25%.[112]

Bonds can be purchased individually. Alternatively, a diversified mix of bonds can be purchased within an actively managed mutual fund or a bond index fund.

Fixed income investments should form part of everyone's investment portfolio in some measure that ought to increase with age. As a general rule, fixed income investments such as bonds move in opposite

---

[111]    Ferguson book, p. 126.
[112]    Yew article.

directions from the stock market. They will help to keep our overall investment portfolio more stable.

### Options and Futures

Unless you are a very savvy investor, it's best to stay away from investment vehicles such as options and futures. They require constant, knowledgeable monitoring. Detailed discussion about them is beyond the scope of this chapter.

## Investing within an RRSP

We talked in the last chapter about RRSPs and the potentially significant tax savings they provide for wage-earners. Investments such as stocks, bonds, mutual funds, guaranteed investment certificates, and even cash can all be sheltered in a certain kind of RRSP. There is a limit to the amount that can be added to the RRSP each year.

Over the years, I have been told by tax law professors, tax lawyers, and chartered accountants that, next to investing in a home as principal residence, maximizing investment in one's RRSP each year is the smartest tax move working Canadians can make. RRSP contributions and their growth are not taxed until funds are withdrawn (perhaps decades later).

Employed young adults can be encouraged to start investing each year in an RRSP as soon as they are able. The earlier they start, the better the position they will be in many years down the road. If young adults contribute even small amounts every year, those amounts will add up and, if wisely invested, will likely generate compounded, tax-sheltered increases over the long haul.

## Spiritually Responsible Investments

Business schools are now teaching their students about societally responsible investment (e.g. investing in "green" corporations). In a similar vein, many Christian organizations are now advocating *spiritually* responsible investment i.e. investment that lines up with Christian moral values.

In the U.S., about $17 billion is now invested in "faith-based" funds. These funds include Christian foundations, Christian college endowments, denominational pensions, and evangelical mutual funds such as the Timothy Plan.[113] One of the biggest players in "faith-based" investments is an organization called Guidestone, which manages more than $8 billion. The overall potential market for "faith-based" investment is about $100 billion.[114]

In December 2009, Tom Phillips and Garrett Stevens launched five ETFs called FaithShares. Those ETFs, (designed for the investments of faith-based organizations, but also available to any investor with a brokerage account) avoid industries that profit from gambling, alcohol, tobacco, war, pornography, and abortion. The first year MER is .87%.[115] While these ETFs don't yet have a long track record, they are perhaps worth keeping an eye on.

At times, spiritually responsible investments have performed better than "sin stocks." In the 1990s, a man named Rusty Leonard managed $3.5 billion at Franklin Templeton Investments. One of his Christian clients in those days was the DeMoss Foundation. Although this Foundation instructed Leonard not to invest in any companies that made money off of "sin stocks," their account was Leonard's second-best performing account in that era.[116]

Christians cannot count on this happening consistently. In the five years prior to the global financial crisis of 2008, the Vice Fund (which invests in gaming, tobacco, alcohol, and military manufacturing) produced an annualized 20.2% return, much higher than the S&P return of 11.3%.[117]

Once the 2008 meltdown began, however, the tables turned again. In mid-November of that year, at the point that the Dow Jones had

---

[113]   Moll article ("Overturning…").
[114]   Ibid.
[115]   Moll article ("Taking stock").
[116]   Moll article ("Overturning…").
[117]   Watson article.

plummeted 33%, something called the ISE SINdex had dropped a whopping 43%. (The SINdex, appropriately named, specializes in alcohol, gambling, and tobacco stocks.)[118]

We can see that in any one window of time, spiritually responsible investments may or may not outperform "sin stocks." Investors who invest on the moral high road must be prepared to pay a price at times. But isn't that what our faith requires of us? To pay whatever price is necessary to abide by our principles and values?

I am challenged to take spiritually responsible investment more seriously. This is easy when buying individual stocks or bonds. It gets more complicated when buying mutual funds because funds keep changing their mix of assets and usually report their holdings only twice a year. (In contrast, ETFs report their holdings every day.)

At a minimum, any of us can at least avoid investing directly in stocks and corporate bonds relating to products and services that we do not approve of.

## Risky Investments

King Solomon once offered this timeless advice: "There is a grievous evil that I have seen under the sun: riches were kept by their owner to his hurt, and those riches were lost in a bad venture" (Ecclesiastes 5:13–14a). Here is the same passage again in a different translation: "There is another serious problem I have seen everywhere—savings are put into risky investments that turn sour, and soon there is nothing left to pass on to one's son. The man who speculates is soon back to where he began—with nothing" (Ecclesiastes 5:13–15 TLB).

In contrast, Proverbs 8:12 asserts: "I, wisdom, dwell with prudence…"

Greedy people are more likely to take heavier risks than others. They are more easily dazzled by the prospect of higher returns. Even financial institutions can fall prey to a spirit of greed. Many experts believe that the global financial crisis was caused by greedy banks, investment firms, and other companies taking excessive risks.

---

[118] Kielburger article.

We should not take unreasonable risks with our investments (although every investment carries *some* inherent risk, even if the risk is simply that the rate of return will not beat inflation). It is imperative that our financial advisors understand the level of risk we can tolerate. In our financial portfolios, risk factors need to be carefully evaluated and managed.

We should not be quick to act blindly on a stock tip from a friend. We should also be careful about borrowing money to leverage our investments; if a bear market comes along, we can find ourselves in a disastrous situation.

## Investments in Depreciating Assets

We all need to "invest" some of our money in assets that we know will depreciate, such as cars, computers, and clothes. I prefer not to think of these kinds of assets as "investments" at all and think of them instead under the category of spending. The money spent on those kinds of assets will generally, over time, eventually be worth nothing or close to it.

## Prayer

As Christians, we can seek God's counsel regarding our investments. We can ask Him for wisdom, knowledge, discernment, good judgment, understanding, and common sense. We can ask God to help us find one or more suitable advisors. We can also ask for clear insight into our own personality and emotional make-up so that we can choose a comfortable level of risk.

My prayer for all of us is that we become like the wise and faithful servants in the two parables of Jesus, diligently increasing a portion of what we have been given.

*Know the state of your flocks, and put your heart into*
*caring for your herds...*

Proverbs 27:23 (NLT)

*...divide your investments among many places, for you do not know what risks might lie ahead.*

Ecclesiastes 11:2 (NLT)

*In everything the prudent acts with knowledge...*

Proverbs 13:16

# SPENDING

# 21

---

# CONSIDERING OUR SPENDING FREEDOM

*It's true that money talks. It often says "Good-bye."*

Author unknown

*It's not the high cost of living that gets you—*
*it's the cost of high living.*

Author unknown

Trillions of dollars of goods and services are up for sale every day. We can choose to buy goods in dollar stores or we can shop in high-end boutiques. As Christians, how do we decide where to spend and what to spend money on? Can we spend whatever we want to spend?

On the issue of spending money, Watchman Nee once wisely wrote: "Presumably God has drawn somewhere a line of demarcation."[119] He believed we are safe if we stay within the line but in danger when we cross it. In this chapter, we will grapple with how we can draw an appropriate line between reasonable spending and not-so-reasonable spending.

---

[119]   Nee book, p. 74.

It's difficult to figure out precisely where to draw that line. I know I have probably crossed the line from time to time. God is still working on certain areas of my spending habits. Some Christians simply spend to meet their basic needs, others buy items far beyond those needs. We all need to spend *some* money. What principles can guide our spending?

## Spending within Our Means

Whether we have a little money or a lot, we *all* need to learn to spend within our means. This principle is absolutely fundamental to financial health.

The best way to learn how to live comfortably within our income involves creating and following a detailed monthly budget. I have heard that a budget is a scheme to live below our *yearnings*. It is also, of course, a practical plan to live below our *earnings*. The teen and young adult years are the perfect time to acquire basic budgeting skills.

Here are some simple instructions regarding developing a budget. They can be simplified even further for wage-earning teens.

### *Calculating Monthly Net Income*

We can begin the budgeting process by calculating our anticipated annual income *after* taxes and other payroll deductions have been taken into account. We can also subtract, up front, the amount we plan to systematically tithe over the year. If we divide the resulting net income figure by twelve, we can arrive at our monthly net income. It is crucial that we become aware of our monthly net income if we want to live within our means.

Some people think they will feel too constrained if they make a budget. A paper budget, however, is *not* what limits what we can safely spend. In reality, it's our net monthly income that limits our expenditures. Blame your income, not your budget, if you cannot purchase something you want!

### Listing Expenses

On the expense side of our budget, we can create three sections.

In the first section, we can list all of our *necessary* monthly expenses pertaining to items such as: groceries, rent or mortgage payments, utilities, insurance, and transportation.

In the second section, we can list how much we aim to set aside each month for saving and investment.

In the third section, we can list what we would like to spend our money on *if* we have anything left over *after* the items in the first and second sections have been taken care of. Whatever amount is left over can be considered discretionary funds. We can decide to either spend that left-over discretionary money on ourselves/our family or on further saving or additional giving.

Large-ticket items such as a new TV or a vacation can be planned for in the monthly budget and listed in that third section. Even though these expenses might actually be incurred in one particular month, they can be spread out over the year. The best practice is to have the money saved and set aside from month to month *before* this kind of expenditure occurs, rather than planning to pay it off in the months *after*. No one can guarantee that we will be receiving the same income-stream months from now.

### Tracking Income and Expenses

A budget is simply a reasoned prediction of what we plan to earn and to spend each month. Actual income and expenses can be tracked each month using financial software such as Quicken. Free on-line budget templates are available on websites such as www.moneyproblems.ca. The ongoing tracking process is just as important as the initial budgeting process.

My husband and I outgrew the need to formally budget and track our money once we became familiar with what we could reasonably expect to earn each month and what we could reasonably afford to spend on various areas of lifestyle. After several years, a person or a couple eventually develops an informed sense of what they will earn and what they can realistically spend.

### Budgeting as a Couple

The disciplines of budgeting and tracking both income and spending will benefit newlyweds who have to blend their incomes and expenses along with blending tastes, habits, and values. It is eye-opening for a couple to track where money is actually being spent from month to month.

The process of budgeting and tracking spending will no doubt challenge most newlyweds. Added to the emotional issues surrounding money is the fact that many spouses (even those long-married) don't always 'fess up to what they spend. A 2007 survey revealed that 22% of Canadians hide purchases from their mates and other family members. For women, the hidden pleasure is usually an item of clothing (32%) or beauty products/treatments (14%). Men are more prone to not divulging expenditures on electronics (13%).[120]

It is prudent for couples to begin openly and honestly talking about financial issues, including spending, as early as possible. The processes of formally budgeting and tracking income and expenses can facilitate regular discussion. Failure to address spending decisions candidly can result in a build-up of resentment in one or both spouses, especially if one significantly outspends the other.

The discussion might eventually involve more than personal/couple spending. As time passes, couples increasingly need to discuss broader issues such as how much money to spend on growing children, adult children, aging parents, and perhaps other family members or friends. It's so important to be in sync on spending decisions. Consider Amos 3:3: "Can two people walk together without agreeing on the direction?" (NLT).

If arguments arise and persist over particular spending patterns, a couple can seek the counsel of an agreed-upon third party such as a pastor, an older mentor at church, or a respected friend—any sensible

---

[120]   RD Money columnist's article.

person whom both marriage partners trust will be neutral. The goal is to find a fair compromise in spending so that the needs of both spouses are met and the good desires of both are also reasonably and somewhat equally accommodated.

God can also help couples as they work out spending decisions. Sometimes He will teach one or both partners a lesson. Early in my marriage, for example, I strongly believed that Sam and I should spend the bare minimum on the cars we needed to drive to work. At my insistence, my first car was a small, second-hand vehicle that we paid only a few thousand dollars to purchase. Sam tried to talk me into buying something safer and sturdier that would last longer. I was determined to prove that this inexpensive car was all I needed.

One day, as I was driving home from work on the highway, I glanced into my rear-view mirror to change lanes. A few minutes later, while trying to look in that same rear-view mirror again, I noticed it had vanished! Inspecting the outside of the vehicle later, I realized that the hinge connecting that mirror to my car had rusted right through and the mirror had fallen right off! After a few more problems with that car (such as not being able to start the car while away from home late one night), my husband did not have to argue much to convince me to buy a better quality vehicle.

In later years, driving kids around in winter ice and snow, I was thankful that Sam was willing to pay more than I had once thought reasonable for a car. Some better vehicles I purchased over the years lasted almost a decade without any problems or need for repairs. I learned that buying the cheapest item is not always the wisest decision over the long haul. I learned to give an ear to my husband's point of view.

For couples, it is not worth frequently arguing about spending. Perhaps you have heard this modern saying: marriage may be grand, but divorce is one hundred grand.

## Principles Beyond Budgeting

Along with learning to live within our means, we can apply other biblical principles to our spending decisions. We can consider the various attitudes of heart we have already discussed in this book, such as avoiding greed, excess, and the world's spirit of materialism. I will not repeat what has been said about issues such as greed, but I do wish to highlight the importance of cultivating biblically sound attitudes of heart; such attitudes ought to impact our spending behaviour. Spending decisions also need to be balanced with other money-related activities we have talked about, such as investing for the future and giving generously. In other words, let's remember to *integrate* our spending decisions with all of the other money principles taught in the Bible.

If we are living with a wise set of attitudes and behaviours regarding our money and material possessions, I believe we can safely possess some measure of spending freedom. By referring to spending freedom, I'm not suggesting for one moment that we all run out and spend as extravagantly as we can afford! I am suggesting that we can feel *some* freedom in spending if we are handling our money wisely. All freedom has necessary boundaries. Spending with freedom is not the same thing as spending with reckless abandon. We must remember that we are stewards of our money.

Let's now consider some further concepts that can influence our spending decisions.

## Spending As Investment

Some kinds of spending create investment. One example is the purchase of a home to live in. Quality higher education can also be considered an investment of sorts. These kinds of expenditures will hopefully bring financial returns in the future. Such expenditures need to be distinguished from spending on items such as cars (which steadily depreciate over time) or holidays and restaurant meals (that immediately burn the money spent). A wise person will deliberately prioritize spending on things that will offer a future return or at least maintain their value. They will not overspend on those things and experiences that lose value.

## Spending According to Our Station in Life

Where we believe God has called us to live and work will affect what we spend. A pastor of a church in an upscale community will need to spend more on clothing and housing than a missionary in a very poor country. Similarly, a professional woman has to spend more on clothing than a woman who stays at home with her children all day.

Pertinent to our station in life, here is an excellent question to ask ourselves: will what we are spending on our lifestyle help us or hinder us in what we believe God has called us to do? Will what we are spending on our lifestyle help or hinder our witness as Christians in our particular community?

## Spending within a Closed Circle

Authors Hill and Pitts suggest that we draw a closed circle on a sheet of paper. Inside the circle, we can list our genuine needs and good desires. (We will talk more about our desires in the next chapter.) We can safely spend on the items within that closed circle. The circle ought not to automatically expand every time our income grows.[121] We should not mindlessly spend more simply because we have more.

## Evaluating the True Cost of an Expenditure

Instead of casually spending money on things or experiences just because we can afford them, we can pause to consider how the proposed expenditure will affect us spiritually and relationally. In his thought-provoking book, *Love Not the World*, Watchman Nee advised that, whenever we "touch" the things in this world, we need to ask ourselves how these things will impact our relationship with God.[122] We can also pause to think about how the things and experiences we want to purchase will affect our close relationships with other people. Our purchases can potentially seduce us away from God and from our loved ones, thereby costing us much more than money.

---

[121] Hill and Pitts book, pp. 169–171.
[122] Nee, book p. 16.

Take, for example, the purchase of a television. There is nothing inherently wrong with owning a TV, provided we are discerning about which programmes we watch and how many programmes we watch each day. Some rest and relaxation can benefit our physical, mental, and emotional health. We can enjoy favourite shows in the company of our marriage partner and/or our children. But what if a person watches so much TV that they have no time for personal devotions? What if watching TV seriously diminishes the amount of time a person spends with their spouse or children, in effect alienating those relationships to some degree?

The same is true with regard to purchasing a set of golf clubs, a tennis racquet, or a membership at a club. Golf and tennis can provide exercise, fresh air, and social time with other people. But what if a person begins skipping church every Sunday morning to play golf or tennis? What if the player's spouse feels continually neglected?

Perhaps the purchase of the television, the golf clubs, or the tennis racquet will end up costing a lot more than intended.

We all need to honestly evaluate whether the thing or the experience we want to purchase has the capacity to draw us closer to God and our loved ones, or whether it will draw us away from those vital relationships. What we spend our money on is very closely tied to that on which we spend our time, affection, and energy.

## Being Wary of Worldly Attachment

The apostle John wrote: "Do not love the world or the things in the world. If anyone loves the world, the love of the Father is not in him. For all that is in the world—the desires of the flesh and the desires of the eyes and pride in possessions—is not from the Father but is from the world" (1 John 2:15–16).

I don't think this verse means we can't ever handle *any* possessions in this world or can't ever enjoy good experiences. The crux of the issue is whether these things or experiences create a worldly attachment. Does the world captivate us more than God stirs our heart? Do we spend to indulge our every passion, to satisfy every desire of the flesh, or to boost our pride? Have we become addicted to things or experiences? Have they got their hooks into us? Do we emotionally crave certain things and experiences?

Watchman Nee counselled that it is not necessary for us to remove ourselves physically from the materialistic world around us. God does not want us all to become hermits living in caves in the wilderness. Efforts to remove ourselves *physically* from the allure of the world will not guarantee *spiritual* separation from the world. Conversely, Nee also argued that simply remaining in physical contact with the material world does not have to result in our hearts being *captured* by the things and experiences in the world.[123] We can enjoy things and experiences without loving and adoring them. We can also learn to starve whatever appetites threaten to control us.

We must sincerely look into our own hearts. Has God truly captured the whole of our affection? Or has some part of us remained in captivity to the world?

The things and experiences (beyond necessities) that we can most readily spend on are the things and experiences that have the greatest potential of becoming ensnaring idols in our hearts.

### Seeing the True Worth of this World's Attractions

Watchman Nee suggested that we cultivate a proper perspective on the true worth of things and experiences in this world. We have already talked about what things and experiences *cost* in terms of money, time, energy, and perhaps relational closeness. But what are the things and experiences we are drawn to *really worth*?

John observed, in 1 John 2:17, that this world is "passing away." Aside from humankind, everything in this world is temporal. Nothing else has been built to last. Earthly experiences are fleeting. Our own journey on this planet will eventually end. When we really grasp these truths, the things and experiences in this world are thereby significantly devalued. We can see them for what they are truly worth.

---

[123]  Ibid., p. 43.

Things and experiences in this world are not worth much at all compared to our relationships with God and others, both now and for all of eternity.

After we become Christians, we still have to go on living in this world. Nee believed that we can safely do so if we recognize that temporal things and fleeting experiences don't offer us any ultimate hope or true future.[124] They are not the essence of our lives.

Nee suggested that, like Jesus, we can overcome the world, *not* by giving up every single thing in the world or by denying every experience, but by being other-worldly-minded in the way that we value things and experiences.[125] We can own things and use things and yet remain somewhat detached from them. We can still enjoy things and experiences, in some measure, without assigning them undue worth. Recognizing their true worth in the light of eternity will make us think twice about what we are willing to spend on them.

This flies in the face of how the world at large thinks. People venerate even the most ordinary consumer products. Consider deodorant, for example. Teenagers in particular buy big-time into the billion-dollar industry that peddles scents and deodorants—an industry that seeks to convince consumers that smelling right will lead to social popularity and sexual allure. A twelve-year-old boy in Britain so badly wanted to smell just right that he died of cardiac arrhythmia from spraying too much deodorant on his body. He had fatally inflated the worth of a can of deodorant.

## Pondering Prophetic Warnings

Paul warned, in 2 Timothy 3:2, that as the world nears its end people will increasingly become boastful and proud lovers of money, lovers of pleasure, and lovers of self. The Book of Revelation warns about the coming of a wealthy, commercially-oriented, luxury-consuming world-order called Babylon. Some future day, Christians will have to make a key decision: whether or not to turn their backs on God to receive an

---

[124]   Nee book, p. 43.
[125]   Ibid., p. 54.

official mark on their hand or forehead that will allow them to buy and sell. Many will fall away from Christian faith, unable to resist the magnetism of materialism.[126]

Perhaps we need to consider such prophetic warnings here and now. Do we spend like the world all around us? Will we get increasingly entangled in the spirit of materialism that will dominate global culture more and more? If the coming empire of Babylon arrives in our lifetime, will we be spiritually strong enough to refuse the mark of the Beast, thereby losing our ability to buy and sell?

I have just finished reading a book called *Operation World* (the 2010 edition). Updated every ten years, this book tracks what is happening in over 180 countries, analyzing such matters as what percentage of each nation's population is Christian and what particular challenges Christians face in each country. I was sad to discover that the Christian populations in many nations have become increasingly nominal in their faith and commitment, deeply affected by the materialism that has spread everywhere, including much of the Third World. Money speaks fluently in every language these days.

As individuals, we need to decide whether we will allow materialism to dominate our ongoing spending choices.

## Deliverance from the Grip of Things and Experiences

Nee wrote about the possibility (indeed, the necessity) of being delivered from the grip of things. He said that, for Christians, the solution to the problem is not to get rid of all of our things, but to get rid of the grip they have on us. Once we are delivered from that grip, with God's help, we can engage in present buying and selling with some inner freedom.[127]

If you believe that certain kinds of things or experiences have a grip on you, make this a matter of prayer. Ask God for deliverance. Ask Him for His help.

---

[126] See Revelation chapters 13 and 18 and Matthew 24:12.
[127] Nee book, p. 77.

If you feel compelled to always wear the latest fashion, if you are obsessed with driving the newest model of car, or if you unduly care what people think about your home, then it's time to start praying. Most of us are gripped by *some* things or by *some* experiences. Most of us could use a little deliverance.

I recently read about "mall girls" in Poland, a country known to be conservatively Catholic. These young teen girls (mostly from middle-class homes) prowl malls, willing to sell their bodies in exchange for consumer luxuries such as designer clothes, cell phones, perfume, and sushi dinners. These girls are feeding an emotional addiction to high-end consumables. It is officially estimated that 20% of teen prostitutes in Poland are in that business to feed their materialistic spending habits.

I am challenged when I see people who do not even profess Christian faith who are able to resist the grip of the material world. Warren Buffett is one of the wealthiest men in the world. In his second book, Barack Obama (at that time a U.S. Senator) talked about meeting Buffett for the first time in 2006. Buffett still lived in the same modest home he had purchased in 1967. Buffett chose to send his children to public schools in Omaha even though he could have sent them anywhere.[128] Buffett has given more than $30 billion of his personal money to help the poor, the sick, and the uneducated. If he can live this way, can't we Christians keep some sensible rein on our spending?

### Addressing Emotional Issues Affecting Our Spending

According to psychologists and sociologists, many modern consumers have become psychologically dependent on buying things. Their sense of emotional well-being is based on how often they visit the mall. They can't easily control their want-it-now spending impulses. If you took away their credit card, they would feel disoriented, depressed, and maybe even physically unwell. Shopping has become a real addiction for too many people.

---

[128]  Obama book, p. 193.

Some people recklessly and compulsively spend all their money. Luke 15:11–20 tells the story of the prodigal son, who took his inheritance money, journeyed to a far country, and "squandered his wealth in wild living" (v. 13 NIV). A famine struck soon after. Destitute, he found work feeding pigs. He made such little money, however, that he could not even eat as well as the pigs. Swallowing his pride, he returned to his father.

In contrast, some other people can't spend money very easily. (Yes, you read that correctly!)

I made an interesting discovery while writing this book. Many mature Christians confided that they often feel guilty when they spend on themselves. They may not feel guilty buying something they *need* such as new underwear or laundry soap or meat and potatoes for dinner. But they *do* feel guilty when they buy something they *want*, such as a new outfit for a special occasion or a holiday away from home.

Other people are afraid to spend. Some have developed an intense level of anxiety, perhaps even a phobia, in relation to spending money. I came across stories of people who had accumulated millions of dollars in savings over their lifetimes but who could not shake the habit of ardent penny-pinching. Despite their wealth, they continued to: drive old clunkers, wear shabby out-of-style clothes, hoard everything, and otherwise live with pathological frugality. After one such gentleman died, his relatives found rolls of money secured with elastic bands in old cake boxes he had kept even though they still had traces of icing and crumbs in them. Ironically, the dollar bills stashed in those sticky boxes had literally fused together and become worthless.[129]

According to psychologist James Gottfurcht, we can know when we are unduly avoiding spending, or spending too much, when the act of spending (or not) interferes with our healthy daily functioning.[130] We should be able to spend reasonably without remorse, guilt, self-flagellation, or anxiety. This assumes, of course, that we can afford

---

[129] Roseman article ("Pinching pennies...").

[130] Hampson article.

what we are purchasing. We should also be able to stop ourselves from going on a shopping binge designed to soothe unpleasant emotions.

Some people need counselling to help them deal with their over-spending or underspending. We all need to find a happy middle ground in our spending habits, aiming to spend in self-controlled moderation. Self-control is listed in Galatians 5:22–23 as one of the fruits of the Spirit.

The ultimate goal, posited throughout this book, is to find a wise and reasonable balance between saving, spending, and giving away the money that passes through our hands.

## A Spending Checklist

By way of summarizing some points made in this section, and by way of integrating some concepts from other sections of the book, here is a checklist of matters we can consider before making a major expenditure:

- Does the expenditure involve a need or a desire? If it is a desire, has it been prayerfully yielded to God?

- Can you afford the expenditure?

- Do you have to go into further debt to finance the expenditure? Will your overall debt load still be manageable?

- Will you still be able to take good care of your family?

- Will you still be able to tithe and to give generously?

- Will you still be able to set aside reasonable savings for future needs?

- Will you still have a large enough emergency fund?

- Does the expenditure seem wise? Are you spending on impulse or have you given this some thought?

Have you considered the opinions of others? What does your spouse think?

- How will this expenditure affect others? Will it positively or negatively impact your relationships with God and loved ones?

- Does the expenditure duplicate something you already have? Do you really need more of the same? Are you getting into the realm of excess?

- What are your motives? Are you spending to feel better emotionally?

- Is the expenditure out of proportion to other expenditures?

## Freedom for the Faithful

I do believe that if we give diligent thought to our spending, and if we faithfully honour all the other key principles about money discussed in the Bible, we are left with a considerable degree of spending freedom. The more we focus on serving God instead of gold, or on giving, or on valuing relationships, or on joyfully awaiting eternity, the more freedom we will likely feel when we find ourselves spending. That degree of inner freedom will be very closely tied to the degree that we are confident, at any point in time, that our hearts and behaviours are rightly set when it comes to money. That degree of peace-filled inner freedom will also be tied to how unshackled we have become from selfishness, greed, pride, guilt, fear, and anxiety.

I pray that God teaches each one of us how to spend with appropriate freedom.

*In all your ways acknowledge him, and he will make straight your paths.*

Proverbs 3:6

# 22

---

# SATISFYING GOOD DESIRES

*The Lord will withhold no good thing from
those who do what is right.*

Psalm 84:11c (NLT)

*You have given him his heart's desire and have
not withheld the request of his lips.*

Psalm 21:2

*...the desire of the righteous will be granted.*

Proverbs 10:24b

We established many chapters ago that God has promised to meet every one of our needs. God does not, however, want us to just barely survive. I believe that God also wants to grant us our good desires. You can see some verses above that support my proposition. In this chapter, we will focus on our material desires for both things and experiences, desires that go beyond our basic material needs. We will contrast good desires with self-indulgent desires.

## Looking at Some Common Desires

Let's look at a few common desires that exist within contemporary Christian culture. Each of these desires can be considered good desires in certain scenarios and self-indulgent desires in other scenarios.

### *A College Education*

We don't need an advanced education for physical survival. No one *needs* to go to college, as a matter of life or death, the same way we need food, drink, and shelter from the storm. Some must acquire a college degree, however, to fulfil what they believe God wants them to do with their lives (for example, those who feel called to be in a profession such as nursing, medicine, dentistry, law, or accounting). These days, because the best work is often knowledge-based, it is arguable that a college education is becoming increasingly advisable for most young adults, whether a specific degree is strictly required for a chosen vocation or not. A higher education can be a wise and solid stepping-stone en route to a good career.

Others go to college out of pure desire, for the sheer enjoyment of learning, to develop artistic talents, musical gifts, writing abilities, biblical knowledge, or computer know-how, even if they do not intend to use those skills in their core career.

I believe that God wants us to make the best use of our God-given intellect and talents. He wants us to achieve our potential in all areas of our lives, career-related or not. We are not just stewards of our material possessions. Even more importantly, we are stewards of our rich inner gifts. He would not have given us such gifts unless He wanted us to develop them and use them in some fashion.

Do the finest colleges and universities in the world exist only for the ungodly? Is it wrong for a Christian to aspire to go to Harvard or Oxford? I don't think so. Many Christians seek degrees from the most prestigious (and most costly) academic institutions in this world. I say all power to them if they use those degrees to honour God. In this book, I have included examples of individuals who have used degrees from Ivy League universities to benefit Christian ministries whether by working for them or giving money to them.

Could a college education ever be considered a self-indulgent desire? What about those who spend year after year in college, aimlessly acquiring degrees, avoiding having to work for a living? The daughter of a friend obtained four very different degrees (at our friend's expense) before our friend finally put his foot down and told his daughter to go out and get a job. She was almost forty by that point!

Even this brief analysis demonstrates that we should not categorically label something as always a good desire as opposed to a self-indulgent desire.

### Celebrations

God loves for us to celebrate significant occasions. Moses, for example, instructed the Israelites: "When you arrive in the land...you must present to the Lord at his sanctuary the first sample from each annual harvest...Afterwards, go and feast on all the good things he has given you. *Celebrate...*" (Deuteronomy 26:1–3a, 11 TLB).

I suspect that God delights in us celebrating Christmas, Easter, Thanksgiving, weddings, birthdays, and anniversaries, although admittedly feasting, decorating, and gift-giving can get out of hand.

Jesus performed His first recorded miracle at a wedding celebration, choosing to turn water into the finest wine. He made the celebration even more special than it had been before. He chose to be present at the celebration and did not condemn it; instead, He enriched it and presumably enjoyed it. God has told us that He plans to have a great wedding feast in heaven to honour His bride, His church.

I've heard of some modern weddings, however, that cost hundreds of thousands of dollars. The recent wedding of the daughter of a former U.S. President allegedly cost millions. The wedding industry makes billions every year. So do the commercial industries profiting from Christmas, Easter, Thanksgiving, birthdays, and anniversaries. Each person has to decide for themselves at what monetary point a good desire, such as wanting a wedding celebration or any other kind of celebration, crosses over into something excessive.

### Owning a Home

No one needs to own their home. All around the world, it is usually possible to rent living space. Many desire, however, to own the place they call home.

Many years ago, my pastor and his wife were renting a house. One day their landlord informed them they would have to move. They began looking for another place to rent but were having trouble finding something suitable.

God spoke to the pastor's wife, impressing upon her that He was going to provide a home they could own. At that point in time, the pastor and his wife had about fifty dollars in the bank. Believing that God would provide them with a home of their own took great faith!

Soon after, funds came to them from a variety of unexpected sources. Around that same time, a home was put up for sale, catching their attention. The asking price was out of their league, however, well beyond the funds that had come in. Wishing to purchase that home, they put in a modest offer anyway, in an amount they could afford, not realistically expecting that the vendor would accept the low-ball offer. Surprisingly, he did. In a short time, they went from renting a home, and having only fifty dollars in the bank, to living in a home they owned.

I believe that owning a home is generally a good desire. We have already seen that buying a home can be a wise financial investment under the right circumstances. We can turn our homes into places of rest, refreshment, beauty, warmth, nourishment, love, laughter, celebration, hospitality, fellowship, prayer, work, and play. Of course, we don't need to own our home to enjoy any of the above results. If we own our own home, however, we are more likely to make the investment of time, effort, and money to optimize the various functions a home can facilitate. A person is not likely, for example, to create a well-planned garden sanctuary or a dry-walled, carpeted basement room if they are only renting a place.

The desire to own one's own home can cross over into greed if a person wants to keep moving up and up to bigger homes on larger properties with more luxurious features. Every person desiring a new home needs to pray and ask God where the line should be drawn between healthy desire and wise investment on the one hand, and discontent and greed on the other.

Then there's the matter of what we purchase to place inside our home. Many North Americans have several computers and TVs in their homes. I confess we have a few of each. Can one computer be justified for each teen or adult in the home? How many TVs can be justified in one family?

To cook meals, it's not unusual for the average home to have a stovetop, oven, microwave, toaster, sandwich press, and perhaps a backyard barbecue. To eat the meals cooked on all those appliances, it is also not unusual to have a kitchen table and chairs, more formal dining furniture in another room, and a garden dining set (with sets of dishes, utensils, and linens to suit each venue).

Many of us paint our walls in colour, not satisfied with the blah builder-beige. Our floors get adorned with carpets. Plain light bulbs get replaced with more ornate lighting fixtures. We invest in artwork, accessories, and picture frames.

I'm not suggesting that we stop equipping, decorating, or enjoying our homes. I'm challenging each one of us, however, to question when enough is enough. At what point do good desires go awry? Just as the healthy and necessary act of eating can at some point turn into gluttony, trying to create pleasant surroundings can at some point turn into the kind of self-indulgent luxury that James 5:5 warns about.

### Travel

Travel can, in some cases, be a genuine need. For example, it is sometimes necessary for our jobs or ministries.

Can travel for other reasons be considered a good desire?

Travel can be a means of keeping in reasonable touch with those we love who live somewhere else.

Travel can be an important dimension of education, especially in these days of global interconnection. Travel abroad can liven up an employment résumé.

Travel can also potentially offer rest, relaxation, perhaps even restoration, benefitting our spiritual, physical, mental, and emotional health.

Travel can be a way of spending continuous quality time with our spouse and children or other relatives and close friends who come with us. At various points, my husband and I have had very demanding and stressful careers; the only way we could *really* get away from our work was to physically get away. For many years, we also found that our free time after work was not always spent together. For a long season of our lives, for example, my husband used to take our son to the hockey rink a few times a week while I took our daughter to another rink for her figure skating lessons. While physically in our home, Sam sometimes spent time working in the basement while I worked in the garden. Going away somewhere *together*, as a couple or as a family, allowed us to reconnect more deeply. Modern life too easily pulls marriages and families apart on a daily basis; vacations can bring us back together. Enjoying adventures together can add a lot of spice to a marriage, providing a great antidote to the hum-drum of everyday routine.

Travel can be a form of spiritual retreat. The concept of making a spiritual pilgrimage has existed for centuries. Away from our regular daily chores, we are able to spend more time than usual in reading, reflection, and prayer. If a big decision has to be made, such as quitting a job or changing careers, we can focus better if we get away somewhere to think and pray about it. Other times, we can consider going on a retreat with others. A marriage retreat, a church retreat, or a stimulating Christian conference can re-ignite us spiritually and relationally.

Travel enables us to bear witness all over the world. I have had interesting discussions about my faith with local people in places like Algeria, Liberia, Mexico, Ecuador, China, Israel, India, Malaysia, and many other countries, some of them not receptive to formal Christian missions. Have you ever stopped to think about how much time Jesus, His disciples, and the apostle Paul spent on the road? Travel facilitated the spread of God's Kingdom back then and it still does today.

Travel can be a way of enjoying God's creation. I have occasionally asked myself: did God make the unbelievable beauty of places like Bora Bora only for the wicked? The Bible teaches us that the earth is the Lord's and the fullness thereof. Is it wrong for His children to take the time and money to enjoy this incredible world He created? Must we restrict ourselves to seeing it only on the Nature channel?

Of course, once again, a line needs to be drawn. Travel can become excessive, obsessive, purely hedonistic pleasure-seeking. The potential benefits of travel need to be balanced with what is written in the Bible about issues such as selfishness, greed, pride, and unduly loving the material world.

We cannot label the desire to travel as good for everyone all the time, but neither can we label it as not good for everyone all the time. It is another personal matter with which to wrestle in our own consciences whenever we consider travelling somewhere.

### Looking and Feeling Our Best

Most of us desire to look and feel our best. Generally, these are probably good aspirations. We want our spouses and children to look and feel their best too. I don't think it honours God if we eat poorly, never exercise, don't care what we wear, and never brush our teeth or style our hair. We are ambassadors for Christ. If we wish to reach people, we should be careful not to turn them off by practicing poor grooming or dressing habits.

Investing *some* money in nutritious food, vitamins, fitness, nice clothing, skincare, make-up, toiletries, and haircuts is probably reasonable. In our present North American culture, however, this can all get crazily out of control. How many lipstick shades and body scents should we invest in? What about pricey health club memberships, spa treatments, or plastic surgery? Once again, let's give some thought and prayer to where we set a limit, not just in the amount of money we invest, but also in the time and energy we pour into the modern beauty, fitness, and wellness industries.

## Dialogue with God

If we are not certain whether a particular material desire is good or not, we don't have to hastily abandon it. We can talk to God about it. How much He would love that!

God wants to give us His guidance and counsel regarding *every* aspect of our lives. Pertinent to this chapter, He can help us to sift through our desires and discern which ones have been inspired by Him and which ones come from our self-indulgent nature. He can tell us whether or not He approves of the desire.

As the first step, we must sincerely yield the desire to God. We can regularly disclose our current desires in our prayers.

How does God communicate with us? How does He let us know what He thinks? I believe that He speaks to us in many ways. In a nutshell, God primarily speaks to us through: His Word; the Holy Spirit; the counsel of trustworthy people; our unfolding circumstances; and the wisdom we accumulate over years of living our lives in right standing with God. (On a tangential note, this discussion about the ways in which we can communicate with God does not just apply to our spending decisions. We can apply these principles to all of our financial activities. God surely wants to communicate with us about all of our money-related actions, including our career choices and changes, our investments, our giving, and our decisions about debt.)

God speaks, first and foremost, through His Word, the Bible. We can consider our material desire in light of biblical truth. Can our desire be affirmed by any specific biblical passage or biblical example? Or, on the contrary, does our desire violate any biblical principle?

Let's look at two different examples to illustrate this. A married person may desire to book a weekend getaway at a nice hotel to celebrate the anniversary of their wedding. Lots of biblical principles would arguably support spending money on that desire. God wants us to maintain loving marriages. In contrast, consider a single person wanting to spend a weekend in a room at that very same hotel to get to know their boyfriend or girlfriend better. This latter expenditure of money, although it seems so similar to the first example, would violate biblical principles regarding sexual morality. The same room at the same price might be a biblically sound expenditure in one scenario but not scripturally commendable in the other scenario.

In addition, the Holy Spirit can speak directly to our inner being. The apostle Paul told us that we are to be led by the Spirit. What the Spirit says will always be consistent with biblical principles. To tell whether or not a specific material desire is good, think about whether the pursuit of that desire would give rise to the fruit of the Spirit (see the list in Galatians 5:22–23). If you pursue the desire, would you be acting in love toward all of the people who will be affected? Would your expenditure likely generate a loving response in the others affected? Does the thought of proceeding give you a sense of deep peace? Would the fulfilment of the desire produce long-lasting joy instead of fading short-term pleasure or self-centred instant gratification? Can you act in faith? Do you have a strong sense that God wants to help you fulfil the desire? Are you able to conduct yourself with self-control? Can you pursue the desire in a kind and gentle manner with respect to, for example, your spouse? Can you be patient and wait? Can you be humble about the fulfilment of the desire or can you hardly wait to boast about it?

Or, in sharp contrast with *Spirit-infused* kinds of fruit, does the pursuit of the particular material desire generate selfish ambition, strife, stubborn obsession, impatience, pride, a disregard for others, or feelings of guilt? These are not fruits of the Spirit.

God also speaks to us through mature Christians in our lives such as our spouses, our adult children, our parents, our siblings, or our close friends. Are you willing to discuss your material desire with them? What do they have to say about it? Your spouse is the most important person to consult because any money you spend will affect them too, especially if you pool all of your earnings. If your spouse has the *same* burning material desire, however, you might consider asking someone outside the marriage to give you objective feedback.

Our evolving circumstances can perhaps offer some clue as to whether or not God approves of our material desire. Let's say we have been praying for a while about whether or not to book a particular vacation. Let's say we are not certain we should spend the amount of money it would cost. Perhaps we are wondering if we should look for something less expensive or if we should go away at all. What if, one day, we find out that our dream vacation package has just been heavily discounted for the very week we can take off? We need to consider whether or not this is potentially a sign from God that He approves of what we have prayerfully yielded to Him.

Or God might respond to our prayer about the proposed vacation with a very different circumstantial clue. Let's say we try to book the vacation we have been considering. We find out the hotel or the flight is full. Those circumstances suggest that God may not be in our plan and we may need to go back to the drawing board and prayerfully investigate other options (including whether or not to go away at all).

In our years of marriage, God has clearly—and sometimes remarkably—eased the way for Sam and I to go on particular trips; He has thwarted other plans in various ways. He has also taught us some lessons. On a few occasions, we have gone on a vacation and have encountered enough problems that, after the fact, we have realized that we would have been better off staying home. Those kinds of experiences have encouraged me to be even more prayerful the next time around! Sometimes God allows us to experience the thorns and snares associated with worldly wealth and worldly pleasure so that we are more inclined to yield future material desires to Him in prayer.

After a while, we develop a bank of acquired wisdom and insight. We can draw on how we have heard from God in the past about various material desires. Getting to know all of the verses about money that are contained in the Bible will help to enlarge our wisdom bank with regards to our financial activity. Becoming acquainted with the *whole* Bible will give us even deeper understanding.

We can also think about whether the specific material desire we are entertaining fits in with what we believe God's plans and purposes are for our life. If we believe, for example, that God wants us to serve on our worship team at church, then purchasing a guitar would help advance that purpose. If we believe God wants us to take a job position across the city, and the commute by public transit would take an unreasonably long time, then the desire to purchase an affordable car makes sense. On the other hand, if we believe God wants us to move to India to work with the poor, then buying a yacht in the Caribbean would be nonsensical.

Once we feel some sense of certainty that our surrendered desire is good and God-approved, we can move forward with boldness and confidence. If God shows us our desire is greedy and self-indulgent, we must be ready to freely abandon it. If we are not yet very certain of where God stands on the matter, we can maintain a questioning, yielded attitude until we have greater clarity. What's the rush?

> *May he give you the desire of your heart and*
> *make all your plans succeed.*
>
> Psalm 20:4 (NIV)

> *Delight yourself in the Lord, and he will give you the*
> *desires of your heart.*
>
> Psalm 37:4

> *If you…know how to give good gifts to your children,*
> *how much more will your Father who is in heaven give*
> *good things to those who ask him!*
>
> Matthew 7:11

> *He fulfills the desire of those who fear him…*
>
> Psalm 145:19

> *The desire of the righteous ends only in good…*
>
> Proverbs 11:23

# 23

---

## DEALING WITH DEBT

*When you think no one cares you're alive, try
missing a few car payments.*

*When your spending exceeds your income, your
upkeep will be your downfall.*[131]

*...the borrower is the slave of the lender.*

Proverbs 22:7

I came across so many humorous comments about debt that I couldn't resist beginning and ending this chapter with a few of them. Although people like to joke about debt, it is, in fact, a very serious issue. For too many, debt has become destructive.

**Runaway Debt**

According to the Federal Reserve Board, revolving U.S. consumer credit-card debt totalled an astounding $800 billion in 2004. By 2009, it crossed the $1 trillion mark. Home mortgage debt also increased over

---

131    Authors of two quotes are unknown.

those same years, from $7.8 trillion to over $10 trillion. Indebtedness is on the rise.

Canadian statistics for that same time period also escalated to alarming levels. In 2008, average household debt topped $90,000. As of mid-2010, total household debt in Canada (including mortgage and credit-card debt) was close to $1.5 trillion.

In better economic times, debt was driven by the craze for the latest tech toys, designer clothes, big-screen TVs, and restaurant life-styles, all helped along by a mindset of instant gratification. That level of consumer debt rose higher in recent years as a result of people losing their jobs. The unemployed no longer borrow for fun; they now borrow for survival.

We know that there is a real problem out there when a popular television programme is called *Till Debt Do Us Part*. In that show, a financial planner helps people overcome spending habits that have created excessive debt.

I read that the late Ken Lay had racked up *personal* debt to the tune of almost $100 million in his last year as CEO at Enron.[132] Mind-boggling, isn't it?

Not everyone is able to properly manage their debt load. In 2008 in Canada, personal bankruptcies increased by 13.5 percent, out-numbering business bankruptcies by a ratio of fifteen to one.[133] In the U.S., between one and two million people file for bankruptcy each year.[134]

Even nations have taken on manic levels of debt that threaten to spiral out of control. As of early 2011, the U.S. national debt had exceeded $14 trillion, and it was still advancing at the rate of almost $2 billion each and every day. This wins the prize for being the largest amount of national debt ever amassed in world history. The Americans have basically mortgaged themselves out to foreign lenders. For years, a National Debt Clock displayed the U.S. debt (and each family's share of it) in Times Square, New York City. The Clock only had space for

[132]    Johnson article.

[133]    Popplewell article.

[134]    Ferguson book, p. 60.

ten electronic digits—not enough for the current eleven-digit debt. It won't likely be modified. Today's numbers are too depressing.

As Barack Obama and John McCain duked it out for the Presidency in the fall of 2008, the U.S. comptroller general of that time criss-crossed the nation advising people that the greatest enemy of the American people was not hiding in a cave in Afghanistan—the greatest enemy was America's own fiscal irresponsibility.

Americans continue to spend far more than they make, leaving future generations to clean up the mega-trillion-dollar mess. Debt levels also reached critical heights in many European nations in 2010. The debt problem threatens to get worse as the baby boomers age and the tax base shrinks in Western countries.

## Limiting Personal Debt

For most people, it is not realistic to avoid all debt in life. With college and university tuitions rising, borrowing money is the only way that many students can complete a quality education. With the high cost of real estate, most people have to carry a mortgage on their home for several years. Those who absolutely need a car to get to work might have to take out a car loan. The majority of those who start their own business need some bank credit. Along the way, my husband and I have incurred debts across those four areas. Over the long term, those debts helped us to earn income and eventually create a strong balance sheet.

Aside from those four major categories of expense, it is generally not wise to get into personal debt, *particularly* for items that depreciate over time or for consumables that disappear almost instantly.

Even in those four areas, we must limit our borrowing to the amount that we can realistically expect to repay. Millions of people took on mortgages they could not repay in recent years. By mid-2010, more than 2.3 million American homes had been repossessed by lenders in less than three years.

## Credit Cards

In our modern world, credit cards are very convenient—perhaps too convenient. I only carry two credit cards: one that I actually use and a back-up card that is available if the first one has been compromised. Regularly using more than one principal card can make it very difficult to keep track of what is being spent.

As a general rule, credit cards should only be used routinely *if* we have the means to pay all of them off at the end of each month. Otherwise, they can be a fast track to financial ruin. If we cannot resist buying on credit and we cannot promptly pay our bills in full every month, then we should probably cut up our cards. Warning signs of trouble include applying for a new credit card to pay off the balance on an old one and getting cash advances off of a credit card to pay other debts.

It is all too easy to get into credit card debt over our heads. If a person charges $1000 on their card and thereafter only pays off the minimum monthly payment required by the average credit card company, it will take about nineteen years to pay off that $1000. At the end of the nineteen years, the person will have paid $1900 to the credit card company, almost double what the original purchase was worth. This demonstrates how quickly credit card interest compounds from month to month and how much of each minimum monthly payment goes towards paying off interest, not principal. Now imagine if the same person racked up *more* debt after that $1000 purchase. Imagine the deep hole of debt they would have to crawl out of!

Credit card companies have been called modern-day loan sharks, extracting ridiculous rates of interest from those least able to pay. The wonder of compound interest helps our savings and investments to grow; unfortunately, the same compound interest can cause our debts to grow at the same velocity. In our financial lives, compound interest can be our best friend or our worst enemy.

As of 2009, out-of-control credit card debt had become the prime factor in 80% of personal bankruptcies. Early in my career, I assisted with legal proceedings in bankruptcy court and saw firsthand the devastating results that unmanageable credit card debt can have on couples and families.

In his medical practice, my husband, Sam, has seen how debilitating unmanageable debt can be to a person's mental, emotional, and physical health. In a recent U.S. poll, more than 10 million people reported negative health impacts from their debts. About 51% complained of muscle tension, 27% had digestive tract problems, 44% suffered from migraines or other headaches, 29% lived with severe anxiety, 23% struggled with severe depression, and 6% had already sustained at least one heart attack. Those statistics provide us with further incentives for avoiding too much debt—a crushing load of debt will cost us much more than money over the long haul.

## Being Cautious About Co-Signing for Someone Else

We should also be very hesitant to co-sign a debt for someone else. Proverbs 6:1–5 warns and instructs: "…if you have put up security for a friend's debt…if you have trapped yourself by your agreement and are caught by what you said—follow my advice and save yourself… Now swallow your pride; go and beg to have your name erased. Don't put it off; do it now! Don't rest until you do. Save yourself like a gazelle escaping from a hunter, like a bird fleeing from a net" (NLT).

In today's legal environment, it is not so easy to get off the hook after you have co-signed a debt. Better to pray about the matter *before* signing on the dotted line. We need to carefully think through this kind of commitment and exercise the best of our wisdom and good judgment. It's one thing if the friend or family member can reasonably repay their debt within a short time. If not, one is setting oneself up for potential frustration, resentment, and strain in the relationship.

We ought to be particularly cautious about co-signing credit for our teens and young adult children. We need to think twice about giving them a credit card that we will be on the hook for unless we are willing to spend time setting the ground rules and teaching them about wise spending habits. We need to be diligent in enforcing those rules and tough enough to take the card away if it is not handled maturely.

**Christmas Debt**

The Christmas season can so easily jeopardize our budget. We can feel obligated to buy a lot of Christmas presents, perhaps some we can't really afford. When the bills arrive in January, a fresh cycle of discouraging debt can begin. Even if we don't follow a budget the rest of the year, let's take the time to make one before Christmas and stick to it! We can make a list of who we will buy for and consider a reasonable price limit for each gift. We can also set a budget for decorating and entertaining. If we do so, we will be thankful in the new year that we have not ratcheted up our debt load.

**Rising Up and Out of Debt**

The next best thing to avoiding debt in the first place is making a firm decision to get out of debt. It is possible. Millions have done it. It will take strong resolve, hard work, courage, and faith.

God wants to help us. Philippians 4 promises that He will supply *all* our needs through Christ Jesus. If one of your present needs is to get yourself out of debt, He will supply the resources to help you.

Consider the story of Elisha and the downtrodden widow in 2 Kings 4:1–7. The woman's husband had recently died in debt. The deceased husband's creditor came calling on the widow, telling her that if she did not pay the outstanding debt he would take her two sons as slave labour.

The widow appealed to Elisha for help. Elisha asked the widow what resources she had. She told him she had one jar containing a small amount of oil. Elisha instructed her to ask her neighbours for several empty jars. He then told her to pour the oil from the original jar into all the empty jars. In faith, she did so. She poured and poured and the oil did not run out. When all the jars were full, Elisha told the widow to go and sell some of the oil so that she could pay the debt.

You can choose to believe that God wants to help you with your debt too. Your resources may almost have run dry, but God's resources never run out. Every day, ask God in prayer for His help in rising up and out of debt. I believe that He wants to help you honourably repay what you owe.

Various non-profit organizations exist that can help. In Canada, we have Credit Counselling Canada (CCC). This non-profit umbrella organization can refer you to other non-profit groups in your area that will offer advice on such matters as credit card interest rates, planning a long-term budget, developing a debt-reduction strategy, consolidating debts, and setting attainable payment goals. Their member organizations offer advice over the phone or through in-person counselling.[135]

In Psalm 37:21 we are told: "The wicked borrows but does not pay back…" In contrast, the good man is honourable about his debt. Today is a *new* day and a fresh opportunity to be wise and honourable with present debts.

## Forgiving Those Indebted to You

The Bible also speaks to those who are creditors. Leviticus 25:35–36 states that if our brother becomes poor we should help him and not charge interest on our loan. When we charge interest on loans to others, it should be reasonable, not exorbitant.

We can even consider cancelling debts owed to us. I am not talking about business debts so much as I am talking about debts owed by family members or close friends who have encountered hard times. I am not suggesting we forgive *every* debt, but in certain circumstances we can consider being compassionate and merciful.

I have always been fascinated by the biblical concept of Jubilee, which includes cancelling old debts at certain points in time. It is an Old Testament concept, but one that Jesus spoke about in some of His first public words. In Luke 4:18–19, Jesus quoted a passage from Isaiah proclaiming the Year of Jubilee. It is also interesting that some of Jesus' most powerful words about forgiveness were spoken in the context of a parable about forgiving debt (see Matthew 18:23–35).

Some voices in our modern world are crusading for rich countries to forgive the debts of poor countries. Rock star Bono addressed those

---

[135] www.creditcounsellingcanada.ca.

who attended the 2006 National Prayer Breakfast in Washington, D.C. A professed Christian, Bono challenged rich and powerful nations and individuals to embrace the concept of cancelling old debts. If it is within our power to do so, we can set others free.

*Wife: There's a guy at the door who wants to talk to you about a bill you haven't paid.*

*Husband: What does he look like?*

*Wife: He looks like you had better pay him now.*

*Don't withhold repayment of your debts. Don't say "some other time," if you can pay now.*

Proverbs 3:27 (TLB)

*And you shall lend to many nations, but you shall not borrow.*

Deuteronomy 28:12b

REMEMBERING THE POOR

# 24

---

# God Cares About the Poor

*The needy shall not always be forgotten, and the hope of*
*the poor shall not perish forever.*

Psalm 9:18

*He raises up the poor from the dust; he lifts the needy for*
*the ash heap to make them sit with princes and inherit a*
*seat of honor.*

1 Samuel 2:8a

*As for me, I am poor and needy, but the Lord*
*takes thought for me.*

Psalm 40:17

Certain experiences can help us to see the poor through the light-dispersing prism of God's love and concern for them. Such experiences have the power to shake us out of the donor fatigue to which we too easily succumb. Many of us also suffer from "photigue," an emotional numbness that besets us after we have seen too many photographs of starving children we have never met.

In the summer of 1990, Sam and I travelled with our preschool children to a town in the far north of Ivory Coast, West Africa. Sam volunteered his medical services in a mission hospital for one month. While Sam worked, I kept Darrin and Samantha happily occupied with some inexpensive playthings I had brought from home.

One windy day, we decided to fly our two-dollar kite in the empty soccer field nearby. Within minutes, a crowd gathered. Within the hour, the local school had emptied, the police station had closed, and stores had locked their doors. Pretty much everyone from the local village had shown up to watch us fly our kite. We let many of the African children take turns jubilantly running up and down the soccer field with the magical kite. By the end of the afternoon, our two-dollar toy was in tatters.

The next day, as a gesture of honour and thanks, the local people invited our kids to come play with their kids. The village mothers and kids gathered with us on a patch of dry earth surrounded by dirt-floor huts with conical thatched-grass roofs. The African children proudly offered Darrin and Samantha their communal toy car. It had four wobbly wheels made from the lids of baby-food jars and the tops of tin cans. Its body consisted of scraps of old cardboard, paper, and plastic. The village children laughed with great delight as our kids pulled this toy around with a ragged string. Everyone was having as much fun as they had the previous afternoon.

I stood on the sidelines watching the children play with the patch-work car. I could not help noticing that most of the African children had bare feet, very skinny limbs covered in sores, and clothing full of holes. One little boy had such a big hole in his pants that his buttocks were basically bare. It's one thing to glance for a few seconds at a photo of a poor child in a charity mailing. It's quite another to watch many such children for a number of hours.

I had previously seen terrible poverty all over Africa—in stinky slums, crammed buses, and ramshackle markets. God had previously broken my heart in *some* measure, enough to have brought me back to Africa on this mission of mercy. That morning, as I watched my children play with the village children and their single toy, the poverty of the Third World became *real* in a *fresh* way that particularly touched me. God broke my heart just a little more as I sensed how much He loved those poor children.

Later that month, as we were packing up to leave Ivory Coast, I saw a grown man cry as I gave him what remained of our crayons (worn down to small stubs), our plastic popsicle-making tray, and a few left-over packages of Kool-Aid—items that in total had cost me a few dollars back home. He was emotionally overwhelmed and over-joyed to the point of tears at the thought of passing on those treasures to his own children.

You can imagine how I felt coming back to the overflowing toy box and other luxuries in our spacious home in Canada. Our four-year-old son, Darrin, kept commenting, for many weeks after he came home, about all the nice stuff he had compared to the little African friends he had left behind. Two-year-old Samantha wanted to know when we could go play with the kids in "Akika" again. I could not get our African friends out of my mind either. At least for a while.

I pray that we all have many such encounters, at home or abroad, that cause us truly to *see* the poor in this world. May God shake us out of our emotional numbness. May we stop feeling apathy when we receive donation appeals depicting starving children in faraway places. May we see the poor through His tears and perhaps shed a few of our own. May He chisel away at our hearts, then chisel away some more. I confess that my own heart is still a rough work in progress.

## Some Disturbing Statistics

In one recent year, consumers across the globe spent $18 billion on cos-metics, $16 billon on blue jeans, and $15 billion on perfume. A further $14 billion was spent on cruises. In Europe alone, $11 billion was spent on ice cream. Over a recent Christmas season, Americans spent about $440 billion on retail purchases.

Annual global spending on the military and arms trade amounts to around one trillion dollars. On its own, America has cumulatively spent trillions of dollars on their involvement in the wars in Iraq and Afghanistan.

In 2010 alone, global sales of pet food amounted to $49 billion.[136]

Imagine our world having different spending priorities. If $9 billion could be spent each year on HIV and AIDS, that problem could be brought well under control. Only $13 billion each year would ensure that every person in the entire world received basic health care and adequate nutrition. An annual $6 billion would provide every child on the globe with a primary school education.[137] Pause to compare those amounts with what we collectively spend on make-up, blue jeans, perfume, cruises, ice cream, Christmas presents, pet food, and military campaigns.

The keener pursuit of more noble priorities remains largely in the realm of the imagination. The real world keeps spending money on guns and consumer luxuries while basic health and educational needs remain unmet for so many. It's pretty tough for anyone to climb out of poverty without an adequate level of both health care and education.

According to World Vision, the poorest one billion people in this world live on less than one dollar a day. A further one billion subsist on less than two dollars a day. Websites of organizations such as Free the Children record even higher numbers living on such meagre amounts.

In mind-boggling contrast, in a single recent year Tiger Woods made more than $100 million in endorsement deals, Oprah Winfrey received about $225 million from her media empire, and Steve Jobs took home about $646 million from Apple Computer. The chief of a hedge fund firm on Wall Street personally pulled in $3 billion dollars — that's billion, not million.[138] I am not trying to criticize these particular individuals. I'm simply disturbed that this reality exists while at least one-third of the global population subsists on a dollar or two a day.

---

[136]   Riseboro article.

[137]   Toycen article.

[138]   Maich article ("The $3 billion…").

Recently, World Vision noted that the top *three* billionaires in the world owned more assets than the 600 million poorest people. On a similar note, a World Institute for Development Economics Research study showed that, at the turn of the millennium, the wealthiest 1% of adults in the world owned 40% of all global assets. I keep coming across media articles asserting that the gap between the rich and the poor is growing ever larger. The rich gain exponentially while the downwardly mobile sink even lower.

In light of all these numbers, we delude ourselves when we think that we have come a long way from the days of exploitive colonialism. Maybe we have not come as far as we think.

This is not just about one nation oppressing another. Within nations, too many of the rich turn a blind eye to their own poor. Who can forget the scenes in *Slumdog Millionaire* showing lavish million-dollar condominiums overlooking million-peopled slums? I'm sad to report that homeless people sleep on the streets of my city too.

It is true that, on a global level, *some* effort is being made to help the poor. At the United Nations Millennium Summit of 2000, world leaders together pledged to end poverty by 2015 — a lofty goal indeed. Eight goals were set, called Millennium Development Goals (MDGs), which included eradicating extreme poverty and hunger, achieving universal primary level education, increasing foreign aid levels, changing trade policies, forgiving the debts of the poorest nations, and so on.

As the half-way point to 2015 was assessed in late 2008, however, it was clear that many goals were nowhere near being reached. Along with the other financial woes of 2008, there came a serious food crisis—by the end of that year over 850 million people were chronically hungry. About 25,000 people died each day from hunger-related illnesses. Grain stockpiles were lower than they had been in thirty years and food prices sky-rocketed. Globally, about 100 million people shifted from living on two dollars a day to one dollar a day. In countries like Afghanistan, this meant that some people moved from a subsistence diet of tea and bread to tea on its own some days. It is no wonder that violent food riots occurred all over the Third World that year and food relief trucks had to travel with armed escorts.[139]

Poverty continues to be widespread even within the wealthiest nations. Over 40 million people live below the poverty line in America. In Canada, about half of all single, widowed, or divorced women over 65 live in poverty; so do more than a million children. As of Christmas 2009, about 700,000 Canadians were regularly relying on food banks.

World leaders met again in 2010 to discuss progress on Millennium Development Goals, which had been set back by the global recession. Although the discussions brought fresh impetus to the MDGs, poverty and hunger were still disgraceful blights on our world. The world leaders discovered that over one billion people in the world were at imminent risk of starvation; the total number was increasing, not decreasing.[140] In the spring of 2010, World Vision reported that 8.8 million impoverished children under the age of five were still dying each year, which translates into seventeen preschoolers dying every minute or four hundred bus-loads dying each day.[141]

Does any of this make sense? Do you think the universe is as it should be? When God created this world, is this how He intended for humankind to share the rich resources He bestowed? Is He pleased? Does the world seem financially unbalanced to you to the point of being ridiculous? We're all caught in the middle of this madness. We must all bear some responsibility for the shameful state the world is in.

Let's shift from the macro to the micro. What about our personal worlds? Does anything need to change? Do *our* individual lives make sense in light of the bigger picture I presented above? Are you one of the poor, in need of more money? Or are you one of those who spend on endless consumer luxuries without much thought?

---

[139] Articles by unspecified authors, ("Ending Poverty…"; "Food Crisis…"); Morgan and Phiri article.
[140] Moll article ("Hunger…").
[141] Riseboro article.

Do *you* want to see a shift in the statistics? Do you believe God cares about this? I personally squirm a little when I ponder all these statistics, because I buy my share of cosmetics and ice cream and I've enjoyed cruising.

One would think that we Christians would live quite differently from our neighbours. Yet too often we work, save, consume, and give to others (or not) pretty much on pace with those around us who have other worldviews.

Will you work with me to *change* that?

I do not suggest that all Christian women stop wearing make-up or perfume...or that it is sinful to ever go on a cruise or enjoy an ice cream cone...or that we should starve our pets...or that all wars should be stopped purely because of the economics. We can, however, all play *some* part in shifting the obscene statistics that describe our current world.

## God's Heart in the Matter

Throughout the Bible, we encounter the consistent theme that God the Father loves the poor and cares about them. In fact, the Bible talks about the poor hundreds of times. Aligned with His Father, Jesus had a heart for the poor. Both Isaiah 61:1 and Matthew 11:5 tell us that Jesus came to preach good news to the poor. He cared about them both spiritually and materially. Thankfully, there's *still* good news for the poor who are willing to have faith in the risen Christ today. In Matthew 6:11, He invites everyone to pray each day to the Father: "Give us this day our daily bread." God wants to meet every need of the poor and He wants to grant their good desires too.

Alongside the hope offered to the poor, the Bible offers practical instructions to the rich. As we shift to the next chapter, let's consider some ways that the richer half of humanity can help the poorer half on this globe. We can help the poor both near and far. The Bible offers good news for the rich folk too, if they have compassion on the poor. The commands presented to them—to help the poor—come alongside some amazing promises.

Let's now explore some ways that we can make a difference. May our hearts reflect *more* of God's tender heart for the poor.

*"Because the poor are plundered, because the needy groan,*
*I will now arise," says the Lord; "I will place him in the*
*safety for which he longs."*

Psalm 12:5

*He upholds the cause of the oppressed and*
*gives food to the hungry.*

Psalm 146:7a (NIV)

*He will rescue the poor when they cry to him…He feels pity*
*for the weak and the needy, and he will rescue them.*

Psalm 72:12–13 (NLT)

*You have been a stronghold for the poor, a stronghold to*
*the needy in his distress, a shelter from the storm and a*
*shade from the heat…*

Isaiah 25:4

# 25

---

# PRACTICALLY HELPING THE POOR

*He who oppresses the poor shows contempt for their Maker,*
*but whoever is kind to the needy honors God.*

Proverbs 14:31 (NIV)

*...keep on helping the poor...*

Galatians 2:10 (NLT)

In 2008, I had the great privilege of visiting the place where Mother Teresa based her charity in Kolkata (formerly Calcutta), India. Blue-and-white-robed sisters still run the charity she developed. I walked through the rooms where Mother Teresa ate and slept, prayed and wrote. To honour her memory, many of her personal notes and journals had been put on display alongside her dusty sandals and numerous photographs depicting her many decades of working with the poor. Spending one morning focusing intently on her life, I was blown away by all she had done to alleviate the misery of the impoverished. Her example can inspire all of us.

Mother Teresa understood and lived by some simple yet profound truths. God *does* care about the poor. He cannot help them, however, unless *we* act as His hands and His feet. We can convey His love, concern, compassion, and provision. We can help the poor one prayer at a time, one dollar at a time, one act at a time, one person at a time. We can do whatever we can, however modest the act. Each humble action matters.

The prophet Isaiah recorded this message from God: "Share your food with the hungry, and give shelter to the homeless. Give clothes to those who need them…" (Isaiah 58:7 NLT). This same message is repeated numerous times in Scripture.

Deuteronomy 15 captures these instructions from Moses: "If among you, one of your brothers should become poor,…you shall not harden your heart or shut your hand against your poor brother, but you shall open your hand to him and lend him sufficient for his need, whatever it may be.…You shall give to him freely, and your heart shall not be grudging when you give to him, because for this the Lord your God will bless you in all your work and in all you undertake. For there will never cease to be poor in the land. Therefore I command you, 'You shall open wide your hand to your brother, to the needy and to the poor, in your land'" (vv. 7–8, 10–11).

In Matthew 25:31–40, Jesus promised eternal reward for those who feed the hungry, provide drink to the thirsty, clothe the naked, and invite the stranger in. We have *all* been clearly charged with this mission and this mandate from God: to help the poor in tangible, practical ways.

This mission is not minor and it is not optional. I invite you to consider what Jesus went on to say in Matthew 25:41–46: if we do *not* feed the hungry, clothe the naked, and visit the sick, we will *not* inherit the Kingdom. We will not spend eternity with God. These are some of the most sobering words in the New Testament. It is true that we are justified by faith; but it is also true that faith without works is dead.[142] One of the tests Jesus sets forth to determine whether our alleged faith in Him is really authentic and truly sincere involves examining how we treat the hungry, the thirsty, the naked, and the sick.

---

[142] See, for example, Romans 3:28, Romans 5:1 and James 2:24–26.

The ideal of eradicating poverty will not be fully achieved in this world before Christ returns. Yet we can still work toward that ideal. Most of us will never achieve the stature of Mother Teresa, but we must all do *some*thing. We must balance and integrate the oft-repeated biblical command to help the poor with all of the other biblical principles about money management. We cannot ignore this key command and still expect other principles to work well.

## Giving Our Possessions to the Poor

One of the easiest things we can do in Western society is to give some of our possessions away. We can either give to the poor and needy directly or give to organizations that will help them.

We can look around our homes. We can brave a visit to our basements. We can scrutinize all of our possessions—everything from clothes, to books, to kitchen dishes. Maybe we no longer need the items our children once used, such as cribs, playpens, and strollers. Maybe there are carpets and furniture we have not used since we redecorated or down-sized. We can research local Christian organizations (or other charities) that will accept gently-used items for the eventual benefit of those living in poverty or in low-income brackets.

An organization I have come to respect highly is the BFM Foundation Canada, which operates Bibles for Missions Thrift Stores in dozens of communities in our nation.[143] They accept donations of items such as furniture, clothing, books, and kitchenware, then sell those items at very low prices. A winter coat, sweater, or suit jacket that might have been originally purchased for $100 can be resold for $5 or $10. Books that cost $30 might be marked for sale at $2. Those in need can buy these items at much cheaper prices than they could in a retail store at the mall. They are not being given a hand-out; their dignity is preserved.

The net profits of the BFM Foundation go to another charity called The Bible League of Canada. Its activities include sending Bibles around the world. That same winter coat that resells for $10 ultimately

---

[143]  www.bfmthriftstores.ca.

turns into three Bibles being sent abroad. Many Christians in other nations wait for years (even decades) to receive their own personal copy of the Scripture. Your old clothes can speed up that process.

Looking in my closet, I might notice a jacket that I have not worn for a while and realize it's still in great shape. Initially, I might think that perhaps I will wear it again someday (when I lose a pound or two, when I buy another skirt to match it, when I work in an office again, or when it comes back in style). When I remember that I can turn that jacket into a few Bibles and that someone who can really use that jacket might soon actually begin to wear it, I can part with it more easily.

In 2010, the BFM Foundation Canada gave more than $5 million in net profits to The Bible League of Canada. Over the past few decades, BFM has cumulatively donated over $35 million to The Bible League of Canada. Those old jackets, books, and dishes of ours really add up! Ultimately, the money is used for more than placing Bibles. Some of it goes towards training evangelists, starting up churches, implementing Bible study programs, and other related activities. As part of the overall process, the poor in our own country acquire household items and clothing at very manageable prices. And our homes get de-cluttered without adding to our landfill sites.

If we take the time to look with a fresh perspective all around our homes, we will likely be amazed at all the things we have that we do not need, do not use, and would not miss. I guarantee that most of you have treasures in drawers, closets, cupboards, and other storage places. Take steps this week to begin giving items away. Clean house. Pare down. Simplify. And bless others in the process.

I am challenged anew, even as I write this chapter, by the questions raised in James 2:14–16: "What good is it, dear brothers and sisters, if you say you have faith but don't show it by your actions? Can that kind of faith save anyone? Suppose you see a brother or sister who has no food or clothing, and you say, 'Good-bye and have a good day; stay warm and eat well'—but then you don't give that person any food or clothing. What good does that do?'" (NLT). Maybe our biological brother or sister does not need food or clothing—but what about our brothers and sisters in Christ in our church, our community, and around the world? Let us freshly purpose to give practical, tangible, material aid to them.

We can also be motivated by 1 John 3:17–18: "…if anyone has the world's goods and sees his brother in need, yet closes his heart against him, how does God's love abide in him?...let us not love in word or talk but in deed and in truth."

Jesus sums it up so simply: "Whoever has two tunics is to share with him who has none, and whoever has food is to do likewise" (Luke 3:11).

## Giving Money to the Poor

We can do more than give away our excess possessions. We can also give money to help the poor.

We can open our wallets to the poor we encounter on our streets, helping beggars and homeless people as the Spirit prompts us. I have heard, however, from those who work with the homeless, that it is better to give money to an established ministry that helps them rather than to the homeless directly. Although we must be careful not to give in to stereotypes, money given directly to someone on the street might be spent on alcohol, drugs, or cigarettes. Reputable ministries can invest our donations in food, drink, clothing, blankets, mobile medical aid, shelter, and counselling. Our concern and compassion for those living on our streets should be balanced with wisdom and prudence.

We can also donate money to organizations such as World Vision, Samaritan's Purse, and many others that help the poor in places and in ways that we cannot, those both near and far. World Vision provides food and clothing for the poor along with medical, educational, vocational, and community aid. I encourage you to browse through their Christmas gift catalogue; for surprisingly small amounts, donors can choose to fully stock a medical clinic, fund supplies for an entire classroom, send farm animals, provide farming tools, shelter children rescued from prostitution or child soldiering, help a family start a microbusiness, etc.

Check it out! World Vision International currently raises more than one billion dollars each year, but great need still remains around the world.

We can regularly support an individual child through organizations such as World Vision and Compassion. We can become their angel investor. You might ask: What good does it do to help one child when billions in this world are poor and a billion of them are on the brink of starvation? The cause can seem hopeless and the numbers overwhelming, but we can fight the temptation to give in to that kind of thinking.

Mother Teresa dealt with that issue by repeatedly reminding herself that we help the poor one person at a time. No one person can help everyone, but we can all do our part. I admire those who can inspire others to jump on this bandwagon. As a result of the efforts of two dynamic women, my church now supports 340 children through a Christian organization called Childcare Plus.

While still students, my son, Darrin, and his future wife, Alicia, began providing monthly support for poor children growing up in Third World countries. I have been even more impressed and humbled by stories of homeless people donating some of the proceeds of their panhandling to others rendered homeless by Hurricane Katrina, the earthquake in Haiti, and the recent tsunami in Japan. If those with such limited funds can scrape up the money to help the impoverished, so can the rest of us.

Gandhi is believed to have coined this saying: The rich need to learn how to live more simply so that the poor can simply live. If we put our minds to it, I am sure that all of us can save some money by finding something we can cut back on or live without; then we can give that money so that others can simply live.

## Advocacy for the Poor

There is one kind of "lip service" that actually benefits the poor—using our voice to advocate for them as we have opportunity. In Proverbs 31:8–9, we are invited to do this: "Speak up for those who cannot speak for themselves…Yes, speak up for the poor and the helpless…"(NLT).

Maybe you cannot give a lot financially. This need not stop you from speaking up for the poor, so that those who can give more financially are encouraged to do so.

We can also raise awareness by our actions, not just our words. Prince William, heir to the British throne, slept one night in below-zero temperatures on a hard concrete sidewalk near some dumpsters. He spent that night on the street to better understand the homeless and to raise awareness of their plight. In similar fashion, many teens participate each year in World Vision's 40 Hour Famine. By sleeping on their school's gym floor and not eating for forty hours, those students begin to identify with the poor and to draw attention to their needs.

## Social Activism

Many Christians feel called to become social activists on behalf of the poor on a much more committed level. A recent survey in Canada ranked Tommy Douglas as the greatest Canadian hero of all time. Douglas started his adult life as a Baptist preacher. In the 1930s, when so many around him became unemployed and impoverished during the Great Depression, Douglas became a passionate social activist. He created snow-shovelling jobs for the unemployed. He arranged for food and clothing to be shipped from the better-off provinces to his own needier province of Saskatchewan. He eventually became the Premier of Saskatchewan and later the first federal leader of the New Democrat Party. He created the first medicare system in Canada, available to all Canadians (a system now regarded as one of the best in the world). Seven decades later, his exemplary life is remembered, respected, and admired by so many (regardless of political party affiliation) because he worked tirelessly to create practical programmes that would benefit the poor, the sick, and the unemployed.

## Working for the Poor

Of course, the greatest example of working for the poor *is* Mother Teresa. She worked amongst the poor in India for several decades. We typically hear about how she held the suffering and the dying in her arms, but she did much more than that. She waited for hours at government offices, asking for water pumps, electrical hook-ups, garbage removal, and other practical services for the slums she worked in. She sought food and medicine for the needy. She raised funds. She trained those who came to work alongside her. Her selfless, indefatigable spirit challenged many others to help the poor.[144]

I have come across numerous other impressive examples of individuals who have dedicated their lives to working with and for the poor. I have space here to share two brief stories.

A Christian woman named Ruth Goodwin, who earned her Harvard MBA in 1992, could have worked for any number of blue-chip companies or prestigious banks. Instead, she chose to work with Women's World Banking, which extends aid to women in development projects in many nations.[145]

Kevin Bradley traded his profitable career as a stockbroker for work ministering to the homeless. At first, he and his wife lived off their savings. He remembers times when he had less food in his pantry than some of the people his ministry was helping.[146]

### Churches, Companies, and Communities

So far we have been discussing mainly what we can do individually to help the poor or how we can contribute to the missions of Christian charities. Beyond these important efforts, we can also encourage our churches, our companies, and our communities to get corporately involved.

Many of the poor need a place to sleep. In California, some churches and businesses permit their parking lots to be used at nights by people who live/sleep in their cars because they can no longer afford their rent or mortgage payments.

---

[144]   Le Joly book.
[145]   Monroe book, p. 219.
[146]   Bishop article.

In some communities, churches rotate (each taking one night of the week), allowing the homeless to sleep in their basements. This matters because, increasingly, the homeless are being deprived of the one thing they could formerly count on—the street. In Manhattan, the homeless are now bussed to the outer boroughs so that tourists can enjoy a sanitized urban core. In many cities, the old neighbourhoods (where the poor once slept undisturbed on sidewalks) have been reclaimed by property developers; the owners of the new urban lofts, shops, cafés, and art galleries drive away the homeless. In most cities, there's a chronic shortage of government-funded shelters. Churches can stand in the gap.

The poor also need to be fed. In my city, lawyers donate both time and money to open up a dining room in the downtown courthouse for the homeless to enjoy four meals a week at times when court is not in session. Many businesses donate left-over catered meals or perishable groceries to charities that will collect and distribute this food to the hungry while it is still fresh. Fire stations collect bags of food for the needy at designated times such as Easter and Thanksgiving. My church has a food bank that accepts donations of non-perishable food items all year round. My church also hosts an annual Christmas feast for the less fortunate in our community and regularly participates in feeding the homeless in the city's inner core.

In agricultural communities near my city, farmers donate blemished produce. Organized volunteers chop up the edible portions, dehydrate and package the chopped pieces, and then ship dried soup packages to the Third World. Food once destined for landfills now nourishes the starving. One farmer on his own could not facilitate this, but hundreds working together as donors and volunteers can make a huge impact.

Communities can also further help the less fortunate in our midst in creative ways. The town I used to live in ran something called a curb-side give-away-day each summer. Instead of holding garage sales, residents could put all their old and unwanted (but still usable) possessions by their curb-side and others from all over town could take away whatever they wanted for free.

One year, as I began packing to move from that town, I became amazed at how much stuff we had accumulated in our basement. We had skates, rollerblades, hockey equipment, bikes, junior-sized golf clubs, and other sporting equipment our kids had outgrown. I purposed to participate in the curb-side give-away-day that summer. (To my shame, I had not made the effort to participate in prior years, hence the full basement.) On the designated Saturday that year, I carted all of our old sports items to the curb-side by the armload and watched each armload disappear almost immediately. After I finished with the mountain of stuff in our basement, I looked in our kitchen—and out came plates, pots and pans, cookie jars, and other sundry items that I no longer used often enough to keep. Then I mined our toy-box for the toys our kids had long ago outgrown. I soon discovered how valuable all those items were to others. They disappeared quickly too.

The number of possibilities as to how our churches, our companies, and our communities can practically help the less fortunate folk among us will be defined by how much we are prepared to collectively imagine and support such possibilities. None of us are able to support *every* initiative, but we can surely try to support *some* of them.

## Supporting Our Government's Role

Throughout history, governments have not always done much to help the poor. This began to change a few centuries ago. In the 19th century, in Britain, a so-called welfare state began evolving, to get past the shame of the horrible poorhouses of that era. Among other goals, the idea was to give better dignity to the poor and to provide them with a minimum standard of living.

This past century, government welfare programmes developed to some extent in other industrialized nations such as America, Canada, Japan, and Germany. As a result of escalating costs, growing tax burdens, and anti-Communist sentiments during the Cold War era, welfare programmes eventually fell somewhat out of favour. In the

1980s, President Reagan and Prime Minister Margaret Thatcher began a partial dismantling of the welfare system in the United States and Britain. Canada did not dismantle it to the same degree.

In most Western countries, there is still *some* governmental safety net for the poor and disadvantaged. Having experimented with a variety of welfare programmes, the perennial question remains in Western nations: how much should our governments help, subsidize, rescue, and support the poor and the disadvantaged? The issues involved are quite complex, because many of the poor and disadvantaged are also sick, disabled, mentally ill, addicted, illiterate, unemployed, or elderly.

While speaking to others as I wrote this book, I was surprised to discover on many occasions that, among Christians, there is as much debate about helping the poor as there is about seeking personal prosperity. All Christians give lip service to helping the poor—of course. But when it comes to voting for political parties that do or do not plan to use tax dollars to help the poor, there are wide discrepancies in Christian voting patterns and intentions. Many Christians are not supportive of subsidizing a welfare safety net through their taxes. Some Christians get quite heated when discussing this issue.

We have two options as the Body of Christ in this present world. The first option involves all of us (individually and corporately) offering practical and monetary aid to the poor. If all Christians around the world faithfully and generously offered enough aid, poverty *could* probably be eradicated without governmental involvement.

The second option (the default) is to let our government deal with whatever shortfall exists in our collective giving. Given that Christians are evidently not stepping up to the plate with enough dollars, we should not criticize our government when they give financial aid to the poor in our own nation and beyond. No matter how it gets done, helping the poor is simply non-negotiable from God's point of view.

Jesus did not tell us to rebel against paying taxes. When asked whether it was right to pay taxes to Caesar, He replied that we should render unto Caesar that which is due Caesar, and unto God that which is due God.[147] *If* we rendered unto God the amount of money we should be rendering to help the poor, Caesar would not have to extract so much from us in taxes to provide a social safety net for the disadvantaged.

Certainly, various thorny issues need to be addressed appropriately, such as government aid recipients becoming too dependent on hand-outs, the development of an attitude of effortless entitlement, and the corruption of some Third World recipient states. I wish I had space to address the *many* issues that complicate the role that governments play when it comes to helping the poor at home or abroad. The complexity of the debate should not deter ongoing discussion, nor should it postpone the search for sound solutions.

## What the Poor Can Do for Themselves

What does God expect of the poor? What can they do for themselves? I believe He asks them to do the same things He asks of all of us, things such as exercising faith, working hard if and when they are able to, and shaking off a poverty mindset (if they have one).

What do I mean by "poverty mindset"? Some people don't expect their circumstances will ever change. Their grandparents were poor, their parents were poor, and they are poor. Feeling hopeless, they do not believe that material blessing will ever come their way. This mindset has been ingrained into many people their entire lives.

Over the years, I have heard some variation of the following sermon illustration. A poor family lived in a shabby house, struggling to farm a dry patch of land. They barely scraped by from week to week, living in ragged clothes and surviving on minimal food. Their kids dropped out of school so that they could contribute to the family's meagre income. All the while, unknown to them, a large reserve of oil existed underneath their property. The family lived and died in poverty without knowing the wealth that they were sitting on, wealth that could have totally changed their lives. It was right there all along, but they had no awareness of it.

---

[147]   Matthew 22:17–21.

And so it is with Christians who do not open their Bibles and read what God has to say about money. Many fail to see or believe that a verse such as Philippians 4:19 (which talks about God meeting *all* of our needs) applies to *their* situation. Material blessing and sufficient provision are near to each one of us, closer than we may think, but we must open our spiritual eyes to see it and our hearts to believe it.

Along with having faith and vision, we must all purpose to be obedient to God. In Deuteronomy 28, Moses talks about how God will materially bless the obedient but inflict poverty and lack on the disobedient.

Poverty is not always the fault of the individual—this point needs to be emphasized. Much of the poverty in this world has been caused by social injustice and other circumstances beyond one's own control. In Proverbs 13:23, for example, we are told: "A poor person's farm may produce much food, but injustice sweeps it all away" (NLT). In James 5:1–4, we read about rich people who defrauded their labourers of their rightful wages. Others struggle financially because they cannot find or keep work due to physical or mental health disabilities. Yet others have been the victims of abuse, abandonment, racial prejudice, crime, accidents caused by others, etc. The many reasons for poverty cannot be addressed in this short chapter. What we can take away from this discussion, however, is that the poor are not always the cause of their own plight.

Whole nations suffer massive poverty. Loren Cunningham, founder of YWAM, and a man who has travelled to literally every nation on earth, believes that three things lead to an entire nation becoming poor: unbridled greed, corruption, and injustice.[148] Anyone who has travelled in the Third World will likely agree that the poor masses in those nations did not create their own dire macro-economic situation. Colonial powers, autocratic political leaders, tribal conflict, wars between nations, an oppressive elite class, and natural disasters must bear a lot of the blame for the wide-spread systemic poverty in

---

[148] Cunningham book, (*The Book...*), p. 144.

many countries. Billions are *born into* impoverished conditions that are not easy to escape without assistance.

Some of the poor, wherever they live, are able to work and want to work. Let's help them help themselves. I am encouraged by the trend of many organizations, Christian and otherwise, to fund micro-enterprises in many parts of the Third World. In Thailand, for example, more than thirty women who once worked in the sex industry now have the opportunity to make jewellery for a small micro-enterprise called Nightlight.[149]

In my own country, I admire ministries that open businesses which offer work positions to those who want to stop living on the street. In my own city, for example, one ministry runs a muffin shop. Facilitating opportunities for the poor to engage in work gives them dignity; they can be freed from relying on humiliating hand-outs. Author Robert Lupton asserts that giving a poor person dignity is as important as offering them a warm coat. It's much better to provide a poor person with the opportunity to work in a thrift store than to simply give them second-hand clothes.

## God's Promises to Those Who Help the Poor

In Proverbs 14:21, we are told: "…blessed is he who is generous to the poor." This promise is repeated in Proverbs 22:9. In Proverbs 19:17, we learn: "He who is kind to the poor lends to the Lord, and he will reward him for what he has done" (NIV).

In Deuteronomy 24:19, Moses instructed and encouraged the Israelites: "When you reap your harvest in your field and forget a sheaf in the field, you shall not go back to get it. It shall be for the sojourner, the fatherless, and the widow, that the Lord your God may bless you in all the work of your hands."

Isaiah 58:8 promises that, if we help the poor, God will be our rear guard. Rock star Bono once commented on that verse: "That is

---

[149]    Maxwell article, p. 27.

a powerful incentive: The Lord will watch your back. Sounds like a good deal to me…"[150]

Isaiah 58:10–11 further promises this: "If you spend yourselves in behalf of the hungry and satisfy the needs of the oppressed, then your light will rise in the darkness, and your night will become like the noonday. The Lord will guide you always; he will satisfy your needs… and will strengthen your frame. You will be like a well-watered garden, like a spring whose waters never fail" (NIV).

In Psalm 41:1–3, we learn: "Blessed is the one who considers the poor! In the day of trouble the Lord delivers him; the Lord protects him and keeps him alive; he is called blessed in the land; you do not give him up to the will of his enemies. The Lord sustains him on his sickbed; in his illness you restore him to full health."

God will bless those who help the poor, both in this life and in eternity. Luke 14:12–14 records this statement of Jesus: "When you give a dinner or a banquet, do not invite your friends or your brothers or your relatives or rich neighbors, lest they invite you in return and you be repaid. But when you give a feast, invite the poor, the crippled, the lame, the blind, and you will be blessed, because they cannot repay you. For you will be repaid at the resurrection of the just."

## God's Warnings to Those Who Ignore or Oppress the Poor

In striking contrast to God's various promises to bless those who help the poor, He has nothing but stern words for those who do not. In Proverbs 21:13 we are told: "Those who shut their ears to the cries of the poor will be ignored in their own time of need" (NLT). Proverbs 22:16 predicts: "A person who gets ahead by oppressing the poor or by showering gifts on the rich will end in poverty" (NLT). Proverbs 22:22–23 warns: "Don't rob the poor just because you can…For the Lord is their defender. He will ruin anyone who ruins them" (NLT).

Ezekiel 16:49–50 describes some of the reasons God destroyed the city of Sodom: "Behold, this was the guilt of your sister Sodom: she and her daughters had pride, excess of food, and prosperous ease, but

---

[150] From Bono's address at the National Prayer Breakfast in Washington, D.C. (2006).

did not aid the poor and needy. They were haughty and did an abomination before me. So I removed them, when I saw it."

For some New Testament perspective on this, I invite you to think about this story Jesus told:

> There was a certain rich man who was splendidly clothed in purple and fine linen and who lived each day in luxury. At his gate lay a poor man named Lazarus who was covered with sores. As Lazarus lay there longing for scraps from the rich man's table, the dogs would come and lick his open sores. Finally, the poor man died and was carried by the angels to be with Abraham. The rich man also died and was buried, and his soul went to the place of the dead. There, in torment, he saw Abraham in the far distance with Lazarus at his side. The rich man shouted, "Father Abraham, have some pity! Send Lazarus over here to dip the tip of his finger in the water and cool my tongue. I am in anguish…" But Abraham said to him, "Son, remember that during your lifetime you had everything you wanted, and Lazarus had nothing. So now he is here being comforted, and you are in anguish." (Luke 16:19–25 NLT)

Is it worth living *this* life in some measure of luxury, without showing mercy to the poor, when we have been warned that one day we will have to account for our selfish actions and pay for them eternally?

## Hope for the Future

I am encouraged by the emerging generation of young adults. Many of them have a strong sense of social justice and a keen desire to help the poor and the less fortunate. My son, for example, has poured energy into designing calendars and T-shirts to help raise funds for an organization ministering to the homeless. My daughter built homes in El Salvador on a Habitat for Humanity trip. Many of their friends volunteer and give. I pray that their generation maintains their admirable compassion for the needy.

Jesus still wants to help the poor. He still wants to feed the hungry crowd. There's one major impediment: too many of us sitting in the front row of the crowd are helping ourselves to second and third helpings of His loaves and fishes before passing the baskets to those waiting in the back rows. One child dies of starvation every six seconds. We, the well-fed, must work together to change that!

*He who gives to the poor will lack nothing…*

Proverbs 28:27 (NIV)

*…let the poor and needy praise your name.*

Psalm 74:21b

*Do the thing in front of you.*

Mother Teresa[151]

---

[151]  Morgan and Phiri article, p. 33.

# REAL RICHES

# 26

———

## LIVING BEYOND MONEY

*There was a man all alone; he had neither son nor brother.*
*There was no end to his toil, yet his eyes were not content*
*with his wealth. "For whom am I toiling," he asked…This*
*too is meaningless—a miserable business!*

Ecclesiastes 4:7–8 (NIV)

*The poorest man I know is the man who*
*has nothing but money.*

John D. Rockefeller

*There is no class so pitiably wretched as that which*
*possesses money and nothing else.*

Andrew Carnegie, from his 1889 essay "The Gospel of Wealth"

*I feel like a man who has no money in his pocket, but is*
*allowed to draw for all he wants upon one infinitely rich; I*
*am, therefore, at once both a beggar and a rich man.*

John Newton

*...having nothing, yet possessing everything.*

2 Corinthians 6:10

In the 1850s, the American economy experienced enormous growth. Unexpectedly, a financial crash occurred in 1857. Banks began to close. Stock values plummeted. Despair went viral. A man named Jeremiah Lanphier, a lay missionary, decided to reach out to the particularly distraught business community in New York City. He advertised the start-up of a weekly lunch-hour prayer meeting. On the first day, he prayed alone for half an hour. Then six people straggled in to join him.

The next week, twenty showed up. By the following month, over one hundred men were regularly coming. Within six months, more than 50,000 people streamed into additional noon-hour prayer meetings occurring in more locations across the city. They learned that God could save, bless, and fulfil their lives in ways that money never could.

Many who struggle with precarious finances in today's troubled economic times are learning these same lessons.

Such truths can be learned in the midst of good economic times too. Some years ago, I joined an outreach team which met with the top few hundred wealthiest and most powerful men and women in Ecuador. One night, I attended a dinner party hosted by a Christian couple. Their dozen Ecuadorian guests were not Christians. The couple and their guests lived in an exclusive gated community. The streets were lined with gorgeous homes surrounded by tropical gardens, large swimming pools, and private tennis courts. The President of their country lived in one of those homes.

The dinner party guests were dressed impeccably, the women in cocktail dresses and high heels, their make-up perfect, their long shapely nails painted vibrant red. Maids in black dresses with white aprons moved silently around the home as they served us. I thought those maid outfits only existed in the movies.

One member of our Canadian team gave a brief testimony, then asked the Ecuadorian guests to bow their heads in prayer. He said that they could pray silently in their hearts, in agreement with the words he was about to pray, if they wanted to accept Christ as their Saviour and Lord. Instead of praying silently, however, literally half of the group began to repeat the words of the prayer out loud. Some started to cry. Some fell on their knees. That evening, it was clear that great material wealth and status could not provide what each human heart sorely needs: a real relationship with God.

Shortly after we were married, my husband, Sam, and I stayed in the home of a senior Vice President of a Fortune 500 company. From a worldly perspective, this distinguished silver-haired gentleman and his beautiful younger wife had it "all." Their Connecticut country mansion, set in lovely woods beside a private lake, showcased prized antiques; their garage sheltered a fleet of polished vintage cars; their handsome sons looked like they had stepped out of a Ralph Lauren ad. Everything seemed picture-perfect.

One evening, Sam and I shared about our faith in Christ. The husband, particularly intrigued, leaned forward as we talked about our individual spiritual journeys. To our surprise, tears began to stream down his cheeks. He confessed, with great sadness, that he had spent his best years pursuing material wealth for the purpose of his own pleasure. He was ready to admit how empty and meaningless that aspect of his life had become. At that late point in his life, he *knew* there had to be something more. I will never forget the intense, hungry look on his face as we answered his many questions about faith in Christ.

## Money Does Not Buy Happiness

I am among those who firmly believe that money does not buy real happiness, satisfaction, meaning, or fulfilment in life. This can be demonstrated by the number of very wealthy people who commit suicide. Two suicides allegedly occurred, for example, in the immediate family of the late shipping billionaire Aristotle Onassis.

Even many secular researchers agree that having oodles of money does not guarantee happiness. In 2009, the University of British Columbia and Harvard Business School jointly conducted a study of over 400 people earning a wide range of incomes. Those being surveyed were asked to rate their level of happiness on a scale of 1 to 100. Surprisingly, those who earned $25,000 averaged a score of 70; those at $55,000 ranked themselves at 76; those raking in $125,000 averaged just 67, while those at the loftier level of $500,000 weighed in at 78 (barely more than those at $55,000).[152]

A 1985 survey compared respondents from the *Forbes* list (of the four hundred wealthiest Americans) with members of the Masai tribe in East Africa (who lived in dirt-floor grass huts, with no electricity or running water). The survey found that both groups rated their level of life satisfaction with equal scores. This is quite astonishing.

Many other research studies, in the fields of psychology and social science, agree with the conclusion that rising income does not necessarily equate with rising well-being. In Western society, the average person currently has more money, a bigger home, better food, more holidays, and more luxuries than their grandparents had decades ago, and yet the average modern person is no happier. Depression, anxiety, divorce, and suicide rates have been escalating over time, not falling. Various researchers have discovered that a person's level of happiness is more positively impacted by a good marriage, serving in the community, meaningful work, and spiritual faith than it is by money.[153] A study by the Pew Research Center in 2006 concluded that people who attend religious services are happier than those who don't.

Tal Ben-Shahar, a psychology lecturer at Harvard, has spent years studying what makes people happy. Although he posits that money can be a factor, money is not nearly as important as people often assume. He personally remembers being "the happiest man alive" when he received his first paycheque as a college intern, but the happiness from his new income only lasted a few weeks. A few years later, he felt elated again when he received a paycheque that was triple the amount. Once again, the spike in happiness was short-lived. The same pattern continued every time he received a substantial raise.[154] Can you relate?

152 Van Evra article.
153 Ibid.
154 Hood article.

Ben-Shahar found his experience was not unique. He concurs with other studies which have concluded that, although the American standard of living has greatly improved in the last several decades, the percentage of those who would describe themselves as very happy has not budged. A higher standard of living has not improved the happiness quotient in American society at all. Ben-Sharar believes that lasting happiness is more dependent on what goes on inside of us than on the state of our bank accounts. Grateful people, for example, are happier than ungrateful people, regardless of the amount of wealth they have accumulated. Simply making a lot of money does not assure happiness—rather, for many, it can paradoxically lead to an impoverished spirit and a diminished ability to enjoy life. No measure of financial reward is enough to compensate a person who is unhappy.[155]

Over the years, I have collected anecdotal evidence that suggests that having material wealth is not all that it is cracked up to be. I read a fascinating article, for example, about the owners of several chateaux in France. From a distance, many of their chateaux look magnificent, with their round towers, conical roofs, exquisite stone façades, and grand windows, all surrounded by acres of genteel gardens. Some of the castles even have moats and drawbridges. I was interested to learn that most of the owners of those elegant chateaux find their properties to be giant headaches.

Many of the chateaux are falling into disrepair and most are ridiculously expensive to maintain. Can you imagine what it costs to re-shingle a castle roof or to heat and air-condition massive rooms? Can you imagine the taxes and the insurance premiums? What about the gardening bills?

Some owners have tried to open their palaces to the viewing public, but in most cases the consequent income barely covers the maintenance costs. Some chateaux have been turned into bed-and-breakfast properties. Their owners have no choice but to commit their entire lives to running their properties, becoming slaves to their guests. Some chateaux are being sold for as little as half a million dollars because the

---

[155]  Ibid.

owners cannot stand the hassles of ownership anymore. They move to more modest homes.[156]

The newly rich also find that their money provides no guarantee that they will live happily ever after. Many lottery winners have discovered that their windfall money does not necessarily improve their lives, emotionally or otherwise, over the long haul. In 1996, a hospital worker from Scotland named John McGuinness won approximately $21 million in a lottery. By 2008, he had spent it all, declared bankruptcy, and moved into subsidized social housing. He ended up worse off than he had been before his big win. Notwithstanding this kind of story, the Canadian government made over $13 billion in revenue from its lotteries and casinos in 2006. In large numbers, people are still looking for the pot of gold at the end of the fantasy rainbow that they believe will magically transform their dreary lives.[157]

In my own life, I have learned that increased material wealth does not bring increased happiness. I have lived on a tight student budget. I have lived out of a backpack, sometimes sleeping in airports, hostels, budget hotels, a dump-truck cab, train stations, and even in a brothel (although my husband and I did not know it at the time). I have travelled on the cheap in some of the most poverty-stricken countries in the Third World. In contrast, over the years I have also lived in large homes in upscale neighbourhoods. I have travelled on an ample budget. And the truth is, I was not any more or less happy… as a child in a family of humble means…as a university student living on a shoestring…as a backpacker with few possessions…as a big-city lawyer married to a busy doctor…or as a guest in a five-star hotel. I can honestly say that I have enjoyed each phase of life equally. I have learned that the words of Jesus in Luke 12:15 are very true: real life and real living are *not* related to how rich we are.

As a lawyer, I have rubbed shoulders with many wealthy colleagues and clients. As a doctor, my husband has known his share of rich peers and patients. No matter how much money these people have

---

[156] Anderson article.
[157] Vermond article.

accumulated, a surprising number have gone through multiple bitter divorces, raised troubled children, or worked so hard that they had no time for their spiritual development or for their family and friends.

The misery that besets so many rich people gets ample attention in books and movies. Most of you are probably familiar with the story of Scrooge in Dicken's classic tale, *A Christmas Carol*. Once obsessed with money, Scrooge finally realizes that loving others matters much more. Maybe you saw the movie *The Nanny Diaries*, in which a rich and snooty Manhattan mom ultimately discovers that her relationship with her child is much more precious than all the hours she once spent shopping on Fifth Avenue or lunching with her girlfriends.

Doesn't the *highest* standard of living involve something above and beyond money and material possessions?

All Christians have the great privilege of discovering that real life and real living are not related to how rich we are. We can live in such a way that the things with price tags attached to them are not worth much at all compared to those things in life which are priceless. Great relationships are priceless—both relationships with others and, above all, our relationship with God.

## A Relationship with God

The Bible teaches that our relationship with God is worth immeasurably more than the sum total of *everything* else we might have. It is above all. Notwithstanding its incomparable value, our relationship with God cannot be bought with money.

Isaiah 55:1–3 makes this invitation: "Come, everyone who thirsts, come to the waters; and he who has no money, come, buy and eat! Come, buy wine and milk without money and without price. Why do you spend your money for that which is not bread, and your labor for that which does not satisfy? Listen diligently to me, and eat what is good, and delight yourselves in rich food. Incline your ear, and come to me; hear, that your soul may live; and I will make with you an everlasting covenant…"

This is echoed in Revelation 21:6–7: "It is done! I am the Alpha and the Omega, the beginning and the end. To the thirsty I will give from

the spring of the water of life without payment....I will be his God..."
Revelation 22:17c offers: "...let the one who is thirsty come; let the one
who desires take the water of life without price."

Peter elaborated on how we enter into a relationship with God:
"You know that it was not with perishable things such as silver or gold
that you were redeemed from the empty way of life handed down to
you from your forefathers, but with the precious blood of Christ..." (1
Peter 1:18–19 NIV). Jesus has already paid the full price for our salvation from our sins and for our rightstanding with God the Father.

In Ephesians 3:8, Paul referred to the "unsearchable riches of
Christ." In Philippians 3:8a, Paul also stated, "...I count everything as
loss because of the surpassing worth of knowing Christ Jesus my Lord."

Entering into a relationship with God is as simple as this: we personally acknowledge that we have sinned and that our sins have separated us from God; we confess whatever sins come to mind (of course
none of us can list them all!); we choose to believe that Jesus is the Son
of God and that He died on the Cross as payment for our sins; we
ask God the Father to forgive our sins in the name of Jesus, His risen
Son; and we ask God to send the Holy Spirit to dwell in our hearts.
The Spirit helps us to withstand ongoing temptations to sin in various
ways and He also urges us to confess any further sins we do commit
so that we maintain our rightstanding with God.

Many wealthy men and women have attested to the all-surpassing
value of a personal relationship with God, obtained and maintained by
taking the steps just described. I love the story of Henry John Heinz,
the ketchup tycoon. He achieved great wealth and success in his life,
but he counted it as nothing compared to his relationship with God.
He wrote this in his last will and testament: "Looking forward to the
time when my earthly career will end, I desire to set forth at the very
beginning of this will, as the most important item in it, a confession of
Jesus Christ as my Savior. I also bear witness to the fact that throughout my life, in which there were unusual joys and sorrows, I have been
wonderfully sustained by my faith in God through Jesus Christ."[158]

---

[158]  Books book, pp. 115–116.

Sam Walton started Walmart, a mega-billion dollar company which has been at or near the top of the Fortune 500 list for years. Yet Walton, like Heinz, valued his salvation in Jesus Christ and his relationship with God far above his business success. Throughout his lifetime, he faithfully served God in his local church and sought to introduce others to his beloved Christ.[159]

We can all find our truest joy in God. In Psalm 4:7, David wrote: "You have put more joy in my heart than they have when their grain and wine abound." He understood that his relationship with God was far better than anything others could attain in the material world. David also wrote, in Psalm 16:5: "Lord, you alone are my inheritance, my cup of blessing" (NLT).

The poorest people in this world are those who consider themselves to be rich but who are not in a true relationship with the living God. Revelation 3:17–20 addresses them: "For you say, I am rich, I have prospered, and I need nothing, not realizing that you are wretched, pitiable, poor, blind, and naked. I counsel you to buy from me gold refined by fire, so that you may be rich, and white garments so that you may clothe yourself and the shame of your nakedness may not be seen, and salve to anoint your eyes, so that you may see….so be zealous and repent. Behold, I stand at the door and knock. If anyone hears my voice and opens the door, I will come in to him and eat with him, and he with me."

Jesus knocks at the door of each of our hearts. If you have never invited Him in, and wish to, please turn to Appendix A. You are one simple-yet-life-altering prayer away from a relationship with the Almighty Living God.

God empowers us to live our lives at their best, as we were meant to live them. Just as our salvation cannot be bought with money, this mighty inner power (the indwelling Holy Spirit) cannot be bought either. In Acts 8:15–21, the story is told of how Peter and John laid their hands upon some gathered believers and those believers received the Holy Spirit. A man named Simon saw this and offered the disciples

---

[159]  Ibid., pp. 160–163.

money to buy this power. Peter replied: "May your money be destroyed with you for thinking God's gift can be bought" (v. 20 NLT).

God's power and presence in our lives cannot ever be taken away from us by others. Corrie ten Boom, unjustly incarcerated in a Nazi concentration camp for part of World War II, was stripped of everything she owned. On some occasions, she was even stripped of her clothes and was forced to stand naked outside for hours, many times in inclement weather. Speaking to a German woman after the war, Corrie said that though the Nazis had been able to strip her of everything materially, they could never take away the inner riches she had in Christ.[160] She could only be rendered physically naked, not spiritually naked like the poor and pitiable souls described in Revelation 3 above.

Of course, all of this assumes that we come to God seeking true relationship with sincere hearts. We cannot come, as some do in this age of the prosperity gospel, seeking Him as a means to material riches. Trying to use God to acquire money is a disrespectful, misguided, and ultimately fruitless avenue of approach to God.

God wants us to come to Him out of our need for Him, willing to love, serve, and obey Him whether we have a little or a lot in the material dimension of our lives, in good economic times and in bad times. Our relationship with God is meant to truly surpass this material world and everything in it.

An Old Testament character named Job lived by that truth. At the beginning of the Book of Job, Satan pointed out to God that God had prospered Job and had protected his wealth. Satan predicted that Job would curse God if God allowed Job's riches to be taken away. God responded to this challenge by allowing Satan to destroy Job's wealth. Job went through a variety of emotions as he dealt with that loss, but here is what Job said (in Job 1:21, after he lost his sheep, camels, servants, and finally, his children): "I came naked from my mother's womb, and I will be naked when I leave. The Lord gave me what I had, and the Lord has taken it away. Praise the name of the Lord!" (NLT). Job understood the supremacy of God over all else.

---

[160]  Ten Boom book, p. 50.

## Relationships with Others

One list of the thousand most frequently used words in the English language recorded "love" at position 387 and "money" at 389. Of course, we don't just talk about loving our loved ones. Considering that we also glibly talk about loving everything from pizza to hockey to pink nail polish, we can assume that we talk much more about money than our love for the people in our lives.

Yet, next to our relationship with God, there is nothing more important, satisfying, and fulfilling in this life than being rich in human relationships. In one of their famous songs, the Beatles reminded us that money can't buy us love. The great news is that even if we have little money at various times in our lives, we can still be very rich in relationships. John Newton (18th century sailor, clergyman, and composer of the beloved hymn "Amazing Grace") once said to his wife: "…we may not be rich—no matter. We are rich in love."[161] On a similar note, American President John Adams once advised his daughter Abigail: "Desire no other riches than the riches of the heart."

It's okay to spend some money on our relationships, but I am sure you will agree with me that it is far more important to give our love, our time, our attention, positive and affirming words, and other gifts of the heart. We can spend ourselves, not just our money, on developing our relationships in life. When we talk about someone having lived a life well-spent, we are not usually referring to the money they disbursed.

I am sad when I encounter people whose lives are bankrupt in terms of relationships. I will always remember one client I represented in court years ago. She had been arrested for shoplifting a cosmetic item worth only a few dollars. This was her *ninth* such criminal charge. She did not shoplift over and over again for lack of money; in fact, she was married to a very wealthy CEO. The Judge asked her *why* she kept on shoplifting. She told him that the stolen items were of no value to her; what she really wanted was her husband's attention. As per usual, her husband had not bothered to show up in court. She begged the Judge to impose a jail sentence, tragically believing that her husband would

---

[161] Petersen book, p. 28.

take notice of her then. She was distraught and disappointed when the Judge instead sentenced her to further psychiatric treatment.

In wonderful contrast, each one of us can be rich in a wide range of relationships: with our parents, siblings, spouse, children, grandchildren, friends, neighbours, work colleagues, churchmates, and even strangers we encounter for a brief time. If a relationship with one particular person does not work out, thankfully we can seek to develop other relationships. We share this world with almost seven billion other people!

With the power of Christ within us, we have much to offer others. Peter said to a man in need of healing: "I have no silver and gold, but what I do have I give to you" (Acts 3:6a). At bare minimum, we can always offer others our love *and* we can be a channel of God's love.

Let's remember always to value our relationships more than we value money. If we don't, we will have much heartache in our relationships. We must nurture our relationships and guard against distractions. Just when we think we have our priorities straight in this area, interesting temptations might cross our path. While writing this book, one such temptation surfaced in my life. Out of the blue, a real estate agent called and said she knew of a prospective purchaser who wanted to live in my neighbourhood. No homes were up for sale at that time. We were happy in our home and had no reason to move. The purchaser was willing to pay us well above market price if they could buy our home and move into it one month later.

It was truly tempting. As Sam and I talked about it, we realized that we could not only make an amazing profit by selling our current home, but we could also probably find a good bargain elsewhere in the sluggish real estate market. Why not do it?

After thinking about it, we encountered several reasons to turn down this enticing opportunity. We would disrupt our lives and relationships. We would put our family through a lot of unnecessary stress. We would put friendships on hold while we packed boxes and searched for a new home. Accepting this unsolicited offer of material profit would jeopardize our true riches. (I also realized that it would be particularly ironic and quite hypocritical to set this book behind schedule because of the unnecessary pursuit of quick money!)

## God's Gifts of Wisdom, Knowledge, and Ideas

In 2 Chronicles 1:7–12, God asked Solomon what he wanted God to give him. Solomon chose wisdom and knowledge. God was so pleased with Solomon's choice that He gave him wisdom and knowledge and then added material riches and honour.

In Proverbs 3:13–15, Solomon wrote: "Blessed is the one who finds wisdom, and the one who gets understanding, for the gain from her is better than gain from silver and her profit better than gold. She is more precious than jewels, and nothing you desire can compare with her." In Proverbs 8:10–11 he re-iterated: "Take my instruction instead of silver, and knowledge rather than choice gold, for wisdom is better than jewels, and all that you may desire cannot compare with her." In Proverbs 16:16, he repeated: "How much better to get wisdom than gold! To get understanding is to be chosen rather than silver."

Speaking of God's laws, precepts, and commandments, the psalmist who wrote Psalm 19:10 similarly stated: "More to be desired are they than gold, even much fine gold…" In Psalm 119:72, the psalmist declared: "The law of your mouth is better to me than thousands of gold and silver pieces."

In Ecclesiastes 7:11–12, Solomon expressed the ultimate superiority of wisdom over money in this way: "Wisdom is even better when you have money. Both are a benefit as you go through life. Wisdom and money can get you almost anything, but only wisdom can save your life" (NLT).

We can obtain much wisdom and knowledge from the Word of God. God can provide us with additional wisdom and knowledge through His Spirit.

God can also inspire us with new ideas. Think about the potential of an idea. Someone came up with the idea of using sand to create a silicon chip. This simple idea turned into billions of dollars for those who developed and advanced it. Silicon chips fuelled the global computer revolution. What started as a simple idea has changed the quality of life and range of opportunities for billions of people.

We can ask God for wisdom, knowledge, and good ideas. These secondary riches can flow from our relationship with Him.

## God's Gift of His Creation

I believe that God wants us to enjoy His creation. We are not to worship or deify it, but we can enjoy its richness. So much of the time, we can do so without spending a dime. We can observe the sunrise and the sunset…the moon and the stars…a rainbow…cloud formations…clear blue skies. We can take the time to look at flowers and grass and trees. We can look at (not just endure) rain falling down or snowflakes sparkling in sunshine. We can admire a pond, a stream, a river, a waterfall, an ocean.

For several decades, I have had the privilege of being able to stay at a cottage in the woods with family and extended family for periods during all four seasons. When our kids were growing up, it was wonderful to get them away (as much as we could) from the electronic distraction and passive entertainment that flowed from television, computers, and certain toys. Instead, we hiked through the woods. We looked for pussy willows in the spring, picked wild raspberries in the summer, and collected red and yellow leaves in the fall. We named the well-worn trails we walked on, fun names like Bear Pass and Poisonberry Path. We often stood on a rock cliff we had named Echo Hill, easily spending an hour at a time listening to the echo of the words we shouted out. At the edge of a sapphire-blue lake, we skipped stones into the water.

We fed almost-tame chipmunks that came close to the cottage. We spied on the red cardinals, blue jays, and hummingbirds that frequented the bird-feeders. We chased butterflies. We watched for squirrels and rabbits, beavers and raccoons, and even the occasional deer. A few times, a black bear wandered onto the property. At night, we could listen for the loons calling or the wolves howling. We marvelled at shooting stars.

Many of our activities cost nothing.

God's creation is a free gift we can step out to enjoy without bringing our wallets. Look out your windows, step outside your door, walk until you notice something God created.

## God's Gifts of Time and Energy

God also enriches each one of us with a measure of time and energy. Some of that time and energy ends up being spent on making money, investing it, spending it, and giving some of it away. Beyond that, we are meant to have much time and energy to spend on more valuable things. Some will hopefully be spent on our relationships with God and others. Some will hopefully be spent enjoying His creation.

Hopefully, we will also save some time and energy for our own selves. How wonderfully rich it is to quietly enjoy a cup of tea, to listen to music (or perhaps to compose it), to read good words (or perhaps to write them), to reflect, to soak in a warm tub, and at the end of the day to fall into a deep and restorative sleep. Most of those activities are either free or cost very little.

Some say that time *is* money. I disagree. Time is worth infinitely more than mere currency. Those who equate the two live lesser lives. I heard about one tough-as-nails Manhattan investment banker who asked her obstetrician to have her baby delivered by C-section even though it was not medically necessary. She wanted to book the delivery in her daily schedule so she could be in control of her lucrative career. If she could deliver her baby over a designated lunch-hour, she could be back to work later that afternoon to supervise the closing of an important business deal. That's what becomes of those flat-lined souls who equate time with money.

## Character

In the midst of his terrible trials, Job resolved this: "…when he has tried me, I shall come out as gold" (Job 23:10). Job was not concerned about his lost wealth. He was concerned that he would emerge from his season of troubles with a golden character, a soul transformed for the better. Our character is worth much more than our money. Inner attitudes of heart such as gratitude, generosity, honesty, and integrity are part of what forges great character.

## All True Riches

All true riches emanate from God. He is worth far more than everything else combined. Let us pursue *Him* above all else…

> *And what do you benefit if you gain the whole world but lose*
> *your own soul? Is anything worth more than your soul?*
>
> Mark 8:36–37 (NLT)

> *Let not the wise man boast in his wisdom, let not the*
> *mighty man boast in his might, let not the rich man boast*
> *in his riches, but let him who boasts boast in this, that he*
> *understands and knows me…*
>
> Jeremiah 9:23–24a

> *Riches I heed not, nor man's empty praise,*
> *Thou mine inheritance, now and always:*
> *Thou and Thou only, first in my heart,*
> *High King of Heaven, my Treasure Thou art.*[162]

> *Turn your eyes upon Jesus,*
> *Look full in His wonderful face,*
> *And the things of earth will grow strangely dim,*
> *In the light of His glory and grace.*[163]

---

[162] From the fourth verse of "Be Thou My Vision," a 6th century Irish hymn attributed to Dallan Fargaill, translated into English by Mary E. Byrne in 1905, now in Public Domain.

[163] Refrain from "Turn Your Eyes upon Jesus," a hymn written by Helen H. Lemmel in 1922, now in Public Domain.

# 27

---

## A RICH BALANCE

As our journey together draws to a close, I hope that we have all developed a greater understanding of God's truth about money. We have considered almost one thousand Scripture verses along the way and have discussed many practical examples of what it means to manage and relate to money from a biblical perspective.

It's not easy—figuring out how to make money in the first place, then figuring out how much to save, invest, spend, and give away while still maintaining time and energy for the higher priorities of our relationships with God and others. We have all been entrusted with a certain amount of money, whether we have a little or a lot. One day we will be answerable for what we have done with the material assets that have passed through our hands. I am thankful that God has given us a wealth of wonderful governing principles that can help us to carry on working through all of the details of our financial lives in the context of our *whole* lives.

I pray that both you and I keep developing and sustaining a balanced approach to the way we view and handle money as we move onward in life. I pray that we will continue to reflect on the many subtopics we have delved into and that we will sharpen our abilities to integrate them into a comprehensive, well-rounded, and well-grounded biblical framework. May we learn how to authentically live within that framework. I pray that none of us will ever again let a particular subtopic form a gospel unto itself. I pray that we all get over the habit of looking at favourite verses about money in isolation or placing our faith in singular palatable principles. I am thankful that God wants to help us in this life-long process of balancing and integrating everything He has said about money (and, indeed, everything He has said about everything).

Furthermore, as we mature in our inner attitudes, God wants to bless us in every area of financial endeavour. God is ready to respond to whatever appropriate faith we apply to our financial lives. He wants to equip and empower us so that we can work hard. God has promised that, one way or another, we will receive enough money and other material resources to meet all of our needs and to fulfil the good desires He approves of. In fact, He will provide a surplus so that we can generously give. As we give, surplus will keep coming back to us. God can help us to wisely save and invest so that we can support ourselves and our loved ones now and in the future instead of ever becoming an undue burden on others.

All that God requires is that we maintain right attitudes of heart toward money as we engage in such necessary activities as working, saving, investing, spending, and giving. Let's purpose to love and serve God instead of money. Let's find our ultimate security in God alone. Let's choose to walk with high integrity. Instead of falling prey to greed, pride, or fear, let's embrace generosity, gratitude, and contentment. From now on, as we walk in step with Him, let's hold onto our money so very lightly instead of tightly. As we nurture all of these wise inner resolutions, let's also continue to carefully consider every emerging cultural trend that threatens to throw us off balance.

If I have missed the mark on any principle or concept in this book, it only proves that I am still a student of God's truth. Perhaps I have not perfectly presented the various principles we have explored or flawlessly balanced and integrated them. But I *am* sure of this: if you have meditated on the almost one thousand verses from God's Word that I have referred to and plan to put them into balanced practice, you will not be led astray. You need not accept every one of *my* words. Some may judge what I have said about this or that. If I have in any way erred in presenting His truth, I trust that He will correct me. I remain a seeker and a student of His truth.

May we all come progressively closer to understanding the truth about money from God's viewpoint. In 2 Samuel 22:31, we are told: "This God—his way is perfect; the word of the Lord proves true..." God alone knows the full truth about money. I pray that He continues to help every one of us in our ongoing journeys, in the financial realm and beyond. May we all learn how to fully and richly balance and integrate the many great principles He has entrusted us with. May He continue to transform *every* aspect of our lives.

> *The sum of your word is truth, and every one of your righteous rules endures forever.*
>
> Psalm 119:160

> *I the Lord speak the truth; I declare what is right.*
>
> Isaiah 45:19b

> *...you will know the truth and the truth will set you free.*
>
> John 8:32

# APPENDIX A

———

The prophet Elijah confronted the people with this challenge: "How long will you go limping between two different opinions? If the Lord is God, follow him…" (1 Kings 18:21)

If you would like to become a Christian, you can pray this prayer today:

> *Father, I believe that You exist and that Jesus Christ is Your Son. I believe that Jesus died on the Cross to pay the penalty for the sins of all humankind. I believe that He has risen and is now seated at Your right hand.*
>
> *I confess that I am a sinner. I confess all my known sins and I desire to turn from them. I confess that my greatest sin has been ignoring You and rebelling against Your sovereignty in my life. I ask You to forgive all of my sins, on the basis of what Jesus did on the Cross for me. Create in me a clean heart! Please remove my sins as far as the east is from the west, as You promised You would. Please give me a fresh, new start in my life.*
>
> *I give my life to You. I ask that You now dwell in me by Your Spirit, empowering me to live as I should. Thank You!*
>
> *I pray in faith, in the name of Jesus Christ, Amen.*

If you have prayed this prayer, you have made a new beginning in your life! The Enemy of your soul will start to attack you with doubts and discouraging thoughts over the coming days. He will accuse you every time you slip up on your imperfect onward journey. Do not listen to him! I encourage you to get a Bible and begin to read some verses every day, starting with the New Testament. Pray each day, talking to God as you would talk to a valued friend. Ask Him to help you to become better acquainted with the Holy Spirit who now lives within you. Find a Bible-believing church and start to make Christian friends. Grow in your ability to trust and obey God.

I will be praying for you.

# Selected Bibliography

————

**Books**

Adams, Moody. *The Titanic's Last Hero*. South Carolina: The Olive Press, 1997.

Alcorn, Randy. *The Treasure Principle*. Oregon: Multnomah Books, 2001.

Bailey, Faith Coxe. *D. L Moody*. Chicago: Moody Press, 1959.

Bailey, Faith Coxe. *George Mueller*. Chicago: Moody Press, 1958.

Books, Borden. *Mothers of Influence*. Colorado Springs. Honor Books, 2005.

Carlson, Carole. *Corrie ten Boom: Her Life, Her Faith*. New York: Jove, 1984.

Clinton, Bill. *Giving*. New York: Knopf, 2007.

Colson, Chuck. *Born Again*. New Jersey: Fleming H. Revell, 1977.

Cunningham, Loren. *Daring to Live on the Edge*. Seattle: YWAM Publishing, 1991.

Cunningham, Loren. *The Book that Transforms Nations*. Seattle: YWAM Publishing, 2007.

Ferguson, Niall. *The Ascent of Money*. New York: Penguin Press, 2008.

Gottherdt, Alan. *The Eternity Portfolio*. Illinois: Tyndale, 2003.

Graham, Billy. *Storm Warning.* Nashville: Thomas Nelson, 2010.

Greene, Mark. *Thank God It's Monday.* England: Scripture Union, 2001.

Grubb, Norman. *Rees Howells Intercessor.* Pennsylvania: CLC Publications, 1952.

Harris, Samuel. *The Scriptural Plan of Benevolence.* New York: American Tract Society, circa 1850.

Hill, Craig and Pitts, Earl. *Wealth Riches and Money.* Colorado: Family Foundations Int'l, 2001.

Kullberg, Kelly Monroe. *Finding God beyond Harvard.* Illinois: Intervarsity Press, 2006.

Le Joly, Edward. *Mother Teresa of Calcutta.* New York: Harper Collins, 1985.

Lewis, C. S. *Mere Christianity.* Glasgow: William Collins Sons & Co., 1986 edition.

Lindsay, Michael. *Faith in the Halls of Power: How Evangelicals Joined the American Elite.* New York: Oxford University Press, 2007.

Loveless, Caron. *The Words that Inspired the Dreams.* Louisiana: Howard, 2000.

Lupton, Robert. *Compassion, Justice, and the Christian Life: Rethinking Ministry to the Poor.* California: Regal Books, 2007.

Monroe, Kelly (ed.). *Finding God at Harvard.* Michigan: Zondervan, 1996.

Montgomery, Leslie. *The Faith of Condoleezza Rice.* Wheaton, Ill.: Crossway Books, 2007.

Nee, Watchman. *Love Not the World.* Great Britain: Kingsway Publications, 1970.

Newton, John. *John Newton: His Autobiography*. (Public Domain).

Norton, Howard and Slosser, Bob. *The Miracle of Jimmy Carter*. New Jersey: Logos, 1976.

Obama, Barack. *The Audacity of Hope*. New York: Three Rivers Press, 2006.

Petersen, William. *25 Surprising Marriages*. Michigan: Baker Books, 1997.

Pue, Carson. *Mentoring Leaders*. Michigan: Baker Books, 2005.

Robertson, Pat. *Right on the Money*. New York: FaithWords, 2009.

Rusten, E. Michael and Sharon. *The One Year Christian History*. Illinois: Tyndale, 2003.

Smith, Adam. *The Wealth of Nations*. (Public Domain).

Ten Boom, Corrie. *Tramp for the Lord*. New Jersey: Fleming Revell, 1974.

Waldfogel, Joel. *Scroogenomics: Why You Shouldn't Buy Presents for the Holidays*. New Jersey: Princeton University Press, 2009.

Wellman, Sam. *Florence Nightingale*. Ohio: Barbour, 1999.

Wiersbe, Warren. *Victorious Christians You Should Know*. Michigan: Baker, 1984.

Woodbridge, John (ed.). *More than Conquerors: Portraits of Believers from All Walks of Life*. Chicago: Moody Press, 1992.

Zacharias, Ravi. *Walking from East to West: God in the Shadows*. Michigan: Zondervan, 2006

## Articles

Anderson, John Ward. "French castles just hassles." *Toronto Star*, August 29, 2006.

Banjo, Shelly. "Check Out Charities." *The Wall Street Journal*, November 8, 2009.

Bernard, Tara Siegel. "A Spending Plan is Like a Diet." *The New York Times*, January 9, 2011.

Bishop, Randy. "From Wall Street to the streets." *Today's Christian*, September/October 2001.

Carrigan, Bill. "Financials, homebuilders have likely hit bottom." *Toronto Star*, August 29, 2008.

Castaldo, Joe. "Give and Take." *Canadian Business*, winter 2008/2009.

Daw, James. "BMO's single-decision portfolios offer more for less." *Toronto Star*, April 27, 2010.

Evans, Kelly. "Hard-hit Families Finally Start Saving." *The Wall Street Journal*, January 6, 2009.

Fatah, Sonya. "India's richest man builds a vanity project to live in." *Toronto Star*, August 16, 2008.

Flavelle, Dana. "Top executives still raking it in." *Toronto Star*, January 5, 2010.

Frank, Robert. "Marrying for Love...of Money." *The Wall Street Journal*, December 14, 2007.

Friedman, Stew. "The First Couple and a New Era of Workplace Flexibility." *http:// blogs.hbr.org/cs/2010/04*, last accessed on April 6, 2010.

Gibbs, Nancy and Ostling, Richard N. "God's Billy Pulpit." *Time*, November 15, 1993.

Gibbs, Nancy. "Persons of the Year." *Time*, December 26, 2005.

Hampson, Sarah. "It makes them sick to spend—literally." *The Globe and Mail*, June 8, 2009.

Hood, Duncan. "Professor of Happiness." *MoneySense*, summer issue, 2006.

Johnson, Carrie. "Enron's Lay Dies of Heart Attack." *The Washington Post*, July 6, 2006, p. A01.

Karlgaard, Rich. "Peter Drucker on Leadership." *Forbes*, November 19, 2004; posted at *www.forbes.com/2004/11/19*, last accessed on December 7, 2009.

Kielburger, Craig and Marc. "Investing for Profit—and for good." *Toronto Star*, Nov. 17, 2008.

Maich, Steve. "The Gospel According to Bill." *MacLean's*, July 21, 2008.

Maich, Steve. "The $3 billion prophet of doom." *MacLean's*, April 28, 2008.

Maxwell, Joe. "The Mission of Business." *Christianity Today*, November 2007.

Moist, Paul. "Creaking Pension System is Failing Canadians." *Toronto Star*, December 16, 2009.

Moll, Rob. "Overturning the Money Tables." *Christianity Today*, July 2008.

Moll, Rob. "Scrooge Lives!" *Christianity Today*, December 2008.

Moll, Rob. "Hunger Can Be Conquered." *Christianity Today*, February 2010.

Moll, Rob. "Taking stock." *Christianity Today*, March 2010.

Morgan, Timothy C. and Phiri, Isaac. "Hunger Isn't History." *Christianity Today*, November 2008.

Moring, Mark. "Hollywood Hellfighter." *Christianity Today,* May 2008.

Newmark, Evan. "Mean Street: Bruce Wasserstein and the Meaning of Life." *The Wall Street Journal*, October 19, 2009.

Popplewell, Brett. "Repeat bankruptcies a rising trend." *Toronto Star,* March 12, 2009.

RD Money columnist. "Are You Fiscally Faithful?" *Reader's Digest*, July 2008.

Renkl, Margaret. "Have A Heart." *Ladies' Home Journal*, December 2007.

Riseboro, Caroline. "8.8 million children die as world spends billions on pet food." *Toronto Star,* April 2, 2010.

Roseman, Ellen. "Profitable reading to stuff in the stockings." *Toronto Star*, December 6, 2006.

Roseman, Ellen. "Pinching pennies all life long." *Toronto Star*, September 10, 2008.

Rosin, Hanna. "Did Christianity Cause the Crash?" *http://www.theatlantic.com/doc/200912/rosin-prosperity-gospel*, last accessed on April 9, 2010.

Smith, Roy C. "Greed is Good." *The Wall Street Journal*, February 7, 2009, p. W1.

Stafford, Tim. "The Evangelical Elite." *Christianity Today*, November 2007.

Stern, Daniel. "Representing Peter Drucker." *http://blogs.harvardbusiness.org/cs/2009/12*, last accessed on December 14, 2009.

Symonds, William C. "Earthly Empires: How evangelical churches are borrowing from the business playbook." *Business Week*, May 23, 2005.

Timm, Jordan. "An insider take on the money men who brought it all down." *Canadian Business*, November 9, 2009.

Timm, Jordan. "Why cold, hard cash is the wisest gift a Scrooge can give." *Canadian Business*, Special Edition, Winter 2009/2010.

Toycen, Dave. "If there's a will, there's a way." *Childview*, World Vision Canada, winter 2006/07.

Unspecified author. "Bankers and their Bonuses." *The New York Times*, February 13, 2011.

Unspecified author. "Ending Poverty: Are We on Target?" *Childview*, World Vision Canada, fall 2008.

Unspecified author. "Food Crisis: A World Apart." *Childview*, World Vision Canada, fall 2008.

Unspecified author. "Numbers." *Time*, (Canada), January 9, 2006.

Unspecified author. "Self-Examination Time." *Christianity Today*, April 2009.

Unspecified author. "U.S. gambling revenue increases 5.3%." *Toronto Star*, May 15, 2008.

Van Biema, David and Chu, Jeff. "Does God Want You to be Rich?" *Time* (Canada), Sept. 18, 2006.

Van Biema, David. "Going After the Money Ministries." *Time* (Canada), November 26, 2007.

Van Evra, Jennifer. "The good life may cost less than you think." *The Globe and Mail*, June 8, 2009.

Vermond, Kira. "No Such Luck." *Chatelaine,* July 2008.

Waisberg, Deena. "Get a Fresh Start on Your Finances." *Canadian Living*, February 2009.

Wartzman, Rick. "A Time for Ethical Self-Assessment." *Business Week*, December 23, 2008.

Watson, Thomas. "Abandoned at the Altar." *Canadian Business*, March 1, 2010.

Yew, Madhav Acharya-Tom. "Balancing Act." *Toronto Star*, November 5, 2009.

## Websites

(website address was accurate at date of last access)

http://blogs.harvardbusiness.org, last accessed on April 19, 2011.

http://online.wsj.com, last accessed on March 27, 2009.

www.alphacanada.org and www.alpha.org, last accessed on November 22, 2010.

www.bbc.co.uk, last accessed on February 8, 2011.

www.bfmthriftstores.ca, last accessed on January 17, 2011.

www.bibleleague.ca, last accessed on November 22, 2010.

www.CharityNavigator.org, last accessed on March 16, 2011.

www.christianlegalfellowship.org, last accessed on November 22, 2010.

www.cra-arc.gc.ca, last accessed on November 22, 2010.

www.creditcounsellingcanada.ca, last accessed on March 16, 2011.

www.crown.org, last accessed on April 4, 2011.

www.druckerinstitute.com, last accessed on April 4, 2011.

www.forbes.com, last accessed on March 16, 2011.

www.GiveWell.net, last accessed on April 4, 2011.

www.goodsenseministry.com, last accessed on April 24, 2010.

www2.guidestar.org, last accessed on March 16, 2011.

www.harvardbusiness.org, last accessed on April 19, 2010.

www.kfc.com, last accessed on June 10, 2008.

www.listenuptv.com, last accessed on March 16, 2011.

www.moneyproblems.ca, last accessed on March 16, 2011.

www.muskokawoodsfoundation.com, last accessed on April 4, 2011.

www.nytimes.com, last accessed on April 19, 2011.

www.opendoorsca.org or www.od.org, last accessed on April 4, 2011.

www.samaritanspurse.ca or www.samaritanspurse.org, last accessed on April 4, 2011.

www.statcan.gc.ca, last accessed on October 18, 2010.

www.theglobeandmail.com, last accessed on April 28, 2010.

www.urbanpromise.com, last accessed on March 16, 2011.

www.worldvision.ca or www.wvi.org, last accessed on April 4, 2011.

www.youthunlimitedgta.ca, last accessed on March 16, 2011.

www.ywam.org, last accessed on November 3, 2009.

# CONTACTING THE AUTHOR

———

I love to hear from my readers. I value receiving feedback and I would be very interested to hear what you have thought about this book. If you have any reactions, opinions, insights, or stories you wish to share, please contact me. I can be reached at karenhenein@gmail.com or via my website www.karenhenein.com. I am honoured that you have taken the time to read this book.